5000 Miles At 8000 RPM

Joe Berk

Copyright © 2015 Joe Berk

All rights reserved.

ISBN: 1517355354
ISBN-13: 978-1517355357

Dedication

This book is dedicated to RX3 riders all over the world. You know who you are...Greg B., Greg M., Tiffany, Eric, Pete, Peter B., Juddy, Abe, Fernando, Anne, Craig, John F., John and his son Jay (who should have taken Spanish in high school), Justin, Reuben, Twin Peaks Steve, Andreas, Duane, Lester, Hugo, Tony, Tso, Kyle, King Kong, Gabriel, Juan Carlos, Baja John, John G., both Robs, Steve S., Gerry, Ryan, and thousands of others. You are the people who make your way around this planet exploring new places and products others fear. Keep making your own decisions and keep riding. I salute your adventurous spirit!

Contents

Chapter 1: How It All Started 1
Chapter 2: The Mustang Story 9
Chapter 3: The 250 Mustang, Zongshen, and the RX3 17
Chapter 4: Why a 250? 28
Chapter 5: The Test Bikes and the Media 34
Chapter 6: The Path to Market 44
Chapter 7: Venom, Viciousness, and Vituperation 59
Chapter 8: You Have Ovens? 66
Chapter 9: Baja! 80
Chapter 10: Another Chongqing Visit 95
Chapter 11: Preparation 100
Chapter 12: We Want to Shoot a Gun 110
Chapter 13: The Departure 117
Chapter 14: The Grand Canyon 125
Chapter 15: Zion 133
Chapter 16: Bryce 143
Chapter 17: It's Okay, It's Okay 152
Chapter 19: Medicine Bow 162
Chapter 20: The Run to Rushmore 171
Chapter 21: Deadwood, Sturgis, and Devil's Tower 179
Chapter 22: Cody, Beijing, and Orange Motorcycles 188
Chapter 23: Yellowstone and the Grand Tetons 194
Chapter 24: Boise, Baby! 204
Chapter 25: Hell's Canyon 213
Chapter 26: The Columbia River, Spit, and a Spat 224
Chapter 27: Tillamook and the Oregon Coast Highway 235
Chapter 28: Willits 244
Chapter 29: San Francisco 254
Chapter 30: Santa Maria 264
Chapter 31: Sweet Home, Azusa 268
Epilogue 273

Acknowledgments

My thanks go to the editors and writers at *ADVPulse*, *ADVMoto*, *Motorcycle.com*, and *Motorcyclist* magazines for the objective press coverage they have provided to CSC Motorcycles and in particular, the RX3. It has helped the company enormously.

More thanks go to my good buddy John Welker for his help in organizing and participation in the CSC Inaugural Baja Run and the Western America Adventure Ride. John also helped me proofread this book so I could eliminate the typos and other mistakes that crept in during long hours at the keyboard. You'll read a lot about John in these pages (I call him Baja John in the book, as we have ridden that magical morsel of Mexico many times on many different motorcycles).

I want to point out to the readers of this book that no one from CSC or Zongshen provided editorial direction, nor did they see any parts of it prior to publication. They did not tell me what I could or couldn't write. The good people in CSC and Zongshen will see this book's contents for the first time when it is published.

Foreword

I've only known Joe Berk for a short time. He's a motorcyclist, engineer, professor and a writer. That's at least four more things than I am. Still, our time-limited relationship has been intense, spanning nearly a billion crankshaft revolutions. That's like 17 hamster lifetimes and I'll be dammed if it doesn't feel like more.

Besides inside baseball stats on what it takes to create a new brand in today's interconnected world, his book, and I hesitate to call such a marvelous construct a mere book, includes stories of our time together as we traveled the American West on small displacement Chinese motorcycles.

Berk's 5000-mile ride was designed to showcase the reliability of the new-to-America, Zongshen brand of motorcycle and it accomplished that well. My job was to write about the bike for *Motorcyclist* Magazine. In other words, it was all an international publicity stunt.

Except that it turned out to be not so simple. None of the five Chinese riders knew each other or anyone else before we rode into the Mojave Desert. The two Colombians knew each other but were strangers to the rest. Add 100 degree heat, 35 degree cold and long days holding the motorcycle throttles wide open and the simple publicity stunt became a study in human nature under stress.

Generations from now motorcycle riders of all stripes will speak reverently of Berk's high rpm trip, calling it the defining, HooDoo-moment when Chinese bikes were taken seriously. The images that once shown bright across America's wide, western screen are too important to fade into oral hearsay. This stuff really happened. Berk commands Righteous Truth to record these flickering images in what at first glance appears to be an exceedingly long slog.

Wait, that was wrong. Berk does the jokes and I try to guess the punch line before he finishes. Nothing made me feel smarter or more worthwhile than guessing right. It's a system that saw us through most of the natural wonders this great country has to offer and hundreds of high calorie meals. Now is not the time to rock the boat.

Read this book in anger. Read it at work. Read it in bed. Then burn the brief, hamster-hours of your life in pursuit of the real smell of rain cascading down the narrow walls of an enchanted canyon. Watch the Tidal Light rise and fall, broadcasting chaotic shadows across an asphalt geometry known only to those who dare travel by motorcycle.

The Earth may spin around the Tidal Light billions of times but our individual allotment is scarce. *5000 Miles At 8000 RPM* is Berk's way of telling us to get out there on whatever motorcycle you have and turn as many revolutions as you can before the final one. I suggest you heed his advice.

Joe Gresh
Motorcyclist Magazine

Preface

I didn't start our Western America Adventure Ride with the idea of writing a book. When we rolled out of Azusa shortly after 5:00 a.m. that first day, pounding out close to 100,000 words on my computer was not on my mind.

Somewhere in the great American West, amongst scenes I had enjoyed in western movies as a youngster and I was now seeing firsthand, Joe Gresh commented on how well the bikes were holding up running at 8000 rpm all day long, day after day. I was feeling the pressure of keeping everybody together and staying on schedule, and Joe sensed my stress. He told me he thought things were going well. I made an offhand sarcastic comment regarding a book about the trip, and I said I was going to call it *5000 Miles At 8000 RPM*. I thought I was being cute. You know, the title sounded like Richard Henry Dana's 1840 classic, *Two Years Before The Mast*.

I forgot about that for the next several weeks, and then a few weeks after our return, I started thinking about it again. Maybe there was a book in this.

Then I thought a little more, and I realized I couldn't just tell the story about the Western America Adventure Ride. The story was bigger than that. It had to be the story of CSC Motorcycles, bringing the RX3 to America, the CSC Baja Inaugural Run, the bike itself, what it's like working with CSC and Zongshen, and the Western America Adventure Ride.

I really liked that title, though. *5000 Miles At 8000 RPM*. So I kept it. But I want you to know the story is bigger than just one adventure tour.

With that as the background, let's go for a ride.

Joe Berk

Chapter 1: How It All Started

November 9, 2009 was not a good day. It started normally enough, with cold cereal for breakfast, a cup of coffee, a hot shower, and me thinking about the 8:00 a.m. computer programming class I was due to start in a couple of hours at Cal Poly Pomona. I'm a teacher in the College of Engineering there. It's my day gig.

Decisions, decisions...back in '09 I owned three motorcycles: A 2006 Triumph Tiger, a 2006 Kawasaki KLR 650, and a 2007 Triumph Speed Triple. They were all magnificent machines and they fit a particular niche. By that time I was a committed adventure touring rider and most of my riding was on the Triumph Tiger or the KLR 650, but I liked the Triumph Speed Triple because of its looks. It was lime green with carbon fiber cans and gold anodized accents. It was wicked fast and I thought it was the most beautiful thing I had ever owned.

The Speed Triple it was that morning. I started it and while it was warming up in the driveway I gathered my things: Helmet (a brand new high visibility fluorescent green Scorpion), gloves, my old leather jacket, and a flash drive with my ME 232 course PowerPoint presentations (ME 232 was the course number for the computer programming course I taught). I only had the one class that day, so I thought it was going to be an easy morning. Little did I know.

My Triumph Speed Triple up on Glendora Ridge Road.
I loved the looks of this motorcycle.

I hopped on the 210 freeway headed west, rode the 8 miles or so to Fruit Street, exited, and turned south. There was a guy exiting the freeway on the eastbound side in an orange Camaro. He was coming to an aggressive stop and it looked like he might pull out directly in front of me. I established eye contact with him and I thought everything was going to be all right. That's the last thing I remembered BTA.

BTA is a significant benchmark in my life. It stands for Before the Accident.

Funny thing is, it wasn't that dude in the orange Camaro who clipped me. The accident was a block further south, and I don't remember anything about it. The doctors call it traumatic amnesia, and from what I've heard, it's fairly common in motorcycle accidents. My last memory is establishing eye contact with the Camaro dude.

My first inclination that something was wrong was a vague awareness of helicopter blades beating the air and the whine of the turbine driving them. Someone was speaking to me and my left hip hurt, and then I was out again. I have a vague memory of being loaded onto the Huey. I thought I was having a dream about the Army. There's another memory of the helicopter circling for a landing on top of a building, and then one more of someone in the emergency room asking for my wife's phone number. I couldn't remember it.

A couple of days later the message was not good. My left femur was fractured in two places, and the accident had broken my back. The doctor was explaining all this to me while I wondered why I was suddenly so lucid. I found out later they slow the morphine drip so you are awake enough to sign the papers consenting to surgery. Sure, I signed it. What else could I do?

A week in the hospital passed, and then I got the word: I was being discharged to a skilled nursing facility (words I now know to fear deeply). I felt like I was breaking out of jail, but it didn't go that smoothly. A private ambulance service would transport me to the so-called skilled nursing facility in Upland.

We left at about 5:00 p.m. from the Los Angeles County USC hospital and I was surprised we were moving along so quickly, especially considering the time of day and the direction we were going. When I finally saw signs for Santa Monica about an hour later, I knew why. The dummy driving the ambulance was going the wrong way. I had to tell him we would run into the Pacific Ocean if he didn't turn around. It took another three hours (after I told him about his mistake) to slug it out with rush hour traffic and get back to Upland. I felt every expansion joint and pothole on the way.

The skilled nursing facility was nothing more than an old folks home. It was the stuff of nightmares. I soon realized I was the only one there who was there to get better. For everyone else, it was their last stop. The place was literally a warehouse for people who were waiting to die.

It was time for another escape...this time to Casa Colina (a real rehab facility). I spent a week in Casa Colina and by then I had mastered the art of putting on my socks, getting around in a walker, and using the bathroom by myself. Well, maybe I had not mastered these things, but I did them well enough to go home, and that's what I did. I wouldn't be able to work for another 6 months, but I no longer needed to be monitored 24/7.

About now, I imagine you're probably wondering why I'm telling you all this and what it has to do with our 5000-mile ride around the western US on Chinese motorcycles. Well, there are two reasons:

- I'm a natural-born story teller, and

- I'm a firm believer in the old adage about every time one door closes, another one opens.

It's that second reason that's the more relevant one in this chapter. If it hadn't been for that accident and me being stuck hanging around the house, I would have never connected with CSC and I believe we would have never imported the RX3.

Let me back up a bit. My good buddy Joseph Lee is another Triumph rider. Joseph and I had ridden together throughout California and Mexico on our Triumphs and we were good friends. There was another cool aspect to my friend Joseph. He worked for Pro-One Performance Manufacturing. And yes, he likes to go by Joseph (not Joe).

Let me back up even more. Pro-One is a California company that manufactures custom motorcycle accessories and big-inch choppers. You know, the kind of bikes you used to see on that ridiculous reality show, *Orange County Choppers*. These were motorcycles I would never be interested in buying, but I was interested in learning more about Joseph's job because he actually worked for a company that made motorcycle stuff. To me, that had to be just about the coolest thing in the world.

Joseph visited me one day during my recovery and he told me that Pro-One had started a new company. This venture was re-introducing the old Mustang. The Mustang was a bike that had been manufactured in California from 1946 to 1962. They are kind of like scooter-sized Harleys. I'd heard of them but I knew next to nothing about the Mustang when Joseph told me about Pro-One's resurrection of this old bike. They were going to call the new business the California Scooter Company, and the bikes would be California Scooters. I'll tell you more about the Mustang and all that in the next chapter.

"They need somebody to respond to comments about the bike on the Internet forums," Joseph said. "Would you want to do that?"

Hell, yeah, I thought. I'm just sitting around the house watching TV or playing on the Internet. Watching *Law and Order* reruns was getting old. Joseph had thought of me because I spent far too much time posting comments on the ADVrider.com forum, and because at that time, I had my own motorcycle travel website. He knew I could find my way around the Internet, and that I could write a little bit.

I had forgotten Joseph had ever asked the question (the effects of the painkillers, I guess), but he called me early in the morning a couple of days later and said he and Maureen wanted to come to the house for an interview. I was watching an episode of *Law and Order* that I had probably seen four times already.

"Who's Maureen?" I asked.

"She's Steve Seidner's wife," Joseph said. "She's real pretty," he added, almost as if he were offering that as an enticement so they could come over to the house. I didn't need it. I was bored out of my mind. Oh, and here's some more background: Steve Seidner is the founder and CEO of Pro-One Performance Manufacturing. He was Joseph's boss. Maureen Seidner, Steve's wife, is the company's Chief Financial Officer.

Joseph and Maureen showed up that morning. We had a nice chat. I guess Maureen was impressed. She asked what I would need in the way of compensation if I came to work for them. I told her 50% of the company and a position as President of the California Scooter Company. She looked at me with a blank expression. She was wondering, I'm sure, if she had heard me correctly. "He does stuff like that a lot," Joseph said. "It's part of his charm."

Maureen and Steve met with me for breakfast a few days later, and I was in. It was an interesting meeting. Steve is a quiet guy and until he gets to know you, he's very reserved. I thought maybe he didn't like me at first, but it's just his way until he gets a register on you. That's in a situation like the one we were in, in which he was deciding if I was a guy he wanted on the payroll. When Steve is with a customer, he's incredible. He is the best closer I've ever known. People just naturally like him because they sense (correctly so) that he is trustworthy. He could sell snow to Eskimos during a blizzard because they would know if there was ever a problem with even just one of the snowflakes, Steve Seidner would make good on it.

So, I started my new job from home sitting in my wheelchair. I responded to comments on the Internet about the new little Mustang, and I guess I did my job well.

I have to back up a bit and tell you that the nearly all of the Internet comments were inane. Stupid and ridiculous stuff, for the most part, written by stupid and ridiculous people. The comments were all over the map. People hated the bike because they thought it was Chinese (it was actually assembled in our plant with parts and subassemblies we purchased in Taiwan, not China, but that distinction was lost on the keyboard commandos). People didn't like the bike's size. People said it cost too much. And on and on it went.

In the past, I might have been one of the jerks posting stuff like this, but now my job was to respond to it as a representative of the company being slammed. I had to be nice. I realized that you can't win arguments on the Internet, so I mostly just thanked people for their views (even the real jerks, and there were a lot of them). I always invited them to stop by for a test ride.

A funny thing happened as a result of all this. The people who had been posting negative stuff on the Internet forums stopped doing so when I was nice to them, and in many cases, they actually became supporters. I don't think any of these people ever bought our bike, but when new jerks emerged and posted negative stuff, some of the former jerks raced to our defense.

Your author with his 150cc California Scooter.
I rode this motorcycle to Cabo San Lucas and back.

One of the recurring things that kept popping up (both on the Internet and when potential customers visited) was confusion about the California Scooter name. We were the California Scooter Company and we called our bikes California Scooters, but they were actually motorcycles (not scooters). The controls were those of a motorcycle. The transmissions required shifting with a clutch and a gearshift lever (unlike scooters, which have what are essentially automatic transmissions and no clutch). The California Scooter looked like a motorcycle. It did not have a stepthrough frame like scooters do. To me, it was obvious that the bike was a motorcycle. We called the bikes "scooters" in the vernacular. That was the intent when Steve named the company the California Scooter Company. It was a throwback to the '50s and '60s, when motorcyclists called their motorcycles "scooters" (as in, "I'm going for a ride on my scooter").

All that notwithstanding, we heard the question a lot: Is it a motorcycle or a scooter?

I kept what I wanted to say to myself. Every time I heard or read that question, my thought was that the person asking it was probably too stupid to ride either a motorcycle or a scooter. I always wanted to tell them that (or write it when the question emerged on the Internet), but I never did.

This scooter versus motorcycle question bothered Steve a lot. He told me after I'd been involved with the company for about a month that he wished he had never called us the California Scooter Company and he wanted to rename the company. I liked the name (the California Scooter Company), but I didn't have a personal fortune riding on the success of the business like Steve and Maureen did. I understood where he was coming from.

I thought about the issue that evening, and it came to me: Just call the company CSC Motorcycles. There's a long tradition in the motorcycle world of three-letter abbreviations for motorcycle companies (BSA, KTM, BMW, AJS, etc.). I sent an email to Steve that night suggesting the name.

The next morning when I saw Steve he was pumped up. He liked the concept. CSC Motorcycles. It was simple, classic, and it sounded like a motorcycle company. There could be no confusion about motorcycles versus scooters. I'm pretty sure I made my bones with Steve that day based largely on my suggestion to call the company CSC Motorcycles. It solved the problem. After the name change, we never again heard the question about scooters versus motorcycles.

Sometimes people ask us what CSC stands for. Steve tells them California Specialty Cycles. I say California Scooter Company, unless I know the person who's asking it really well. In that case, my answer is Chop Suey Cycles.

Chapter 2: The Mustang Story

At this point, I think it makes sense to tell you about the original Mustang motorcycles to add perspective to how CSC Motorcycles came to be. I started to write a chapter about the old Mustangs, and then I realized I had already done that for *Motorcycle Classics* magazine. If you're not interested in the original Mustangs and how they led Steve Seidner to start CSC Motorcycles, skip this chapter. If you'd like to know the history, read on.

This story originally appeared in the January/February 2013 issue of *Motorcycle Classics*. I wrote it with my good buddy Jim Cavanaugh, now in his 80s and still riding both his vintage Mustang and a newer CSC 150. Jim was the former Mustang Motor Products plant manager and he is an advisor to CSC Motorcycles.

The Magnificent Mustang Motorcycles

No one knows with certainty how manufacturing mogul John Gladden, founder of the Mustang Motorcycle Corporation, selected the name. Some say he thought of wild horses. Others say it stems from the P-51 Mustang fighter plane. Both stories make sense, but we like the one about the P-51. Gladden Products made parts for World War II combat aircraft, so it seems logical that the P-51 Mustang could have been part of the calculus that created the Mustang moniker.

Gladden Products had a lot of things going for it, but as World War II was ending, John Gladden knew he needed a new product. Synchronicity struck when he noticed a very unusual motorcycle in the company parking lot. It was scooter-sized, but it was a motorcycle — a miniaturized motorcycle. The bike belonged to Howard Forrest, a machinist and engineer, and a serious motorcycle enthusiast who constructed it using a water-cooled, 300cc 4-cylinder engine he designed and built himself, from scratch.

So this was the time and the situation, Gladden casting about for a new product, one of his engineers riding a personally-designed and fabricated small motorcycle to work, and millions of young men returning from the war. Gladden recognized opportunity when he saw it: His new product would be a small motorcycle.

Gladden challenged Forrest and Chuck Gardner (a fellow Gladden Products engineer and motorcycle rider) to develop a lightweight motorcycle. Forrest's 300cc engine was intriguing, but would be expensive to build. Gladden wanted a lightweight and inexpensive bike; more substantive than a scooter, but not as big as a motorcycle — a scooter-sized motorcycle. What resulted was a family of Mustang motorcycles.

The First Mustangs

Mustang originally planned to use 197cc Villiers 2-stroke engines, but after building a few prototypes with the 197cc engine, Villiers instead offered their 125cc 2-stroke. It wasn't what Mustang wanted, but it was the only game in town. Thus was born the first production Mustang — the 1946 Colt. The Colts had leading-link front forks, a hardtail rear end, tiny 8-inch wheels, a peanut gas tank and twin exhausts. Small, yes, but stunning.

Forrest and Gardner weren't ecstatic about the tiny Villiers engine, however, and Villiers was making noises about cutting off their supply. Gladden recognized that making his own engines would be critical to Mustang's success, so Gladden did what moguls do: He acquired an aircraft engine manufacturer that included Busy Bee, a maker of small industrial engines. One in particular seemed a good fit for a new

Mustang motorcycle. It was a 320cc flathead single-cylinder 4-stroke, and it became the basic engine that would power future Mustangs.

Vintage Mustangs from Steve Seidner's collection.

Forrest and Gardner went back to the drawing board. What rapidly emerged in 1947 was the Mustang Model 2, a completely new Mustang and the first with what we now recognize as the classic Mustang appearance. Bigger than the Colt, it had Mustang's new engine and 12-inch disc wheels. The intake and exhaust ports faced rearward, with a finned exhaust manifold. The cast aluminum primary cover was adorned with the Mustang logo, and it had a 3-speed Burman transmission, a tractor seat supported by big coil springs, a rear brake, a rigid rear end and telescopic front forks. It weighed just 215 pounds.

The Model 2 was not without its problems, however, including rod knocks and noisy timing gears. Mustang handled the issues with special production actions, and to make sure only good bikes left the plant, the production foreman had to personally start, run, listen to and approve each engine.

More Models

Looking to expand the market, in December of 1948 Mustang introduced the Model 3 DeliverCycle, a three-wheeled, low-cost commercial vehicle. Police departments used DeliverCycles for parking enforcement — the city of Huntington Beach, Calif., was the first to use trikes for this purpose.

Addressing the Model 2's problems, in 1950 the Mustang team rolled out the Model 4 (known as the Standard). The newest Mustang engine incorporated Micarta timing gears for quieter running, a new magneto and alternator for improved ignition and lighting, forward-facing intake and exhaust ports to simplify the exhaust design, and a stamped steel primary case. The frame was also cleaned up and it got an improved 3-speed Burman transmission. The new Model 4 sold for $346.30. Mustang rolled these changes into a new DeliverCycle, too, the Model 5.

The Model 4 was a home run, and Mustang used it as the basis for several models over the next decade — the Special, the Pony, the Bronco and the Stallion. The Model 4 Special was a factory performance upgrade with higher compression and hotter cams. The standard Model 4 evolved into the Pony (the base model), which was the best-selling Mustang. Output climbed to 9.5 horsepower. Mustang also offered a 5 horsepower version of its iconic bike to meet some states' requirements for junior riders.

The Model 4 Special morphed into the Bronco (Mustang had a practice of referring to their bikes with model numbers, which sometimes were offered as Specials and sometimes evolved into other designations). The Bronco kept the Pony's engine and transmission and added a front brake as standard equipment.

Mustang upgraded the line again with the Stallion (the Model 8). It added a 4-speed Burman transmission and horsepower climbed to 10.5. The Stallion had a chrome flywheel and two-tone paint with pinstriping. The first Stallions had Amal carburetors; later models went to a 22mm

Dell'Orto.

The market started to change for Mustang in 1956. DeliverCycle sales fell and Mustang dropped it. Perceiving a need for a lower-cost motorcycle, Mustang introduced a new Colt in 1956, but it was a bust. Value-engineered to reduce labor costs, the new Colt had a 9.5 horsepower engine, no transmission and a centrifugal clutch. The front suspension reverted to an undamped leading-link arrangement. The kickstarter was awkward and the centrifugal clutch wore the crankshaft prematurely. It wasn't liked within the factory and build quality was poor, resulting in rework that offset any hoped-for savings. Mustang killed it just two years later.

An original Mustang badass: Willie Nelson in the 1950s.
No, he's not that Willie Nelson. This one was a Mustang factory test rider.

Things improved in 1960 with the Mustang Thoroughbred. In a first for Mustang, the Thoroughbred incorporated swingarm rear suspension, a dual seat and an optional storage compartment under the seat. It had the Stallion's 4-speed Burman transmission and a bump to 12.5 horsepower. This was good stuff, but the 1960s would not be good for Mustang. By the time the Thoroughbred rolled out, Howard Forrest had left the company. The Mustang organization was not without its politics, and for reasons few understood, the company had fired Forrest. Chuck Gardner took his place to lead development.

Offroad Expansion

In 1961, Mustang introduced the Trail Machine, the last in a legendary line of Mustang motorcycles. In a break from Mustang tradition, Trail Machines used Briggs & Stratton 5.75 horsepower engines. Staying with the Burman 3-speed tranny, the Trail Machine looked like the illegitimate child of a motorcycle and a lawn mower, with the standard Mustang diamond tread front tire and a more aggressive tractor tread rear tire.

While the machines were functionally excellent — weight was only 169 pounds dry — the rigid rear Trail Machine was tagged with the uninspiring "Rigid Frame" designation, and when Mustang introduced the swingarm Trail Machine in 1964 it was similarly (and boringly) named the "Rear Suspension" model. These bikes were initially offered only in yellow, but Mustang later added blue. Not many sold, and they are rare today.

Mustang resumed Model 5 DeliverCycle production in 1963, and then quickly upgraded it to the Model 7 in 1964. The Model 7 DeliverCycle incorporated the Stallion's 12.5 horsepower engine and 4-speed transmission, but time was running out for Mustang. In 1965 production of Mustang motorcycles came to an end.

No one who's talking knows with certainty why Mustang stopped production. Some say it was because Burman wasn't supplying transmissions at the required rate. Some say there were management problems. Some believe it was all those nicest people you kept meeting on Hondas, motorcycles that offered electric starting, better performance and lower prices. There were a few revival attempts using residual Mustang parts inventories, but only a handful of bikes emerged. The Mustang saga, one of the most intriguing stories in our magnificent motorcycling world, was over. (Or was it? See **Mustang Reborn: California Scooter Company** following this article.)

Today, original Mustangs are highly prized, routinely selling for $10,000-plus in concours condition. Even "beater" Mustangs — when you can find them — typically bring more than $5,000. There's an active fan base (check out www.mmcoa.org), and enthusiasm in Mustang circles runs high.

Mustang Reborn: California Scooter Company

Ed Seidner founded one of the largest motorcycle superstores in the country, Bert's Mega Mall in Covina, Calif., which today sells new Hondas, Ducatis, Triumphs and many more. Son Steve ran that operation until he branched out on his own, starting motorcycle accessory company Pro-One Performance Manufacturing.

Steve Seidner with a modern Mustang in front of a P-51 Mustang.

Ed never had a Mustang, but his friend Billy Buster had one when they were kids and Ed always wanted one. Steve grew up hearing stories about Billy Buster and his Mustang, so he decided to do something about it. He bought an unrestored 1954 Mustang on eBay and took it home to the Pro-One production facility to restore it, a surprise gift for Ed. Steve quickly discovered three things: Customers walked right past ultra-sleek Pro-One V-twins for a better look at the unrestored Mustang; the Mustang was a simple design; and the little bike was solid. In fact, after Steve drained the stale gas, cleaned the fuel lines and filled the bike's peanut tank, the old Mustang started on the first kick.

Steve's response was swift. With the 56-year-old Mustang as a template, he started California Scooter Company, making the bikes he believes Mustang would build today. The new CSC motorcycles are EPA and CARB approved with modern amenities like electric start, turn signals, speedometer, hydraulic disc brakes, etc.

The bikes are built in La Verne, Calif., about 30 miles from the original Mustang factory, while the engines are sourced from Asia. Three years after introducing the 150cc CSC 150, CSC introduced the 250cc P-51, taking the P-51 designation from the World War II Mustang airplane. With its larger 250cc counter-balanced single overhead cam engine, the P-51 absolutely rips. The Mustang formula — short wheelbase, light weight and 12-inch wheels — still works.

So how does the new compare to the old? Fully broken in, my 150cc red CSC Classic tops out at about 66mph. With their 320cc engines, the original Mustangs were crazy fast. My geezer buddies tell me a stock Mustang would do 70mph (how they knew that is beyond me, as Mustangs didn't get speedometers until the late 1950s). I've touched 80mph on the new P-51.

I've ridden vintage Mustangs, but because of their value I was afraid to push them too hard. The old Mustangs feel a little wobbly to me, but of course they have old forks and old tires. The new bikes benefit from more than 50 years of advancements in technology. When I take my CSC on Glendora Ridge Road, the bike is light, tight and an absolute delight through the twisties.

Which bike is faster or better is moot. Both are awesome, and each offers a riding experience like no other. There's one fact, though, that riders of vintage Mustangs and new California Scooters both have to accept: You can't go anywhere without drawing a smiling crowd.

— *Joe Berk*

Chapter 3: The 250 Mustang, Zongshen, and the RX3

We learned about the RX3 almost by accident, which is sort of the same way my first visit to Zongshen came about. I was in China on an engagement with Zebra Technologies, a US printer company that does its manufacturing in China. You might think you don't know Zebra, but you know their products. Zebra makes commercial printers, and their product line includes the printers governments use to make driver's licenses and identification cards, the little printers that print your gas receipts when you pay at the pump, and the belt-worn printers guys in rental car places use when you return a rental car. How I got hooked up with those guys is a lesson in serendipity that's not important here, other than the fact that I found myself in Guangzhou presenting a failure analysis course to a group of Zebra engineers.

This was around the same time we were looking for a 250cc engine for the Mustang. We had originally introduced the modern Mustang as the CSC 150 (so named because of its 150cc engine). Of course, as soon as we did this, all of the experts told us we should have had a 250cc engine for a variety of reasons (all of which were bunk):

- The Mustang purists didn't like the 150cc engine because the original Mustangs had a 322cc engine (which was originally designed for a cement mixer). The purists said we needed at least a 250cc engine to be as fast as the original Mustang. Folks, I've ridden the original Mustang, and I'm here to tell you the CSC 150 would kick its butt in either a drag race or in the twisties. And to all you guys who want to tell me your original Mustangs would go 70 mph, all I can say is this: How could you have possibly known that? Most of the original Mustangs didn't have speedometers.

- The next set of experts told us that we needed a 250cc engine for the bike to be freeway legal. It was more bunk. I called a couple of local police departments to ask them the requirements for freeway use in California, and they didn't know. I called our local California Highway Patrol office, and they didn't know. Finally, I called the CHP Academy in Sacramento and spoke to the guy in charge of Motor Officer training. He didn't know, either, but he said he would research it and get back to me. To my surprise, he called me the next day and delivered the verdict: As long as a motorcycle or scooter has a 150cc engine (or larger), it's freeway legal. Which was, I guess, a good thing because I rode my CSC 150 on the freeway regularly.

- And finally, another set of experts told us the bike would sell a lot better with a 250cc engine. That argument seemed to be the most compelling, but after we introduced the 250cc engine we found that the CSC 150 and the CSC 250 sold in equal numbers.

Zongshen was on our radar because our research back in California indicated that they had an air-cooled 250cc engine that was externally identical (at least where it mounted to the frame) to the 150cc Taiwanese engine we used in the CSC 150. We already had purchased a Zongshen 250 engine, fitted it in the CSC 150 frame, and we were working through the details of incorporating it into what would become the CSC 250.

I called Steve on Skype and told him I was one hour away from Zongshen by air, and for the cost of an airline ticket, I could put my eyes on the company and the people running the factory. "Do it," Steve said, and that weekend I was wheels in the wells headed to Chongqing.

One of many buildings on the Zongshen manufacturing campus.

I think the easiest way to describe that visit is to share the email I sent to Steve while I was in Chongqing. The first part of the letter addresses some of the issues we were working through on the air-cooled 250cc Mustang engine, and the rest describes my tour of the Zongshen campus.

Steve:

I had a good visit with Zongshen yesterday. We discussed many topics. Here's how our day went:

- *I met with four Zongshen managers. These include Deng Wei (Vice Supervisor of the Inland Sales Company), Li Fei (Vice-Director of the Technical Department), Shen Haibo (Vice-Director of the Technical Department), and Miss Deng (a less senior sales manager). Deng Wei spoke English. The other three spoke very little English.*

- *I told the Zongshen people about our interests, and they agreed to provide pricing in a follow-up email. I explained* to them what we wanted during the meeting (and I will send them an email requesting pricing in these areas later today). I told them we were interested in prices in several areas:

1. The OHC 250cc counterbalanced engine.
2. The OHV 250cc engine.
3. The exhaust pipe, muffler, and catalytic converter (I left our drawing for this assembly with them).
4. Complete subassemblies (as we currently buy for our motorcycle).
5. I told them we had an interest in being Zongshen's U.S. distributor.

- Miss Deng and a driver picked me up in a Mercedes mini-van in the morning. It was about a 1-hour drive to the Zongshen campus. Chongqing is a massive and scenic city (it just seems to go on forever). Imagine mid-town Manhattan massively larger with taller and more modern buildings, built in a lush green mountain range, and you'll have an idea of what the city is like. We took a circular freeway around the edge of town, and the views were beyond stunning. It was an overcast day, and every time we came around a mountain we had another view of the city in the mist. It was like something in a dream. Chongqing is the Chinese name for the city. We in the US used to call it Chun King (like the noodle company). We drove for an hour to get to the Zongshen campus, and we were still in the city. I've never seen anything like it. The city is awesome. I could spend 6 months here just photographing the place.

- The Zongshen campus is similarly huge, and completely modern. It is on a landscaped campus (all fenced off from the public) in the city's downtown area. We were ushered into their office building complex, which is about as modern and clean as anything I have ever seen. You can probably tell from this email that I was impressed.

- When we met in the conference room, Mr. Deng (the

marketing Vice Supervisor) appeared to be in charge. I explained what we wanted, and he said they could do nearly all of it. Specifically, he readily agreed that they would be interested in building the 10 major subassemblies for our bike. He said doing this was "no problem at all."

- I asked about the coil, the CDI, the harness, the regulator, and the stator. I explained to them what we did to make the 250cc Zongshen engine run in our bike. As we anticipated, they could not answer questions about the performance characteristics of their engine using the current components, as they are not familiar with the specifications of the current devices. Mr. Li (their engineering manager) thought that the performance of their engine would probably be better when used with their components. They had not heard of our current engine manufacturer.

- I explained the engine misfires we experienced after running the 250cc OHC engine at high speeds for an hour (as occurred during my test rides); again, they could not answer because they do not know the current engine components' specifications. Mr. Li volunteered that we might be damaging the engine mechanically by mixing and matching components due to firing at the wrong time (which would likely be occurring with the mismatched components). They said the best thing to do was to modify our harness to work with their components, rather than the approach we took (mixing components to work with our existing harness). They said they could design an appropriate harness for us, and they would do so if we buy from them.

- I asked if their CDI incorporates a rev limiter. It does not.

- Zongshen has a few motorcycles and scooters that have received EC (European Community) certification. They do not have any motorcycles that have received US EPA or CARB certification. They do have scooters, though, approved in the US (see the next paragraph).

- *Zongshen manufactures scooters, and they have two models that have EPA and CARB certification. I explained that we would be interested in these as possible powerplants for a potential Cushman or Salsbury-type CSC vintage bike. These powerplants include CV transmissions (no shifting). Unfortunately, these would not be directly available to us, as Zongshen has a marketing contract with the current buyer restricting their ability to sell to others.*

- *I asked about our becoming a Zongshen distributor in the US. They explained again that their motorcycles are not US certified (DOT/EPA/CARB). I said that we have expertise in this area, and we could assist in this effort. Mr. Deng said they would be interested in exploring such a relationship. I think there is a great opportunity here.*

- *I asked about a drive train for our trike. Mr. Deng explained that even though they show several ATVs as Zongshen offerings in their catalog, they do not make the ATVs (they only make the engines and transmissions for them). Zongshen provides the engines and transmissions to ATV manufacturers in the Chongqing area, and those companies make the complete ATVs. Mr. Li told me that the ATV companies that make the complete vehicles use rear ends/differentials with chain drive (not shaft drive), and if we had an interest, they would work with us and these suppliers to develop and procure a drive train. Chongqing is apparently the motorcycle capital of China, so there are several companies in the area making motorcycles, engines, ATVs, scooters, and other vehicles.*

- *Zongshen has onsite die casting capabilities, so they can make covers without the Zongshen label (and with a CSC logo).*

- *In order to provide a meaningful quote to us, they will need our drawings and product samples. I know we have intellectual property concerns, but I don't see any way to get a quote without disclosing our design information to them.*

- I asked about their lead times and production capacities. They can tell us the lead times after they receive enough information on the subassemblies to provide a quote. They have enormous capacity, so I don't think anything we order will significantly impact their production load (you'll see more on this in the photos below).

- I explained that one concern we had is that we are relatively small, and we did not know if Zongshen would be interested in our orders because the quantities would be low compared to their other production activities. Mr. Deng told me that they are interested, and addressing our requirements would not be a problem.

The above covers our business conversation related to the air-cooled 250cc engine. I asked to see the factory, and they took me on a factory tour.

In a word, their production operation is awesome. I was thinking the entire time what fun it must be to run this kind of a facility.

Zuo Zongshen is the name of the man who started the business. The company is about 20 years old. Mr. Zuo is still actively engaged running the business. There are photos of him in various places in the plant's different buildings. I noticed that he was not wearing a beret. I asked one of the people showing me around what the Chinese characters beneath his photos said and he told me "I want Joe to write our blog..."

The Zongshen office building is very modern and very nicely decorated inside.

The Zongshen campus was huge. I would estimate that it covered maybe 8 or 10 acres. My guess is that they have something in excess of 1.5 million square feet of manufacturing space. They have several machining centers, all running modern CNC equipment.

There were several buildings like the machining centers on the Zongshen campus. It was overwhelming. This is a big company.

The people who work here live on the Zongshen campus (Zongshen provides apartments for these folks). The average Zongshen factory worker earns in the range of 2000 to 3000 Yuan monthly, which converts to $316 to $475 US dollars. They work a 5-day, 8-hour-per-day week, which pencils out to a range of $1.85 to $2.80 per hour. It looked like a pretty nice life. Zongshen employs about 2,000 people.

In addition to all of the motorcycle work, Zongshen makes power equipment (like Honda does). They have a complete facility dedicated to just that product line.

I next visited one of their engine assembly buildings (they had several buildings dedicated to engine assembly). The building I saw was modern, clean, and the assembly work appears to be both automated and manual (depending on the operation). Note that we were in the factory on a Saturday, so no work was occurring.

Zongshen makes something north of 4,000 engines every day.

Yep, 4,000+ engines. Every day.

The engines enter an automated engine test room after assembly. They had about 100 automated test stations in there.

Zongshen makes engines for their own motorcycles as well as for other manufacturers.

I observed engines of several sizes, including 500cc, water-cooled Zongshen motorcycle engines.

Zongshen can make engines in nearly any color a manufacturer wants. I saw a large display highlighting the different colors they can provide.

They do their own die casting in house.

Quality appears to be very, very high. They have the right visuals in place to monitor production status and to identify quality standards. Visual standards are posted throughout the factory, as were production status boards and assembly instructions.

I also visited the men's restroom to see if it was clean. When I assist manufacturers elsewhere, I always want to see the restroom. You can tell a lot about a company's management based on the condition of the latrines. Not surprisingly, they were immaculate. There's a humorous sign in the Zongshen men's room: Be happy in your work, don't take too long, come in here in a rush, and don't forget to flush.

We then briefly ducked into another machining center. It was dark so I only grabbed a couple of photos. They use statistical process control in manufacturing their machined parts, which is a sign of an advanced quality management approach.

I also have (but did not include here) photos of their engine testing area. They test *all* engines (a 100% test program), and the test approach is automated. I was impressed. I believe their quality will be as good as or better than any engine made anywhere in the world.

Miss Deng took us next to a factory showroom at the edge of the Zongshen campus.

I saw about 50 different motorcycles and scooters that Zongshen manufactures. The bikes were really nice. I looked at the price on one and it was 8980 RMB (or Yuan). That converts to (get this) a whopping $1470 US dollars. I want one.

The Chinese postal service uses Zongshen motorcycles….as do Chinese Police departments, and a lot of restaurants and other commercial interests. They make green bikes for the Chinese Post Office, and the red ones are for commercial delivery services. These are seen everywhere in China.

Zongshen also has a GP racing program, and they had their GP bikes on display.

That's it for now. I will send an email to the Zongshen team later today confirming what we want from them and I will keep you posted on any developments.

Thank you for the opportunity to make this visit. As you can probably tell, Chairman Mao would be proud of me...I am happy in my work.

If you wouldn't mind, please let me know you have received this email. I want to make sure you received it.

The above email pretty much captures the spirit of my first visit to Zongshen in December 2011. To say I was impressed would be an understatement. These guys clearly had their act together, and they had everything a modern manufacturing facility should have. I don't say this lightly. I teach advanced manufacturing methods at the California State Polytechnic University, I've written several books in this area, and I teach manufacturing methods to US and international clients. All that notwithstanding, I felt the guys in Chongqing could teach me. I was that impressed with their operation.

To make a long story a little less long, we incorporated the Zongshen 250cc air-cooled engine into our Mustang, and the bike did well. That little motorcycle would hit an honest 80 mph with the 250cc engine (the 150cc CSC bike does might see 66 mph on a good day). Sales didn't jump (another marketing prediction that failed to materialize), but the Zongshen engine was bulletproof. We've used that engine for several years and we never had any problems with it.

All the while we were buying the 250cc engine for our little Mustangs, we kept an eye on the other things Zongshen was doing. We were surprised and excited the day we inadvertently tumbled to the RX3 project. When we first saw it, we knew it was a game changer. The styling was world class, and the market niche was spot on. I am an adventure touring kind of guy and I loved the concept. The fact that the RX3 was a 250 made it even more attractive. Oh, I know there are lots of guys who think a 250 is too small, but they really don't know. They only think they do. The reality of it is they've been brainwashed (more on that in the next chapter). To my way of thinking, a 250 is the perfect size for a real word adventure touring motorcycle.

Steve immediately recognized the RX3's potential, and he's the guy with the bucks who makes the decisions. The direction was clear: We would go after the RX3 in earnest and bring it to America.

Chapter 4: Why a 250?

One question we sometimes hear is why we went with the 250cc engine for the RX3. The answer is similar to the one Jesse James gave when they asked him why he robbed banks (which was, of course, "That's where the money is"). In our case, the 250cc RX3 is the bike Zongshen offers. Zongshen knew what they were doing when they selected this engine size. A 250cc engine makes a lot of sense for a lot of reasons.

To understand all of this better, particularly from our "bigger is better" American perspective and our predilection with enormous motorcycles, let's take a trip down memory lane.

The motorcycle craze in the US really started in the mid-1960s. I know motorcycling goes back way before that, but motorcycling was essentially a fringe endeavor until Honda came on the scene. We met the nicest people on Hondas, if you remember, and that ad tagline was a winner (as would be "Don't Miss The Boat," which I'll explain in a subsequent chapter).

Honda's sales model was a good one. They roped us in with small bikes and then convinced us we needed larger and larger bikes. Many of us started with a Honda Cub (the 50cc step-through), we progressed to the Super 90 (that was where I jumped in back in the day, as you can see in the very grainy photograph included here for entertainment purposes only), then the 160cc baby Super Hawk, then the 305cc Super Hawk, and at that point in about 1967, that was it for Honda. They didn't have anything bigger (yet). After the 305cc Super Hawk, the next step for most folks was either a Harley or a Triumph.

1965, yours truly, and a Honda Super 90. Those were the days!

You know, back in those days, a 650cc motorcycle was considered a big motorcycle. And it was.

But Honda kept on trucking…they offered a 450 that sort of flopped, and then in 1969 they delivered the CB-750. That bike was so far in front of everyone else it killed the British motorcycle industry and, with a lot of self-inflicted wounds in Milwaukee, it almost killed Harley.

The Japanese manufacturers piled on. Kawasaki one-upped Honda with a 900. Honda came back with a 1000cc Gold Wing (which subsequently grew to 1100cc, then 1500cc, and is now an 1800cc). Triumph now has a 2300cc road bike. Harley gave up on cubic centimeters and describes their bikes with cubic inches. And on and on it went. It seems to keep on going. The bikes keep on getting bigger. And bigger. And bigger. And taller. And heavier. And bigger. In a society where everything was being supersized (burgers, bikes, and unfortunately, our beltlines), bigger bikes have ruled the roost for a long time. Too long, in my opinion.

Weirdly, today many folks think of a 750 as a small bike. It's a world gone nuts.

I've done a lot of riding. Real riding. My bikes get used. A lot. I don't much care for the idea of bikes as driveway jewelry, and on a lot of my rides in the US, Mexico, and Canada, I kind of realized that this "bigger is better" mentality is just flat wrong. It worked as a motorcycle marketing strategy for a while, but when you're wrestling with a 700-lb bike in the soft stuff, you realize it doesn't make any sense.

Don't get me wrong. Big bikes can be fun, and I've had some killer big bikes. A Triumph Daytona 1200. A Harley Softail. A TL1000S Suzuki. A Triumph Speed Triple (often called the Speed Cripple, which in my case sort of turned out to be true, as I explained in Chapter 1). All the while I was riding these monsters, I'd see guys on Gold Wings and other 2-liter leviathans and wonder…what are these folks thinking?

Maybe it was time to dial it down a bit.

I'd always wanted a KLR 650 for a lot of reasons. The biggest reasons were that the KLR 650 was inexpensive back then, and they were lighter than the two-wheeled armored vehicles I had been riding. I liked the idea of a bike I could travel on, take off road, and lift by myself if I dropped it.

To make a long story short, I bought the KLR and I liked it. I still have it. But it's tall and it's heavy (well over 500 lbs fully fueled). Even with its height and weight, though, it was a better bike for real world riding than the behemoths I'd been wrestling on my road trips. And the KLR 650 just seemed like an honest motorcycle. Nobody buys a KLR to be a poser, nobody chromes out a KLR, and nobody buys leather fringe for a KLR. If that's what you want in a motorcycle, hey, more power to you…go live to ride and ride to live, save lives with your loud pipes, and, well, you get the idea. Me? I just wanted to get out and see the world, and do it on a motorcycle that made sense. I wasn't trying to prove anything to anybody with my motorcycle.

More background on my riding: I love to ride in Baja. It is one of my favorite places in the world. I talk about it all the time when I'm around other riders. My friends tell me I should be on the Baja Tourism Board. Whatever. Baja has some of the best riding in the world.

I was talking up Baja one day at the First Church of Bob (the BMW dealership where I hang out with some of my buddies on Saturday mornings). There I was, talking about the road to San Felipe through Tecate, when my good buddy Bob (who owns the dealership) said, "Let's do it."

Baja it was...the other guys would ride their Harleys and uber-Beemers, and I would be on my "small bore" KLR. The very next weekend we pointed the bars south, wicked it up, and rode to San Felipe.

The Boys in Baja...bound for San Felipe with my KLR 650 leading the pack.

That was a fun trip. I took a lot of ribbing about the KLR, but the funny thing was I had no problem keeping up with the monster motos. In fact, most of the time, I was in the lead. And Bob? Well, he just kept studying the KLR. He sold BMWs, but the KLR was speaking to him. I could see it.

On Saturday night at dinner in a restaurant overlooking the Sea of Cortez, Bob opened up a bit. Bob is the real deal…he rode the length of Baja before there was a road. That's why he was enjoying this trip so much, and it's why he was so interested in my smaller bike. In fact, he announced his intent to buy a smaller bike, which surprised everybody at the table.

Bob told us about a months-long moto trip he made to Alaska decades ago, and his dream about someday riding to Tierra del Fuego. That's the southernmost tip of South America. He'd been to the Arctic Circle, and he wanted to be able to say that he'd been all the way south, too.

I thought all of this was incredibly interesting. Bob is usually a very quiet guy. He's the best rider I've ever known, and I've watched him smoke Ricky Racers on the Angeles Crest Highway with what appeared to be no effort whatsoever. Sometimes he'd do it on a BMW trade-in police bike standing straight up on the pegs passing youngsters on Gixxers and Ducksters. Those kids had bikes with twice the horsepower and two-thirds the weight of Bob's bike, and he could still out ride them. Awesome stuff. Anyway, Bob usually doesn't talk much, but during dinner that night on the Sea of Cortez he was opening up about some of his epic rides. It was good stuff.

Finally, I asked: Bob, what bike would you use for a trip through South America?

Bob's answer was immediate: A 250.

That surprised me, but only for an instant. I asked why and he told me, but I kind of knew the answer already. Bob's take on why a 250: It's light, it's fast enough, it's small enough that you can pick it up when it falls, you can change tires on it easily, you can take it off road, you can get across streams, and it gets good gas mileage.

Bob's answer about a 250 really stuck in my mind. This guy knows more about motorcycles than I ever will, he is the best rider I've ever known, and he didn't blink an eye before immediately answering that a 250 is the best bike for serious world travel.

It all made a lot of sense to me. I had ridden my liter-sized Triumph

Tiger in Mexico, but when I took it off road the thing was terrifying. The bike weighed north of 600 lbs, it was way too tall, and I had nearly dropped it several times in soft sand. It was not fun. I remembered another ride in Mexico with my friend Dave when he dropped his FJR in an ocean-sized puddle. It took three of us to get the thing upright, and we dropped it a couple of more times in our attempt to do so. John and I had taken my Harley and his Virago on some fun trips, but folks, those bikes made no sense at all for the kind of riding we did.

You might be wondering...what about the other so-called adventure bikes, like the BMW GS series, the Yamaha Tenere, or the Triumph Tiger? Good bikes, to be sure, but truth be told, they're really street bikes dressed up like dirt bikes. Big street bikes dressed up like dirt bikes, that is. Two things to keep in mind...seat height and weight. I can't touch the ground when I get on a BMW GS, and my days of spending $30,000 on a motorcycle are over. Nice bikes and super nice for freeway travel, but for around town or off road or long trips into unknown territory, these bikes are just too big, too heavy, and too tall.

There's one other benefit to a small bike. Remember that stuff above about Honda's 1960s marketing strategy? You know, starting on smaller bikes? Call me crazy, but when I get on bikes this size, I feel like a teenager again. They are fun.

I've thought about this long and hard. For my kind of riding, a 250 makes perfect sense. My invitation to you is to do the same kind of thinking.

Chapter 5: The Test Bikes and the Media

We ordered three RX3 motorcycles from Zongshen to start the certification process in the United States. Based on the RX3 colors we had seen online and in Chongqing, I knew one of the bikes had to be orange. I wanted that one for myself. We ordered one bike in orange, one in red, and one in blue. We didn't order a white one, although that became one of our more popular colors once we started bringing the bikes to the US.

We had to submit a letter to the EPA to allow the bikes to enter the United States. The EPA subcontracts this function to a consulting organization, so we submitted the letter to those guys and we had a quick answer. We were good to go. The EPA letter didn't allow us to sell the bikes; it only allowed us to bring them into the US for testing and for limited street use (you know, so we could evaluate the bikes),

The process of getting a bike certified in the US is not an easy one, and it isn't cheap. You have to get that EPA letter I describe above, then you have to purchase the bikes, then you have to arrange for shipping through a shipping broker, then you need a customs broker to bring them through the US port and inspection process, then you have to transport them to your facility, then you have to build the bikes, and then you submit them to another consultant organization that does the actual testing. That takes weeks, as the test guys have to run the bike for close to 10,000 kilometers on the dynamometer. If the test results are good on the dynamometer, the bike goes into shed testing. That's where it's tested for volatile emissions escaping from the crankcase or the fuel tank, and this is usually the most difficult test to complete successfully. The bike can fail the shed test if the chain has too much oil on it. It's not an easy process. If you get through all the above, then you fill out a multipage EPA form appropriately titled the Oppressive Questionnaire (no kidding; that's its actual name), Then you submit it to the federal government and hope for the best, And, if you want to sell bikes in California, you get to do the same thing all over again with the California Air Resources Board.

All of the above is not cheap. The cost approaches $100,000 for each motorcycle. That's a part of the business most people don't know about, but it's there and it's real, and it had to be factored into the cost of the motorcycle.

From time to time, I have friends ask me or I see comments on the Internet about buying bikes directly. The gist of these comments is that you can just buy a couple of bikes on Ali Baba (it's sort of a Chinese Amazon.com) and bring them into the US, Whoever is selling those bikes will take your money, but lots of luck getting them through the port and US Customs. You'll need even more luck if you ever try to register such bikes. Trust me on this: It's not going to happen.

When our three test RX3 motorcycles arrived, it was both exciting and messy. It was exciting because they were new and exciting; it was messy because there were no assembly instructions and everything was packed tightly into the crates. There were lots of fasteners (nuts, bolts, and washers) and we had no idea what went were. The engine guards were complicated, the luggage mounted to the engine guards, the front wheels were not installed, the windshield and handlebars were not installed, and in general, the bikes were giant three-dimensional jigsaw puzzles.

We laid out everything that came with the bikes in our service area and after scratching our heads for a while, we managed (after much trial and error) to get one of the bikes assembled. It was a thing of beauty, and the ergonomics were perfect. We built a second bike and we were on the road. Steve and I took the bikes up to Crystal Lake. They were awesome. I must have taken 500 photos that first day. The bikes were perfect. I knew that our only challenge would be getting people to ride the bike; once anyone rode it, the sale was a given. No one could see and ride the bike without buying it. It was that good.

Ah, but that setup! We would clearly need to do better on the production bikes regarding the setup process, and it was obvious we'd have to provide instructions to our customers when we started selling the bikes. We've done that. What we have found since is that RX3 distributors in other countries go to our CSC website to find out how to put their motorcycles together. It's pretty funny when you think about it.

When I first rode the RX3, I was blown away by the power and handling. It's a torquey little bike, and truth be told, it wasn't too much slower than my KLR 650. The handling was light years ahead of the KLR. The RX3 was nimble and responsive. My KLR always felt like the frame was made of rubber. The RX3 felt like a sportsbike with a sensible seating position. The shifting was buttery smooth, and the gears were evenly spaced. The instrument cluster was impressive, with an analog tach, a temp gage, a fuel gage, a clock, an odometer and a trip meter, a gear position indicator, and a digital speedometer. I loved it.

The coolest aspects of the bike, for me, were its power, its comfort, and its handling. The seating position was perfect for me. The power was a nice surprise. I had ridden 250s before and I was expecting low power and a struggle to get up to cruising speed, but the RX3 wasn't like that at all. It rowed through the gears nicely, and it had no problems getting up to an indicated 80 mph quickly.

We found that the speedometers on the first three test bikes were wildly optimistic (I knew we'd have to get that addressed with Zongshen), but the bikes were solid. The handling was very, very impressive. The bike has a fairly short wheelbase and the suspension is taut. I knew the thing would positively shred through the corners up in the San Gabriel Mountains behind the CSC plant (something I proved that day). It was a great machine.

We knew that the bikes were a go as soon as we unpacked and

assembled them, and we issued a press release to let the rest of the world know.

CSC Announces New 250cc Adventure Touring Motorcycle

AZUSA, Calif. - Aug. 25, 2014 - CSC Motorcycles announced this week that it will offer a new 250cc dual sport, adventure touring motorcycle. The new bike, named the CSC RX-3 Cyclone, is the first fully-equipped 250cc bike of its type to be offered in the United States.

"We are serious adventure riders," said Steve Seidner, President and Chief Executive Officer of CSC Motorcycles. "We've done very well with our line of 150cc and 250cc Mustang replicas. Our niche is ultra-high quality, sensibly-sized motorcycles. The riding community asked us to offer a 250cc fully-equipped bike designed for adventure touring. These are folks who might ride anywhere in the lower 48 or head to places like Alaska, Canada, or Mexico. It's our kind of riding."

"The current crop of adventure bikes," Seidner continued, "all seem to be designed for folks who are 7-ft tall. The big adventure bikes are nice, but they are huge. We think they weigh too much, and we think they are not a good solution for exploring the world when the riding is off-road. We wanted to bring an adventure touring bike to the US market that makes sense for both on and off road exploration, and for trips that might last for weeks or months. We've ridden extensively through Mexico, and when your bike goes down in soft sand or deep mud, you don't want to struggle with something that weighs 700 lbs. Our new CSC Cyclone is perfect for exploring out-of-the-way places like the old missions south of the border and beyond. This is a bike that can go around the corner or around the world, and we're proud to be the company taking it through the certification process in America."

The new CSC RX-3 Cyclone is a 250cc, water-cooled, single-cylinder motorcycle with all road amenities, saddlebags, a luggage case, engine guards, and electric start. It has high ground clearance and tires designed for both on-road and offroad riding. The motorcycle weighs slightly over 350 lbs and it has an extended touring range.

CSC expects the US certification process to be complete within the next three months. The motorcycles will be offered in metallic blue, metallic red, orange, and pearlescent white color themes. Pricing will be announced shortly.

More information is available on the CSC Motorcycles website at www.CSCMotorcycles.com.

The reactions to the press release were good. We immediately had two magazines contact us (*ADVPulse*, and *ADVMoto*). They both ran our press release on their websites, and the word was officially out. I sent thank you notes to Rob Dabney at *ADVPulse* and to Paul Smith at *ADVMoto*, and both guys responded by asking for test rides.

Whoa, this was getting good. I invited Rob and Paul to visit with us that weekend. They showed up loaded for bear, as the saying goes. They had photographers and other people with them, and they all showed up on BMWs and KLRs. I rode my KLR 650 because we were only using two of the RX3 motorcycles on the street (it was all that the EPA exemption letter allowed us to do at that time).

I had a route in mind that would give the guys a good feel for the RX3 on freeways, on surface streets, in the dirt, and in the twisties. I didn't think the route was such a big deal, because it was what I would have wanted to do had I been writing an article. I took the guys east on the 210 from Azusa, north on the 15, west through Lytle Creek on surface streets, north again over the mountains on Sheep Canyon Road (a fairly gnarly dirt road), southwest across the mountains on Angeles Crest Highway (one of the world's great motorcycle rides), and back to Azusa on the freeways. It was about a 140-mile ride.

We stopped for lunch at the Grizzly Café in Wrightwood, and as we were arriving my KLR's rear brake felt unusually weak. The KLR's brakes are not exactly powerful (the RX3's brakes are better), so I didn't think that much about it until we pulled into the parking lot. To my amazement, the rear caliper on the KLR was hanging below the swingarm, attached only by its hydraulic line. Wow, that's never happened before, I thought.

We all had a good laugh about my KLR. The only bike with a failure on our press expedition was the tried-and-true KLR. The Chinese RX3s were holding up just fine.

I called Steve Seidner from the Grizzly Café to let him know where we were and what time we'd be back. He asked how the bikes were doing and if the magazine guys liked them.

"Well, we had one failure," I said. "The rear caliper came off a bike."

"Oh, no," Steve answered. "That's not good. Are the magazine guys upset?"

"It was on my KLR," I said. "The RX3s are doing just fine."

The magazine guys had a ball. We had a great ride and both magazines gave the bikes great reviews. Superlative reviews, in fact. I was really pleased with the results, and I especially liked this part in Paul Smith's *ADVMoto* story…

> For the day's demo, I was expecting an hour or two light ride around the city streets and perhaps a little freeway. But Joe surprised us with a realistic and rigorous test route that included a cross section of many of the environments one is likely to encounter when out there.
>
> It was everything from freeways, dirt and gravel roads, and steep inclined dirt track, to debris-infested mountain road twisties at high altitudes. In other words, he had no intention of babying us or the bikes.

The ride went well. I finished it on my front-brake-only KLR (I always said I didn't use the rear brake much, but trust me on this, when all you have is the front brake, it makes for a stressful ride). The magazine guys were impressed, and interest in the bikes picked up sharply.

We were soon contacted by *Motorcycle.com*, an online motorcycle magazine that is one of the largest in the world. When the oldest and biggest online motorcycle magazine gives you a call, you pay attention. Hell, we pay attention whenever a magazine calls us, but I had been following *Motorcycle.com* for 20 years (yep, they started in 1994). When they called, it was an especially good feeling. Tom Roderick (the writer) and Evans Brasfield (the photographer, who also does a lot of writing) came over to the CSC plant on their monster KTMs, and I led them out on my now standard magazine test ride (the same route I used for the *ADVPulse* and *ADVMoto* guys). Freeway, dirt, twisties...we did it all, and meeting these fellows and watching them work was a special treat.

Evans Brasfield capturing a shot of Tom Roderick for Motorcycle.com.

We rode into the little mountain town of Lytle Creek and then I took Tom and Evans up to Sheep Canyon Road for the "in the dirt" photos. After playing on the twisties leading into Lytle Creek and riding across the mountains in the dirt, we headed up Lone Pine Road to the Grizzly Café in Wrightwood.

I told Tom not to be afraid to push the RX3 and he most certainly was not. He and Evans passed me (I was riding my KLR) and that was it...those boys were gone. I couldn't catch even a glimpse of them they were so far ahead. I tried to catch up, consoling myself that Evans was on an 1199cc motorcycle and that's why I couldn't run in the same league. Tom, though, was on the 250cc RX3, and let me tell you, that guy can ride. I watched him lean into the first corner, and that was the last I saw of either of those guys until they stopped a few miles up the road for more photos. I'm a little bit embarrassed to tell you that Tom and the 250cc RX3 left me and my KLR in the dust. It was humbling, but impressive.

The *Motorcycle.com* story was another good one. *Motorcycle.com* has a numerical rating scheme and the little RX3 received a higher score than did the Yamaha Super Tenere. Tom had nice things to say about the bike. I especially liked this quote:

> *The moto world has been scoffing at motorcycles from China, Taiwan and other Pacific Rim Asian countries for years now. Maybe it's time we stopped. The reason behind the arrest is the soon-to-be-available 2015 CSC Motorcycles Cyclone RX3, a motorcycle with a quality of construction, fit and finish to rival bikes from Japan.*

Wow. We were on our way. We started issuing more press releases and more publications started taking an interest in us, including *Motorcyclist* magazine. *Motorcyclist* is one of the largest print magazines in the world, and we were excited when Ari Henning, their road test editor, contacted us. Ari spent a day with us in the mountains, and his article was also very favorable. Here are a couple of quotes from Ari I particularly liked:

> *We've grown accustomed to adventure bikes with big engines, hefty curb weights, and high price tags, so it's refreshing to see a versatile ADV that's less than extravagantly priced. The RX3 is a 250cc, 386-pound (claimed, dry) dual-sport with an astonishing $3,495 price tag. It's by far the most affordable option for a full-featured ADV, and after spending a full day on the bike we feel confident recommending it to anyone looking for an economical adventure.*

…and…

> *Based solely on its function and features, the RX3 is a remarkably good bike for the money. There's not much else on*

the market for that price and nothing that comes close to the RX3's level of amenities.

Every time these magazines mentioned us, they'd put something on their Facebook pages, and that helped us even more. We'd sell another 20 to 40 motorcycles every time a story appeared, and so far, we had spent virtually nothing on advertising.

This business of working with magazines is interesting. The four I mentioned above were all easy to work with and their reporting was accurate.

There were other magazines that expressed an interest, but to be blunt, they were a pain in the butt to work with and we took a pass.

One editor whom I had invited to ride the RX3 sent a condescending email basically telling me that his magazine did not "go for rides." His missive included a list of demands that I thought were outrageous. He wanted us to hire a photographer so that he could have hundreds of high resolution photos to choose from for an article he might write on us, and he wanted a bike provided to him for several weeks.

Another editor told us that he could not give us any editorial coverage unless he had the bike for several weeks and we established a dealer network (I'll talk more about the dealer issue in the next chapter).

Yet another editor told us that he really had not heard of us, but he was willing to consider doing a story if we sent him a bike for a few months. The funny thing, though, was that his advertising people sure seemed to know about us. We fielded calls from them regularly.

Finally, a fourth editor wrote an online story about us with numerous technical errors, factual errors, spelling errors, and grammatical errors. The article looked like it was written by someone in the 6th grade. He wanted to have a bike for several weeks, too. Sure. That's our business model. Give bikes to magazines with marginal writing skills and an inability to get the facts straight.

Even though some of these people were difficult, others were giving us great coverage. The word was out: We were bringing the RX3 to

America, we were getting good coverage in the press, and interest was high.

Now all we had to do was get approval from the US Environmental Protection Agency and the California Air Resources Board, and get the bikes configured the way we wanted them for the US market.

Chapter 6: The Path to Market

Steve and Maureen made the decision to bring the RX3 to America, but there were a lot of details we still had to work out. We were at the very beginning of what we knew was a major undertaking. There were several questions we had to answer:

- How do we sell the bikes? Through dealers, or direct?
- What should the price be?
- What should the warranty be?
- What do we need to keep in inventory for spare parts?
- What should the accessories be?
- How do we advertise, and how much should we spend on advertising?

And on and on it went. There were lots of details to work through, but the two biggest questions were those focused on price and the dealer issue. We attacked the dealer question first, as it would drive the price and many other things.

The dealer question was, in retrospect, relatively easy for us. Steve has extensive experience working as a dealer (he ran Bert's in Azusa for several years, the dealership started by his father and currently run by his brother). Steve had also sold motorcycles through dealers as a manufacturer with his Pro-One line and the CSC Mustangs.

The Pro-One bikes were big factory-produced choppers. Steve produced about 1200 of these monstrous motorcycles. They were huge bikes that cashed in on the Harley mania sweeping the US from the mid-1980s through the 1990s. The Pro-One bikes retailed for something around $40,000 and they had Harley clone engines as large as 124 cubic inches. These motorcycles were essentially show bikes. You could ride them on the street, but to hear others talk about it, after a few miles you were ready for a break. They were nothing I'd ever be interested in, but that's beside the point. The point here is that Steve sold the Pro-One motorcycles through dealers, so he had experience in working with dealers.

Pro-One Performance Manufacturing motorcycles prepped for shipment.

We also sold the CSC Mustangs through dealers, and at the height of the CSC 150 and CSC 250 motorcycles' popularity, I'd guess we had a dozen or so dealers.

The experience in working with dealers for us was not good. It takes a lot to get someone to be a dealer, every bike that sells through a dealer means a smaller margin for us, and most of the dealers required relatively constant hand holding. Speaking for myself (and not for CSC) I was aghast at some of the things we were experiencing with the dealers. They just weren't people I would want to do business with. I could only imagine what it must have been like for the consumers. We regularly got calls from people who wanted a Mustang, but didn't want to buy from their dealer because they had no faith in the dealer. What do you do in a case like that?

We looked at the dealer issue again when we decided to bring the RX3 to America. Part of the decision gets wrapped up in the cost issue, and part of it gets wrapped up in the "do I want to sell my product through these people?" issue. I'll get back to that second part in a minute or two.

Let me preface what I'm about to say by mentioning that in my life, I've known four or five good dealers. One is Laidlaw's Harley-Davidson in Rosemead, California. Those guys treated me fairly when I had my Harley more than 20 years ago and they were always ethical. Another was Cooper's Cycle Ranch in New Jersey (I'm reaching back 50 years on this one); those guys were great when my Dad bought his Hondas and Triumphs there, and when I bought my '65 Super 90 and '72 CB750 Hondas. Sherm Cooper was a former Triumph flat tracker, he was the guy who actually ran the place back then, and it was a real motorcycle shop. Bob Brown's BMW dealership in Pomona, California, is a great place. I know Bob Brown and he's the real deal, an honest man and a straight shooter. I've never owned a BMW, but several of my friends do and Brown's is Nirvana to them. I like Bert's in Covina. I've bought two motorcycles from Bert's (my Honda CBX and my Suzuki TL1000S) and Ron and his guys were good to me. And I like Douglas Motorcycles in San Bernardino. Art Guilfoil owns that place, he is an honest man, and the way he runs his dealership reflects that. I bought two modern Triumphs from Art (my Tiger and my Speed Triple).

But that's it. I'm 64 years old, I've been riding for 50 years, I've owned probably 30 or 40 motorcycles during those 50 years, and I can only name five dealers I'd peg as square shooters.

There are a lot of things I don't like about dealers. I'll try to cover that delicately and objectively in the next several paragraphs.

Dealers need to make money to stay in business; I'm not complaining about that. The typical dealer margin on a new motorcycle is 17%. That may not be what the dealer ultimately agrees to sell you a motorcycle for, but that's the minimum difference they expect between what they pay for a motorcycle and the manufacturer's suggested retail price. If you ignore everything else (freight, documentation, and setup, which I'll address below), that would bump the RX3 price up to about $4100.

You might think you're clever or you're getting a great deal because the dealer shows you the dealer invoice (or you found it on the Internet). Folks, that's all smoke and mirrors. The whole dealer invoice thing is misleading. When you see the dealer invoice and you pay another $100 or $200 (or even if you pay "dealer invoice") you might think you're doing well, but that's not the whole story. The dealers get a significant return from the manufacturer or the importer after the sale to you. You never hear about that part, but that's what occurs.

Dealerships love to pile on freight, documentation, and setup fees. You're getting screwed, blued, and tattooed if you accept what many of the dealers tell you about these fees. Dealers frequently inflate these costs wildly. Let me tell you just how bad this practice is: Some dealerships pay nothing for freight (it's already included in what they pay for the motorcycle), but they still tack on outrageous freight fees. You'd think the bike was shipped from the planet Pluto based on what some of the dealers charge.

Setup fees are equally as bad. Typically, dealers install the front wheel and the handlebars when setting up a bike, put acid in the battery, and they might take it for a short test ride, yet it is not unusual to see $800 setup fees. It's compounded by the fact that many dealers don't even do the setup themselves (they subcontract it out to unskilled labor working a block or two away, and the dealer's cost might only be $25 per bike).

Documentation fees are another rip. Most dealers charge around $80 to $100 for the documentation fee. Their actual costs are much lower.

If you tack all of this nonsense on to the price of the RX3, plus that 17% margin I described above, the price jumps up to a whopping $5,839. Not surprisingly, that's very similar to what the Japanese 250cc bikes sell for. And they're not really made in Japan anymore, but that's another story for another time.

Let's put this in perspective in case you think the above fees are somehow reasonable. We charge $195 for the setup fee on a new RX3. When we do the setup, we install the handlebars, the guards, the luggage, the windshield, we drain the oil and install new oil, we check and adjust the valves, we install the front wheel, we adjust the chain and align the rear wheel, and we test ride every bike (and we do all this for $195). We charge actual freight on the motorcycle from our Azusa facility to your place, and we don't charge you freight from Zongshen to Azusa because it's already factored into the motorcycle price. And our documentation fee is $35 because that's what it costs.

If you want to sell through dealers, you have to have a national advertising program. That gets expensive. It's a significant expense that, in reality, gets passed on to you in the motorcycle's price. If CSC did that, it would raise the price of the motorcycle even further.

There's another aspect to all of this that you'll never hear about from a dealer (and you'll never hear about from a motorcycle manufacturer) and that's warranty fraud. When I consulted for a motorhome manufacturer, they had a full time guy (his name was Paul) who called every recreational vehicle owner after the dealer submitted an invoice to us for warranty work. Paul always started by telling the RV owner he was calling to find out if they were satisfied with the work performed on their vehicle. My thought when I first observed this was that it was a nice touch (you know, the manufacturer following up to find out if the customer was satisfied).

I mentioned that to Paul and he laughed. "We don't care if they're satisfied," he said. "We're just trying to find out how bad the dealer is screwing us. About 80% of the calls I make are to customers who have no idea what I'm talking about. They tell us there was never any warranty work done on their motorhome." When Paul saw my puzzled look, he continued. "The dealers submit fraudulent claims all the time." Wow. That was a surprise to me. Paul went on to tell me that they didn't go after the dealers that did this; the company just denied the warranty claim. The dealers never called to find out what happened to their claim (they knew they'd been caught). It just went on, sometimes succeeding and sometimes not, but when it did it was a windfall for the dealer.

If you think warranty fraud doesn't go on in the motorcycle world, think again. It isn't just you the dealer is lying to with inflated freight, setup, and documentation fees; it's likely at least some of them are doing the same thing to the manufacturer through fictitious warranty claims. The manufacturer has to temporarily bear these expenses when the dealer succeeds with fraudulent claims. Who do you think ultimately bears the cost of this practice? It's not the manufacturer, my friends. It's you, the consumer. That cost is factored in to what you pay for a new motorcycle.

There was another issued we were worried about, and that was the RX3 getting the attention it deserved in the dealers' showrooms. The concern here was simple. If you're a salesperson working in a motorcycle dealership, to which motorcycle would you steer potential customers? The $3,495 RX3, or other motorcycles that cost much more? Our fear was that the dealers would use the RX3 to bring in foot traffic, and then turn customers toward more expensive models. It's where the bigger sales commissions would be.

Finally, we were worried about the dealers' technical expertise in the service area. I'd be willing to bet that of all the times I had a dealer touch anything on any of my bikes, I had to bring it back at least half the time to have the dealer fix things they had done incorrectly, or missed, or screwed up in the process of fixing something else. I haven't been back to a dealer with any of my bikes in years for just that reason. I don't have confidence that their maintenance technicians will get it right.

The bottom line to us was that it didn't make sense to sell through dealers. We'd have to include the expense of a national advertising campaign, potential warranty fraud, and all the rest, and then hope the dealers would give our bikes the attention they deserve.

You know, it's a funny thing. Most riders don't have nice things to say about dealers. In fact, the parlance in the riding community is to call these places "stealerships." But when we announced that we would not use dealers, that was one of the most often-heard criticisms we heard on the Internet forums. I have no doubt some of it came from dealers or their employees (who did not identify themselves as such when posting their comments on the Internet). But some of it came from riders, too.

The decision for CSC was a simple one. Our strategy would be to build the business on reasonable profits and looking out for the best interests of our riders. To be as blunt as I can about this, if you need a dealer we're not for you. You can whine about that on the Internet until the cows come home, but it's not going to change. If you want to buy something like the RX3 from a dealer (there isn't anything else like this bike, but let's assume for the sake of argument there was), you would need to be prepared to buy it with a negotiation starting point of around $6,000. That's not what we wanted to put you through.

The next question for us, then, was what should the price be?

Ah, but that was a much more difficult question. There are many things that go into determining the price of anything, including actual costs, what the market will bear, and what your competitors are doing.

CSC was in a good spot from that last perspective. The other 250cc motorcycles out there are all in the $5000 to $7000 range without the accessories that are standard equipment on the RX3 (and they are all sold through dealers). None of them are competitors to the RX3. *Motorcycle.com* said it clearly in their review of the RX3:

> As the only one of its kind, the Cyclone RX-3 owns the 250cc adventure-touring category. Comparably sized competitors

include cruisers, sportbikes, nakeds, standards and retros from Honda, Kawasaki, Royal Enfield, Suzuki and Yamaha, as well as some lesser known OEMs. But when it comes to a motorcycle resembling a BMW R1200GS or Triumph Explorer in size 250cc, the Cyclone's the only game in town.

So, from a competition perspective, we were golden as long as we kept the price at or below our competitors' prices (and again, there really are no competitors).

I will tell you that our vision for the RX3 price is that it will stabilize somewhere below $5,000. The bike is $3,495 today, but it will not stay there. That's not the old "impending doom" sales close. The price will go up. We're adding overhead to serve our customers better, and that's not going to come out of profits. The RX3 will still be the best deal in town when we raise the price, but it's not going to stay at $3,495 forever.

The next consideration was: What will the market bear? We really didn't know, and actually, we didn't care. We didn't want to charge as much as we could. We wanted to base our price on our costs plus a reasonable profit, and still offer a hell of a deal to our riders.

And then there's the main consideration in pricing the bike, and that's our cost. You know, you can read all kinds of stuff on the Internet from self-appointed experts about what a motorcycle should cost, but the fact is most of the people posting these comments have no idea what they are talking about. One guy posted that our cost on the RX3 was $1,200, which is absurd. I responded to that poor ignoramus and told him he should quit whatever job he had (assuming he actually had one) and start a motorcycle company if he could buy RX3s for $1,200.

Our challenge was far more complex. We needed to factor in the cost of the bikes, how many bikes we would sell in a year, the freight from Zongshen to California, our shipping broker fees, our rent, our employees' salaries, our utilities costs, our insurance costs, the costs of getting the bikes approved by CARB and the EPA, and all of the other expenses that go into a venture like CSC. Then we had to use that to determine the bike's true cost to us, and finally, add to that our profit expectation.

When we did that, we assumed that profits the first year would be low. We were more interested in volume and giving good support to our customers. If people liked us and the bike, the motorcycle would sell itself. We knew the bike was golden (people who see it love it); we just needed to prove we would be there to support it. I think Steve, Ryan, Gerry, and the rest of the CSC team are doing exactly that. But don't take my word for it. Look at what others have said about CSC on the Internet. Those comments are accurate.

Based on our spreadsheet analysis of our operational costs, what we pay Zongshen for the bike, and our modest first year profit expectations, it was looking like the number would be $3,495. That's a hell of a deal, but we wanted to make a splash. We wanted to let the world know about the bike. We needed to get the word out.

We talked about spending $50,000 or so on a national advertising campaign. The problem with advertising, though, is that it has a long lead time, and it's not a science. I took a marketing course once and I remember the professor telling me that advertising isn't engineering. There's no advertising equation where you can plug in stuff and predict what your sales are going to be. You spend money on advertising trying different things and you hope for good results before you run out of money. That was his take on advertising, and this guy ran an advertising agency and taught the subject in MBA school.

We knew from our work on the CSC 150 that it was real easy to spend money on advertising (basically, we proved what that marketing professor had told me decades earlier). We knew we could not compete with the likes of Honda or Harley in the advertising world. We also knew we were getting good results with the CSC blog, our press releases, our Facebook page, and by posting things on the Internet.

Maureen said she'd rather forego profits or even lose a little money on the first bikes if doing so would get the word out. She suggested $2,995, and then after she said it, she changed her mind and made it $2,895. "$2,995 sounds like we're just trying to get the price under $3,000," she said. "I like the sound of $2,895 better."

I liked it. A lot. The concept was to let our first riders benefit from our efforts to make a splash. It was elegant. Maureen told me I should blog this right away, and let people know the offer wouldn't last long. "Tell people they don't want to miss the boat on this one."

Don't miss the boat. The bikes were actually inbound on a boat at that moment. Don't miss the boat. It was a perfect tagline, and it was a perfect name for the CSC introductory RX3 offer. Here's the blog that went out that same morning:

Don't Miss The Boat!
Posted on September 3, 2014

> CSC Motorcycles is certifying the CSC Cyclone RX-3 motorcycle in the United States. This new 250cc adventure bike is a great motorcycle, and we're not saying that because we're the folks bringing these bikes here. We know quality, we know manufacturing, we know Zongshen, and we know motorcycles. This is a great machine.
>
> We posted a bit about this motorcycle elsewhere and our plans for bringing it to America. We asked for your input, you responded, and we listened.
>
> **$2,895.**
>
> Yep, you read that right. The first shipment of these bikes will sell for $2,895 each. After the first shipment leaves the port, the price goes up to the bike's normal price of $3,495. The $2,895 price is a one-time offer. Once the ship leaves port, we won't sell any more motorcycles at this introductory price. Kick, scream, yell, call us names, it won't matter. The $2,895 price is for the first shipment only.
>
> We know the RX-3 Cyclone is a superior motorcycle and it's the perfect size for real-world adventure riding. But we need to get the word out. That's why we're selling the first shipment of these bikes for just $2,895.
>
> After the first shipment, we're going to sell the RX-3 for $3,495, which is a hell of a deal. It's a lot of motorcycle for $3,495:

Water-cooled, fuel-injected, overhead cams, counterbalanced, disk brakes, adjustable suspension, 6-speed transmission, rack, luggage, electric start, engine guards, full instrumentation, all the road amenities, a 1-year warranty, and the list goes on. But that's the price <u>after</u> the first group ships to the US. You might not want to wait that long.

You might be thinking a Chinese motorcycle, no dealer network, "just" a 250...why would I go for that? We're going to answer those questions one at a time, but not here. We'll be posting a series of articles on our CSC blog (just go to www.CSCMotorcycles.com and look for the blog). You'll see.

We're not asking for any money now. All you need to do is call us and get your name on the list with the color you want. When the bike completes the US certification process, we'll call you and ask for a $500 deposit. If you change your mind at that point, you're off the list and you won't be able to get back on. That first shipment may be 44 bikes, or it may be 440. It all depends on how many of you recognize the start of a good thing and want to get in on the ground floor.

*One time, folks. Now or never. It's your call, and our advice is simple: **Don't miss the boat.***

The reaction was immediate. I hit "publish" on the blogging software we use, and then I leaned back with a cup of coffee to read what I had just published (like you, I enjoy reading the CSC blog). The phone rang. It was a guy in Alaska calling to order an RX3 (our first bike sale). Three minutes, almost to the second, from the time I posted the blog. We were on to something here.

The next issue was the warranty and the maintenance approach. We knew that people would ask about this because we weren't going to use dealers. We had long discussions on these topics, and again, Maureen said it best. She wanted to use the word "empower" to describe how we would interface with our customers. Her vision was that we would empower our riders to do their own maintenance by providing a copy of the service manual for free with each bike, and by posting a series of maintenance tutorials on the blog about how to do normal maintenance things like changing the oil, adjusting the valves, changing a tire and all that.

I liked the idea of the tutorials and the free service manual. I didn't like the term "empower" because I thought it had too much of a New Age ring to it and the market wouldn't like it. I was wrong on that. No sooner had I used the term empower on the blog when people started mentioning it on the forums in a positive way. That caught me by surprise (it was a good surprise).

Then the issue became how long the warranty should last. Zongshen gives us a 1-year warranty, which would have probably been okay, but Steve wanted to do more. When we received a priced parts list from Zongshen, we were surprised at how low the costs were on nearly everything. Based on those two factors, Steve extended the warranty to 2 years.

Here's the blog we posted explaining the maintenance approach:

> **A Road Less Traveled**
> *Posted on October 16, 2014*
>
> *We're unconventional. You already know that based on how we're bringing the CSC Cyclone to you. After long discussions and much thought, we're taking a similarly unconventional path on the warranty and maintenance approach. We're betting that most of you either do your own wrenching already or, given the right support, you would like to do it yourself.*
>
> *Consider this: When was the last time you took your bike to a dealer for service and came away feeling good? Were you confident that the work was performed to your satisfaction? Did you pay a standard rate for a job that you knew didn't take as much time as you paid for? Did the dealer tack on other "standard" charges that just didn't feel right (for example, the infamous "shop supplies" hit)?*
>
> *Okay, you get the idea. Our intent is not to badmouth dealers. We just want two things: To provide a great ADV bike and to save you money. We know we're already doing that with the*

Cyclone (it's a quality motorcycle at a great price). We want to do the same thing with the service approach. To get to the bottom line, we want to empower you to do your own wrenching.

Think about it. The Cyclone is a bike designed to go the distance. It's an adventure touring motorcycle. If you need to fix something in Panama when facing the Darien Gap, or Baja somewhere south of Guerrero Negro, or even somewhere in the middle of the Mojave Desert here in the good old USA, is there going to be a dealer nearby? Folks, the simple fact is that when a bike needs work (especially an ADV bike), we're on our own. That's especially true for the places we're going on our Cyclones.

So let's get to the details. Here's how our program will be structured:

- *We're extending the Cyclone warranty to 2 years. This is a quality motorcycle with a warranty to back it up. The first year will be parts and labor; the second year will be parts only. You tell us what parts you need, and we'll shoot them out to you.*

- *When you buy a Cyclone, we'll include a service manual.*

- *We'll post detailed maintenance tutorials online. These will include oil changes, valve adjustments, chain adjustments, changing the fork oil, suspension adjustments, lubricating the chain, adjusting the rear wheel for proper chain tension, adjusting the clutch, removing and reinstalling the wheels, changing tires, changing the air filter, using the electronic diagnostic system, and more.*

- *For any work requiring the Zongshen diagnostic test devices (needed for seldom-required adjustments to the fuel injection system or for evaluating the electronics), at your discretion we'll either sell the electronic diagnostic equipment to you, or we'll Fedex one to you on a low-cost rental basis.*

> Our intent is to empower you to keep your Cyclone in tip-top condition, to save you money, and to give you the skills you need to address any maintenance items when you're out in the middle of nowhere.
>
> We realize there may still be folks who absolutely don't want to work on their bikes. We're betting that won't happen too often. But if you're in that category, fear not. We'll find an independent shop in your area and arrange whatever maintenance your bike needs directly with them.

I thought the above was pretty straightforward, and so did nearly everyone who read it. We still take hits on the forums every once in a while from people who don't quite seem to get it. One guy in particular was a real butt about it, and he was one of the guys who had made a deposit for a bike. He called me at home early in the morning one day wanting to know if he could become an authorized service center. I told him we weren't that far along yet, and I suggested he call Steve at work when we opened. Steve spent about an hour on the phone with the guy and his answer was the same: We're not yet designating businesses as authorized service centers. The guy then proceeded to post a series of negative comments on at least a couple of forums, and he essentially called us liars. For some reason, he was also hung up on the fact that our oil filter costs $12. He thought that was outrageous because he believed a KTM oil filter was cheaper. I guess that's okay. That's our price. If you don't like it, don't buy the bike. It's not like we were forcing you to buy health insurance or something.

To be blunt, the guy was difficult. We didn't want him as a customer, we sent him a message telling him that, and we refunded his deposit. I didn't tell him what I really thought. I thought he was nuts, and that if he was hung up on the oil filter, he should spend $20,000 for a new KTM so he could get his cheaper oil filter.

Telling this guy we didn't want his business really lit his fuse, and from time to time he continues to post adverse stuff on some of the forums. But we didn't sell a motorcycle to him and we never will. The bike is not right for all riders, and in this one case, a customer was not right for us. We make no apologies for that. We weren't the only people to reach this conclusion. This fellow was banned from the Chinariders.net site when he turned on the moderators, and when he posts negative things on the other forums, people jump on him and defend us. There are strange people out there, folks, and the Internet has given them a voice. I'll say more about that in the next chapter.

Our riders seem to be happy with us, with the RX3 warranty, with RX3 parts availability (we stock every RX3 part, including all of the engine's components), and with our customer service. We've had people post that CSC is better at supporting its customers than any other motorcycle manufacturer in the world. I believe they are right. And we are doing it without dealers.

As an aside, we are designating independent motorcycle repair shops as authorized CSC service centers, but we are doing it in a controlled manner. We will only use established brick-and-mortar operations with stellar financials, normal working hours, and superior customer feedback. That's for our customers who do not want to work on their motorcycles themselves. For you folks who enjoy getting your hands dirty, we're still providing a free service manual with every bike we sell, and we still have our maintenance tutorials posted online for your use.

I'd like to add one last thing about not using dealers. One fellow was particularly aggressive in condemning our path to market (it later came out that he worked for a dealer). I understand why he would be threatened by what we are doing. His final retort to me was that we must be pretty arrogant if we think we can change the industry. To that I say: We do not want to change the industry. We want dealers to keep offering $25,000, 37-inch seat height, 600-lb adventure bikes. We want dealers to keep their markups, their setup, freight, and documentation fees, their $1,000 valve adjustments, and all of the other things they do. If you're a dealer and you're reading this, please don't stop what you are doing. It gives us one of our strongest competitive advantages.

Chapter 7: Venom, Viciousness, and Vituperation

As you no doubt picked up in the preceding chapter, the Internet brings out the worst in people, but as we are learning, maybe sometimes that's not such a bad thing. We live in a great country in which people are free to express their opinions, even when they're dead wrong. It's worked well for over 200 years here in the good old USA, and it's sure working well for us here at CSC.

Let me start with a bit of background. When we secured approval by the US EPA, I prepared a press release.

US EPA Approves CSC Cyclone Motorcycle

AZUSA, Calif. - Jan. 1, 2015 - *CSC Motorcycles announced today that the United States Environmental Protection Agency approved the new CSC Cyclone motorcycle as compliant with US motor vehicle emissions requirements.*

The CSC Cyclone is a 250cc adventure touring motorcycle that includes engine guards, luggage, a windscreen, 6-speed transmission, a 4.2-gallon fuel tank, water cooling, and a counter-balanced, fuel-injected, overhead cam engine as standard equipment. CSC Motorcycles, an Azusa, California company, will distribute the CSC Cyclone in the United States and Canada (the Canadian approval process is pending).

"We're pleased with the EPA approval," said Steve Seidner, CSC Motorcycles President and Chief Executive Officer. "The CSC Cyclone is an adventure touring bike that makes sense, and we believe its 250cc engine size is a perfect solution to real world adventure touring needs."

Adventure touring is a motorcycle industry segment that is showing sharp gains, as is the 250cc market segment. Adventure touring involves traveling (frequently on an international scale) on both paved and unpaved roads. Adventure touring motorcycles include an upright seating position, tires suitable for both on and off-road use, and large capacity panniers (side bags). The CSC Cyclone is the only motorcycle of its type in the 250cc range.

"The combination of these two emerging markets – the adventure touring and the 250cc segments – represents a tremendous opportunity for CSC Motorcycles and for our customers," Seidner said. "Our CSC Cyclone has had extremely positive reviews from magazines focused on the ADV niche, including Adventure Motorcycle, ADVPulse, and Motorcycle.com. It's good to see that critical experts in this field agree with us; this is a great motorcycle and at its $3495 price, it represents incredible value. We know that the Cyclone's quality is as good as or better than any other motorcycle on the market today, including expensive European imports that cost 8 times as much as the Cyclone."

With the US EPA approval, the Cyclone can now be sold in all 50 states except California. California requires California Air Resources Board (CARB) approval. CARB approval of the CSC Cyclone is expected shortly.

The CSC Cyclone is manufactured to CSC specifications by Zongshen in China. The Cyclone motorcycles will start arriving in the US in February. CSC Motorcycles is accepting Cyclone orders now.

The EPA approval story was picked up by several magazines and websites, and like all of our press releases, it made its way around the Internet. One of the magazines is a technically superficial online publication called *RideApart*. Their story (which was essentially a very poorly written rehash of our press release) and the EPA approval subsequently got picked up by the Yahoo Autos page.

That's when the Cyclone's EPA approval story went viral. I can't imagine that anyone who knows anything about motorcycles (much less the adventure riding crowd) hangs out on the Yahoo Autos page, but as is frequently the case on Internet forums, it didn't stop a flood of more than 300 comments. There were positive and negative comments, but a lot of it was negative. And vicious. And full of venom. And vituperative (that means "sustained and bitter ranting and condemnation"). But mostly, the comments were just the uninformed rants of folks with nothing better to do. Ignorance sure didn't slow these boys down, though. The comments flooded in.

Our first reaction (when we read the first 100 or so comments) was that it was a bad thing.

Boy, were we ever wrong.

Ever hear the old expression about publicity? It goes like this: There's no such thing as bad publicity.

Well, as it turns out, the Yahoo Autos "experts" weighing in with their opinions on the RX3 (please note that none of them had ever ridden or seen the motorcycle) were actually doing us a tremendous service. For every one of these Triple-V folks (the venom, viciousness, and vituperation crowd) who posted their unfounded comments (and I'll list a few for your entertainment in just a bit), there must have been another 100 or so people who read the comments and then went to our website. Our website traffic quintupled that weekend, and that was a good thing. Why? Because that's where people discovered the facts. They saw the independent third-party articles by *ADVPulse*, *ADVMoto*, and *Motorcycle.com* (stories by real experts who actually rode the RX3 and gave it high marks).

The bottom line? Folks, the phones were ringing off the hooks and our email inboxes were full with inquiries that led directly to new orders. Criticism by ignoramuses on an Internet site? Bring it on!

So, about those comments. Here's a sample of some of the negative stuff...and I'm including all of the spelling and other errors (just as they were posted) to give you a sense of the underlying intellect:

> **From David**: *China makes nothing but Garbage*
> **From Larry**: *Just what we need,,,more Chinese #$%$ flooding the American marketplace,,,,*

The anti-China sentiment was a recurring theme in many of the comments. So, here we go with my responses: Um, okay, David and Larry: Does your anti-China sentiment extend to the computers you used when you sent your comments to Yahoo? Or did you submit your comments using your iPhones...you know, the ones made in China? And your clothes...do you leave the house naked because you won't wear stuff made in China? And your helmets and riding gear (assuming you boys actually ride motorcycles)...do you know that these items were almost certainly made in China? I could have gone on, but I think I made my point.

> **From Bobb**: *these engines have been around for many years not very good at all very poorly built motors,If you want a ok 250 enduro get a moto x aircooled way cheaper than 3500*

My response? Okay, Bobb with three b's: The RX-3 engine has been around since 2011. Perhaps when you visited the Zongshen factory you saw something different than I did. I saw a fully-automated, 100%-tested engine assembly line; a production line superior to any assembly operation I've ever seen in any factory anywhere in the world. And what exactly is a "moto x aircooled?"

> **From Izzy J**: *More Chineese junk ! Should probably buy AAA at same time. The people importing this #$%$ for sale should be ashamed of themselves.....or do they work for Walmart ?*

Ah, there's that Chinese thing again. My response: Izzy, I checked, and none of our CSC employees is moonlighting at WalMart. And the AAA thing...dude, I just don't get the reference. The Auto Club? Is that Freudian?

> **From Rich**: *I read this and thought of that scene in Dumb and Dumber where they are riding the minibike across country. This is a waste of money. There is no resale value and they won't last. Being a Harley rider, I'm usually not one to dog on what you are riding, but these are a waste of money.*

My response: Funny thing, Rich, we may have something in common. When I read your comment, that movie is exactly what came to my mind, too! Oh, and one more question...where do you think many of your Harley parts were actually made?

> **From ImMyOwnMan**: *This is NOT an Adventure bike. Sorry guys. There is no way you are going to get a weeks worth of luggage on that bike and have it roll down the road. May be an OK entry level dually, but an Adventure bike it is not. I have 2 KLR 650's and a Super Tenere. The KLR's are working pretty hard with a load. The Yamaha has more power than it would ever need. 250 cc's are laughable for any touring platform.*

My response: ImMyOwnMan, you certainly are! A week's worth of stuff for me when I'm on a motorcycle trip would basically be an extra pair of socks and maybe a pair of clean underwear. And I'd still have room left over for a lot more. Oh, and that thing about a 250 being laughable as a touring platform? You might want to check in with Simon Gandolfi, who went to Tierra del Fuego and back on his 125cc Honda.

> **From JoeSchmoe**: *Chinese garbage made by six year old Tibetan slaves chained to their workstations- YAY!*

Wow, where to begin on this one? Okay, here we go: JoeSchmoe. I don't know why, but I just don't like your name. But let's get past that. Okay, Mr. Schmoe, here's the deal: Unlike you, I've actually been in the Zongshen factory a number of times. There are no Tibetan slaves. Not even 6-year-old ones. And no one was chained to their workstations. Not even the guys installing the Cyclone's drive chains, which is the only place I saw a chain of any kind.

JoeSchmoe? Seriously? You could pick any screen name you wanted and you went with JoeSchmoe?

> **From MFWIC**: *wouldn't want a guy in a chopper to pull up next to me, if I was riding their Mustang bike.*

My response: MFWIC, your comment is one of the few I actually responded to on that Yahoo Autos page. We have folks on choppers pull up alongside us when we're on the Mustangs all the time. I get your point; it is a pain. They constantly ask us if they can sit on the Mustangs for a photo or three. It's a burden, but we bear it lightly.

Brandon, one of many Harley riders who wanted a photo on a CSC 250.

> **From J**: *Chinese junk!!!!!!!!!!!!!!!!!!!!!!!!!! The quality of the alloys and metals used in manufacturing over there is piss-poor at best.the only thing comparable to this bike would be another*

chinese p.o.s.! Which one of you test pilots got sucked into this? You should stick with your chink made scooter and leave real motorcycles to people that know something about them.what idiot pays you for your stupidity anyway? Thinking like that makes #10 for iowa look like a genius!

My response: Ah, yet another student of Chinese culture. J (and I should point out that this J is not my good friend J Brandon, who actually passed his 4th grade English class): The gentleman you are inquiring about (i.e., your question about "what idiot pays you for your stupidity anyway?"), well, that would be Steve. I'll relay your concerns to him.

I could go on, folks, but you get the idea. There are a lot of people who post incredibly stupid things on the Internet.

You know, when I first started doing this gig with CSC, I wondered what made people so critical and just plain mean on the Internet. The psychologists tell us people who criticize irrationally often see themselves in what they are criticizing, and they are really criticizing what they don't like about themselves. Maybe that's the case; I just don't know. Others say that the anonymity of the Internet brings out the worst in people. I sure believe that. And there's a third factor, I suppose: Some people just like a platform because they are powerless everywhere else. Whatever.

I suppose I shouldn't complain too much. If you seek us out on the Internet and look for comments on the various forums, where there are negative ones posted, other folks weigh in pretty quickly to set the record straight. That's happened even on the Yahoo Autos page. And where folks post negative stuff, if we respond politely, it will usually turn the situation around. We have a number of cases where folks who had been badmouthing us became some of our strongest supporters.

When I wrote the blog that became this chapter, I thought it was going to be a short entry. It quickly jumped up to 1500 words, though, and writing it only took about 45 minutes. At that point, I felt I had written enough. It was cathartic, and I had made my point.

Chapter 8: You Have Ovens?

The next move for me was back to Chongqing. We had ordered the first shipment of RX3 motorcycles and it was time for a face-to-face meeting with the folks in Zongshen. It's one thing to send emails and have Skype conversations; it's another to order a million dollars of new motorcycles. There were both contract and technical issues to negotiate, and my experience is that these things are best handled eyeball-to-eyeball.

My wife, Susie, traveled with me in December 2014 to resolve these details, and we knew we'd be spending Christmas in China. It wasn't the first time. The Chinese government discourages religion of any sort, but the folks in China sure love Christmas. This was the third or fourth time we had been in China over the holiday season. There's Christmas music everywhere, all in English, and all with American artists. The same goes for Christmas decorations. It's weird to hear Sinatra, Tony Bennet, and others singing Christmas carols outdoors on public address systems, and to see Christmas trees, Christmas wreaths, and all the rest that goes with the holidays in a place like Chongqing. Very few people speak English here. You have to wonder what they think when they see and hear all of this.

It takes a long time to get from Los Angeles to Chongqing (a 6-hour flight from LAX to Honolulu, a 2-hour layover in Hawaii, almost 13 hours from Honolulu to Beijing, a 2-hour layover in Beijing, and then another 3 hours to Chongqing). It was a good set of flights, though, and the time went quickly. While we were in the air, I read Bill O'Reilly's latest blockbuster *Killing Patton* (it was an excellent book), and when I finished that one, I started re-reading (for about the fifth time) Peter Egan's *Leanings* (it's one of those books every motorcycle rider should read). With the help of the International Date Line, we arrived in Chongqing 2 days after we left Los Angeles.

Our Zongshen point of contact, Bella, was waiting for us at the airport, and then it was another hour to the hotel in downtown Chongqing. Like I said, it was a long journey.

Susie and I were on our second wind by the time we arrived in Chongqing. We didn't feel tired at all, perhaps because we managed to nap a bit on the flight from Hawaii to Beijing. But it was that kind of fitful napping when you wake up every 20 minutes trying to find a comfortable position. And folks, that just doesn't exist in an airline seat designed for the mythical 98-lb weaklings featured in the Charles Atlas Dynamic Tension ads of yesteryear. You geezers and full-figured riders out there know what I'm talking about.

Chongqing was exactly as I remembered it. It was immense, with skyscrapers shrouded in mist peeking up through the green mountains, hills, valleys, and the Chiang Jiang River bisecting the city. Chiang Jiang, in Chinese, means the long river. It runs from western China all the way across the country to Shanghai on the east coast. In fact, it's how our motorcycles would begin their journey to America, in shipping containers on river boats en route to Shanghai. We know the Chiang Jiang as the Yangtze River.

We arrived in Chongqing around noon. Susie and I had a great lunch at a traditional Chinese Sichuan restaurant with Bella. It was good. Chongqing is known for its spicy food. I love the place.

Say what you will, but I've spent a lot of time here and I can tell you the Chinese are not a lot different from us. They admire the US and I've never detected even a hint of animosity. As is our habit when we were in China, we would read the *China Daily* (their English language daily newspaper) over a dynamite breakfast in the hotel every morning. The *China Daily* is like *USA Today*, but better written and with more substance. There's a political lean to it, but I have to tell you, it's more pro-American than either the *New York Times* or the *Los Angeles Times* (two other papers I like to read with breakfast when I am in the US).

The Chinese like all things American. Maybe it's because of the Chinese people's exposure to us in so many different ways. Bella told us that they enjoy most of our TV shows (*The Big Bang Theory* is a favorite, as I also found it to be in Turkey and in Scotland earlier this year). Some of their favorite food spots are distinctly American. Pizza Hut, Kentucky Fried Chicken, Subway, McDonalds and a few US fast food restaurants are everywhere.

Anyway, the food in China was awesome. Like all of the fancy hotels we've stayed in while in China, the one in Chongqing has a breakfast buffet to beat the band. Susie wanted an omelet with egg whites only...try translating that! One of the guys standing around helped us by explaining what we wanted to the Chinese chef, and I actually watched that omelet artist extract the yolks, unbroken, from the pan with chopsticks!

We weren't meeting with the boys from Zongshen until the next day, so we did a bit of sightseeing in Chongqing. Chongqing is not a tourist town, and with 34 million inhabitants, it most certainly is not a small town. It's actually one of the largest cities on the planet. 34 million people! That one city has as many people as all of California. Or, to put it into an even larger perspective, the population of Chongqing is about the same as all of Canada.

So, back to our sightseeing. I wrote a quick blog for CSC early in the morning the next day, and then I looked online to see what was happening in this mega-city. We settled our sights initially on a cable car ride across the Yangtze River. We grabbed a cab but the cabbie spoke no English, so the guy at the hotel had to explain what we wanted. Then he gave us a card so that when wanted to return, we could show it to the next cab driver.

The Yangtze River cable car ride was awesome. It's about 4,000 feet across the river, and we were packed into that little wooden cable car like sardines. Going up to the cable car in the elevator gave a hint of what was to come. We were squeezed in with folks I've never met before, and I was already more intimate with them than I had been on most of my high school dates. I guess that's just a natural consequence of being in a city with 34 million people.

Chongqing in the mist, vaguely reminiscent of a James Bond movie.

Chongqing used to be known in the West as Chun King, and I suppose that's because the way the Chinese pronounce Chongqing it almost sounds like Chun King. When I was a kid, my Mom used to buy Chun King Chinese noodles. Little did I know it was a real place and one day more than a half century later I'd be visiting it.

The downtown area on the other side of the Yangtze was unbelievably crowded. The scenes were straight out of a movie. People were carrying things in buckets hanging from poles across their shoulders, like I'd seen in old movies set in the Orient. Vendors for every kind of thing that's ever been sold were everywhere. Motorcycles were everywhere. Babies, kids, young people, old people...it was a mass of humanity that was almost biblical. We were the only non-Asians in this sea of people, but no one took any notice of us.

Fresh fruit sold the old-fashioned way in downtown Chongqing.

To me, people are the best part of traveling to exotic places, and Chongqing sure was an exotic place. It's usually not a part of China that tourists get to know, other than maybe gliding through it on a Yangtze River cruise. I love doing this kind of thing. It's a benefit to business travel that makes the adventure come alive for me. Some people hate traveling on business. Not me.

I was having a grand time. My Nikon was working overtime. Everywhere I turned I saw another photo opportunity. We couldn't speak the language and I'm guessing the people around us could not speak English, but everyone was friendly. It was a great morning.

I told Susie that I was getting a bit tired (we were still fighting the time change from Los Angeles to Chongqing). I think I said I wanted to stop monkeying around and head back to the hotel. That's when she smiled and pointed to somebody who was doing exactly that (i.e., monkeying around).

Monkeying around in downtown Chongqing.

We wrapped up our day sightseeing. Tomorrow would be our first day of technical and contract discussions with Zongshen. I was excited and I looked forward to it.

Our good buddy Dan, the Zongshen driver, was waiting for us in front of the lobby with his Mercedes van. After arriving at the Zongshen engineering and administration building, we met several of the Zongshen managers and engineers. Bella had a full 3 days of discussions and plant tours lined up for us based on a suggested agenda I had sent to her earlier.

One of the topics I wanted to cover was the motorcycle configuration for the US market. I'll hit just the high points here.

We wanted the headlight to be on all the time. That's a requirement in the US; in other parts of the world, the headlight can be turned on and off at the rider's discretion. The headlight switch on the Chinese domestic model RX3 has an off, parking lights, and headlight position. Steve suggested we keep the switch, label it as O (for off), A1 (for Accessory 1), and A2 (for Accessory 2), and connect it to two 12V accessory outlets we wanted to locate under the seat. As a guy with a KLR (and previously a series of Triumphs), I knew this idea was a winner. It would be a nice thing to have to two built-in, switch-controlled outlets for heated vests, additional lights, or whatever accessories our riders would want to include on their RX3 motorcycles. When I suggested it to Zongshen, the reaction was straightforward: No problem. This would be a recurring theme on nearly everything we wanted. Their engineers are awesome, and they took a lot of pride in being able to custom configure the bike the way we wanted it.

The next issue was the 17-inch rear wheel. Our three test bikes and the standard configuration RX3 have 15-inch rear wheels. The haters on the Internet forums were going nuts on this one, criticizing the bike for its 15-inch rear wheel. I liked the 15-inch rear wheel. The bike rode great with it. The Internet guys were concerned about tire availability. The Zongshen guys told me it would be no problem to provide the bike with the 17-inch rear wheel.

I thought I'd be a smartass on the ADVRider forum. After reading a series of particularly hysterical negative comments about the 15-inch rear wheel, I posted (in what I thought was a sarcastic manner) that I was in China discussing the motorcycle's production configuration. I wrote that there was a possibility we could have the bikes delivered with a 17-inch rear wheel. I asked which wheel the posters would prefer.

A funny thing happened over this rear wheel business. I thought I was being cute with my comment about being in China and being able to change the rear wheel to a 17-inch configuration. That's not the way the guys on ADVRider read it, though. Several people immediately answered that they would prefer the 17-inch rear wheel. I posted that we would do that. This all occurred in the space of a few minutes (the time difference between China and the US notwithstanding). Then a series of complimentary posts followed from the same guys who had been critical about the bike, telling the world that we were great guys for taking their inputs. Imagine that. A motorcycle company that asked for customer inputs and then did what the customers wanted. CSC's reputation as a company who listened to its RX3 customers was born in that little bit of intended Internet sarcasm. Hmmm. We might be on to something here.

We asked about Zongshen's optional dash-mounted accessories outlet. It's the one that has a 12-volt cigarette lighter to the left of the instrument cluster and a 5-volt USB outlet to the right of the instrument cluster. The Zongshen marketing people told us the price, and then the engineers told us that we couldn't simply buy the accessories outlets and install them on the motorcycle. This accessory outlet package (not to be confused with the two outlets we had specified under the seat that were controlled by the O/A1/A2 handlebar switch) required a different main harness. Whoa, I thought. I asked if I understood this correctly: The dash-mounted accessories outlet required a new main harness? Yes, they answered.

That wouldn't fly. I couldn't imagine our customers rewiring their entire motorcycle just to install the accessories outlet pack. But I knew that the accessories outlet would be a popular option if we could make it work.

"Can we just put the compatible accessories outlet main harness on all of the motorcycles?" I asked. The Zongshen people said yes, but the main harness would cost more. "How much?" I asked.

The Zongshen folks started pulling up spreadsheets on their laptops, there was a 15-minute discussion in Chinese, and the answer came back. Susie and I looked at each other and suppressed a laugh. The cost increase was less than a couple of bucks. "Let's do it," I said. "Put that main harness on all of our bikes." I didn't need to check with Steve; he'd be disappointed in me if I even asked the question.

We wanted the cush drive on our bikes. It's the rubber donut deal that fits between the rear wheel hub and the sprocket carrier. It makes for a smoother ride and the guys on one of the Internet forums thought it was a big deal to have it. No problem, said Zongshen.

The RX3 has an optional rear subfender that some people might like, but you couldn't just buy it as an accessory. The subfender requires a different swingarm with a mounting bracket. If you don't install the subfender (which was my preference; I thought the subfender looked a bit goofy), the swingarm would have this big mounting point that looked out of place. Steve and I discussed this and decided to pass on the subfender.

We took factory tours a couple of times during this visit. On one of the factory tours, we saw the complete Zongshen lineup (they make a lot of different motorcycles). We saw the regular RX3 in a couple of colors, and we also saw the police version.

The police version of the RX3 is a stunning motorcycle. It's solid white with blue and yellow accents, and it just looked cool. I've had in interest in police motorcycles for a long time and I've written a bit about them (I wrote a book, *The Complete Book of Military and Police Motorcycles*, a few years ago, and I wrote an article for *Rider* magazine about police bikes). I liked the looks of the police RX3.

When I wrote *The Complete Book of Military and Police Motorcycles* several years ago, I learned that one of the problems the police had was powering all of the accessories on their bikes (sirens, strobe slights, radios, etc.). BMW uses a second battery in their police motorcycles for that purpose. Some of the other marques use a bigger alternator. I asked one of the Zongshen engineers if the RX3 had enough alternator output for all of the accessories used on police bikes. He told me that the standard RX3 alternator has a 220-watt output, and they used a 300-watt alternator on the police bike.

Wow, I thought. That's great news. My KLR 650 only has a 187-watt alternator, and the stock RX3 was already at 220 watts. But that 300-watt alternator was an even better deal. I asked if there was any disadvantage to the 300-watt alternator (more parasitic power drain on the engine, or anything of that nature), and the answer was no. The next question was: Can we specify the 300-watt alternator on all of our bikes? No problem, said the Zongshen folks. This was getting better by the minute.

One group of Internet forum questions on the Chinariders.net site focused on the swingarm bearings. Those posters wanted to know if the swingarm used needle bearings or plain bushings (the needle bearings are more desirable). The RX3 has needle bearings (it was another home run for us).

We wanted to know if the RX3 had a rev limiter. In my riding the RX3 test bikes, I never had the engine cut out when I revved it over its 9,000-rpm redline, so I assumed it did not have a rev limiter. I learned that the engine does in fact have a rev limiter, and it's set to cut power to the engine at 11,000 rpm. I have no idea why it's that high (and I've never revved the engine that high), but it was good to know it exists and what the setting is.

Our next topic was the optimistic speedometer on the three test bikes. By our reckoning, it was a little over 20% optimistic. I told the Zongshen engineers that wouldn't fly in the US and we wanted the speedometer to be accurate. To my surprise, I encountered some resistance on this. The Zongshen engineer in charge of this area told me they could get it to within 10%, but they couldn't do any better than that. I was surprised, and based on the body language I was reading, I didn't think they were going to do anything. I asked if they could get it to 5%, but the answer was a firm no. My belief at the time (again, based on the body language) was that they wouldn't do anything, but they did. When the production bikes arrived, we tested a couple and we found that they are exactly 10% optimistic.

Another topic was the fuel gage. It reads empty when they tank is still half full. When I asked about that, the answer was that our bikes are fuel injected, the fuel pump is in the fuel tank, and the fuel pump needs to stay immersed in fuel for cooling reasons. That's why Zongshen set the thing up to show empty when the tank still has about 2 gallons left in it. I asked if they could change it to show empty when there was only a half-gallon remaining (which, in my opinion, should be enough to keep the fuel pump cool). The answer was a firm but polite no. At that point, I'd thought we'd been doing pretty well with the 17-inch rear wheel, the cush drive, the speedometer error correction, the 300-watt alternator, the new main harness, and a few other things, so I didn't push it. As an aside, that fuel tank gage is annoying, but it is about the same as any other fuel-gage-equipped motorcycle I've ever owned. They all show you're out of gas when there's still a fair amount remaining. The RX3 gets about 70 mpg, and basically the light starts flashing empty at around 140 to 150 miles on my bike. It doesn't bother me because I use the trip meter as my real fuel gage. I know I can easily get close to 200 miles out of a tank and still have fuel left. The other thing is that I need to stop about every 70 or 80 miles on a motorcycle for a stretch break. The bottom line here is that the fuel gage isn't perfect, but it's not a big deal.

Dynamometer testing RX3 motorcycles in the Zongshen plant.

After that, it was time to see the RX3 assembly line, and I enjoyed that part of our visit more than any other. I've been in a lot of factories and I've run a few, but watching the RX3 motorcycle assembly line in action was a real treat. I grabbed a bunch of photos, and I watched the process closely. I had a few recommendations and the Zongshen people incorporated them.

Watching the bikes come off the line was cool, too. Every bike goes into a fixture that checks wheel alignment, and from there it goes to a dynamometer. The Cyclone has a published top speed of 84 mph, but that's not what it's tested to on the dyno. Every bike has to spin that dyno up to 91 mph. That's the minimum. The bikes I watched topped 94 mph on the dyno! That's not real world (on the dyno, the bike doesn't have to fight aerodynamic drag), but still, when I saw this my only thought was "Damn!" Pardon my language, but it was an impressive thing to see.

One of the meetings I had with the Zongshen folks focused on marketing, and for that, a half dozen of their marketing execs entered the conference room. Bella was running the Zongshen folks in and out of our conference room like a drill sergeant and we were making great progress. The way it worked is every time a new group entered, Bella would make the introductions and we would exchange cards. The meeting with the marketing people was no different. She first introduced Mr. He. I said hello and gave him my card. Bella next introduced Mr. Ha. Same thing. Then Mr. Hu. Then Mr. Ho. Bella's family name is Ho, too. And finally, Mr. Ma.

"Let me see if I have this right," I said, looking at each person in turn. "Mr. He, Mr. Ha, Mr. Hu, Mr. Ho, Mr. Ma, and Ms. Ho?" The Chinese all laughed.

"And you're Mr. Ma?" I asked, looking at the marketing guy I would be working with.

"Yes, but you can call me Fred," he answered. Ah, okay. Folks, I can't make this stuff up.

One of the more senior marketing guys looked directly at me and asked, "You have ovens?"

Ovens? The question caught me off guard. We have an oven, I thought, trying to remember who manufactured it. Why did they want to know about my oven?

"You have ovens?" he asked again, obviously wondering why this big dumb American sitting in front of him couldn't answer the question. "We have ovens. We ride around China for one oven. One guy ride from here to Istanbul for another oven. You have ovens?"

Ah, ovens. Events. I got it.

"Yes, we do," I answered. "We ride in Baja a lot, and I want to do a Baja ride as soon as the production bikes arrive."

The Chinese looked at each other and didn't react. Baja didn't impress them.

"What else?" he asked.

"Well," I said, "a big deal in the US is to do a Four Corners run, where you ride to each of the four corners of America, you know, cities in Key West, Maine, Washington, and California." I drew a picture of the US and outlined the route to make it more clear.

"Too far," he said. "Too much freeways. What else?"

"There's another event called the Three Flags Rally, where we ride from Tijuana, Mexico, through the American West, and up into Calgary, Canada," I said.

The Chinese lit up on that one. They liked it. I was on a roll.

"I have a website that shows the photos I took when I did that run on my Triumph," I continued, and I opened up my laptop to show them. The photos were some of my best...magnificent scenery in Utah, Colorado, Wyoming, Washington, Oregon...the American West in all its glory. The Chinese clustered around me, enthralled with the photos I was showing them.

Susie recognized the significance of that moment way before I did. She grabbed this photo with my Nikon. The look of joyous anticipation on the Zongshen marketing guys' faces is obvious.

The instant the Western America Adventure Ride was born in a Zongshen conference room.

The Chinese loved this idea. "We sponsor this ride," one of them said. "We send people to ride with you. Maybe we give you 30,000 or 40,000 US dollars."

I was astonished. I didn't know what to say. Finally, I said, "$40,000 is better than $30,000," and everybody had another good laugh.

And that, folks, is how the CSC Western America Adventure Ride was born.

I had a few more meetings to finalize a few more things, Susie and I did some more sightseeing in and around Chongqing with Bella, and then we were back in the air for the long flight home to Los Angeles. All of the details were worked out, every i was dotted, and every t was crossed. The RX3 was coming to America.

Chapter 9: Baja!

The CSC Inaugural Baja Ride, in which we had 15 riders (all on brand new Chinese motorcycles headed for a 1700-mile ride through one of the toughest environments on the planet), happened almost by accident.

Baja is one of the best places on the planet for a motorcycle ride.

It all started when I was waxing eloquent on the blog about what I would do when I received my RX3. I mentioned that I planned to take my RX3 through Baja the first week I got it.

I thought it would be a cool thing to do. I love riding in Baja, I've written a few articles about the place in various motorcycle magazines, and I only mentioned it in the CSC blog because it was something I intended to do.

Well, that's all it took to get the ball rolling. Steve told me that people calling CSC about the RX3 wanted to know about the Baja ride, and specifically, they wanted to go. It was becoming a bit of a hassle for the rest of the staff. They wanted to sell motorcycles. I wanted to ride mine in Baja. Now we had people calling us asking about the Baja ride.

It didn't take long for us to put two and two together. People were buying the bike because they wanted to ride through Baja on it. Wow. How about that?

I asked people through the CSC blog to let me know if they were planning to join us on the Baja ride. The total number of number of people who wanted to shot up to 15. I capped it at that. Although I've led rides in Mexico for my friends, the largest number of people I had ever ridden with before was 5, and that seemed like a good number.

Our planned total of 15 Baja riders was pushing it, but I didn't think it would be a problem because I seriously doubted most of them would show up. I'd organized Baja rides with my friends before, and when I would first mention my plans for those rides, I'd have a dozen guys say they'd go. On the morning we left, though, it was typically just my good buddy Baja John and me. It was a running joke between us, and I honestly thought it would be the same for the CSC Baja ride. Steve was sweating having that many people go; I figured maybe three or four people would show up.

Boy, was I ever in for a surprise. My first inkling of that came about as the result of a labor riot. About a month prior to the CSC ride, Susie and I did a scouting run in the Subaru through Baja. We didn't really need to, but it was an excuse to get out, get on the road again, and take a few photos. I got some good ones on that trip, too, including an incredible shot of a very cooperative diamondback rattlesnake just outside my car door.

A Baja buddy sampling the air and checking me out.

But I'm digressing. For years, people always told me I was crazy for going into Mexico because of the danger. I always blew them off, believing they were saps for accepting everything they saw on TV or read in the *LA Times*. I'd been down there numerous times and I never had any problems. None. Zip. Nada.

All that changed on this scouting run. Susie and I found ourselves in the middle of a labor riot about 175 miles south of the border, just north of San Quintin. We found out the hard way that the migrant workers down there were not happy with their wages on the farms. A lot of them migrate into the San Quintin area with their families, including their kids, whom they evidently put to work in the fields. The Mexican government was clamping down on child labor, so that affected these people and they were plenty angry about it. Real angry, apparently.

One of the military checkpoint guys on Mexico's Transpeninsular Highway told us the road was closed about 80 km ahead, but he didn't speak English and he didn't tell us why the road was closed. I thought it was most likely because they were working on the road (that happens frequently in Baja), and when that occurs, the roads close for maybe 20 minutes. Amazingly (based on what we found out a few miles down the road) that young soldier let the car in front of us proceed, and then he let us go, too.

About 30 miles later, we started seeing what we thought were small piles of asphalt on the road with lots of wires (you know, like for fixing potholes, which they have a lot of, but I couldn't figure out what the wires were). We saw this for about the next 15 miles. We saw hundreds of people milling around, too; far more than I've ever seen in these little farming towns.

It turns out that we what thought were piles of asphalt were actually the remnants of burned out tires, as in "let's light a fire and shut the main highway down" burned out tires. The ag workers had been having demonstrations (actually, labor riots) in the San Quintin area, and we found this out the hard way. It had been going on for 2 days. The *LA Times* and the US news media were completely unaware of it, which is astounding considering it was happening only about 300 miles south of their offices.

We went a few more miles and encountered a roadblock (more burned out tire remnants and boulders blocking the road) with about 50 very angry men milling about. They immediately surrounded us. They wouldn't let us go forward or turn around. One of them threatened the Subie with a baseball bat. They were all over the car. Susie had the presence of mind to lock the doors. I didn't know what to do, so I fell back on what always seemed to work elsewhere: I asked the guy who seemed to be in charge if I could pay the toll. He seemed genuinely surprised at that, he thought about it for maybe 5 seconds (duly observed by his subordinate seditionists), and then he realized this might be a viable way to make a living. Our erstwhile Mexican revolutionary said, "Hokay," I gave him a ten dollar bill, and he told the insurrectionists, "Let them pass." Crisis averted. Whew!

We were only a few weeks away from the CSC Baja ride, and I was thinking that maybe it wouldn't be such a good idea given the current political climate and labor unrest in the San Quintin area. I posted the adventure described above on the CSC blog and proposed a different route in the United States, and then the emails started pouring in. The message was the same in all of them: I'll go wherever you want to take us, Joe, but I really want to ride Baja.

**Scenes from the CSC Inaugural Baja Run. We had 15 riders.
It was a blast and we are going to do it every year.**

I was genuinely surprised. Usually I was the guy defending the safety of riding in Mexico. This time I was saying maybe we should take a pass, and everyone was telling me, "No, we want to ride Baja." Maybe Steve was right and most of these guys would show up. Baja it would be, then. We were headed to Mexico.

The day before we were due to leave, our Baja-bound riding buddies started arriving in Azusa. All of them, from as far away as Washington state, Washington, D.C., Arizona, Texas, and all points in between. My traveling *compadres* on our epic CSC Inaugural Baja Run were real riders and they were enormous fun to be around. They thought the idea of buying a new Chinese motorcycle and blasting through Baja for 5 days would be a good thing. They were my kind of people, and I was looking forward to riding with them.

Our plan was to get as far south as Santa Rosalia and use that as our turn-around point. I wanted everybody to be able to say they rode to the Sea of Cortez and to experience *La Cuesta del Infierno*, the twisty descent into that town. I wanted to make the experience memorable for everyone. I knew a lot of these folks not only wanted to ride, but they also wanted an adventure that they could describe to their friends.

We also wanted to put our marketing strategy into play. A key part of the CSC marketing strategy is to not just sell the motorcycle, but to also sell the adventure. We wanted people to experience the adventure and the excitement that goes with their RX3 motorcycles. I knew that it would be a big deal to ride a motorcycle into Mexico. The first time I did it 25 years ago I had a lot of anxiety until I actually got down there and experienced for myself how much fun it is. But to just pick up and do it on your own is not in the cards for most people. My job here was to make it easy for people to take that first step, and to be both a guide and a friend on this ride.

Our first day's destination was El Rosario, about 200 miles south of the border. It was a long day, with 360 miles of riding from Azusa, but it was fun and I got to know everyone. It was a great group. Everybody got along and everybody was interesting.

A big part of the attraction on the RX3 is doing your own maintenance, and with Baja John and I providing just a bit of guidance, the bikes had their first service by their new owners that evening in the Mama Espinoza's parking lot. Mama Espinoza's hotel and restaurant is an iconic stop on any ride through Baja; all serious Baja travelers stop here. It was grand fun and everyone was in high spirits. And, we had rolled right through San Quintin (about 50 miles north of El Rosario) earlier in the day with no labor riots.

El Rosario is an important place in Baja from a location perspective. If you're traveling south, it's the last place to buy fuel from a pump for the next 200 miles. There are guys who sell fuel from bottles further down, but nobody passes through El Rosario without filling up at the Pemex station.

Roselda, the prettiest gas station attendant in El Rosario!

Day 2 led us into the Vizcaino Desert, just south of El Rosario. It's one of the prettiest parts of Baja, with numerous cacti and other plant species that grow in Baja and nowhere else on Earth. Our destination that night was Santa Rosalia. Along the way, we stopped in Guerrero Negro for some of Antonio's fish tacos, and everybody loved them. We also stopped in San Ignacio, a small oasis town in the middle of the peninsula dominated by a church built in 1728. There were plenty of photo ops, and it was a fun day.

Day 2 was another high mileage day and we rolled into Santa Rosalia on the Sea of Cortez that evening. We stayed at the Francis Hotel., an ancient wooden hotel that was dripping with authenticity, history, and charm. The rooms have real keys, not those little credit card things you get in most hotels in the US. I like that. Everyone was in high spirits.

One example of how well everyone was getting along and how much fun we were having was when Pete locked himself out of his hotel room. Pete did this at the Frances Hotel, so he left to get another key from the lobby. Pete is a police officer and before he left to get a substitute key, the guys gave him a good-natured ribbing about not being able to get back into his room. A few of the riders on our Baja expedition were standing in front of Pete's room while Pete was off fetching another key when Juddy happened along. Juddy heard what had occurred and he unlocked Pete's door in seconds by using a credit card as a shim.

"Don't tell Pete," Juddy told everyone, seconds before Pete reappeared with a substitute key.

"What's going on?" Juddy asked Pete.

"Ah, I locked myself out of my room," Pete said, "and I got another key from the office."

"Wait," Juddy said. "I have an app on my iPhone that can unlock the door," and with that, Juddy punched a few buttons on his iPhone screen, he held it next to Pete's door knob, and then said, "try it now..."

Pete did. The jury is still out on whether he knew Juddy was having some fun with him. We all had a good laugh, and I've probably told that story 50 times already. It was that kind of a trip.

As I mentioned, Santa Rosalia is about 700 miles south of the border, and it was our turnaround point. We headed out the next morning for Guerrero Negro, about 150 miles north of Santa Rosalia, with an option for the more experienced riders. The choices for our group were to either head directly for the hotel in Guerrero Negro, or to make a side trip to see the ancient cave paintings in Sierra San Francisco. The cave paintings involved a 27-mile ride off the Transpeninsular Highway on an absolutely stunning paved (but deserted) road, and then another 7 miles on a really gnarly dirt road.

Eight riders in our group opted for the cave paintings, and it was spectacular. John (of the father-and-son John and Jay team) told me later that he thought it was the best part of the trip. The paintings were amazing. They were done over 10,000 years ago by a civilization that vanished, and no one really knows anything about them other than that they liked painting in caves. Poof. Gone. Wiped clean off the face of the earth, just like that line in the Indiana Jones movie.

On the way back, we had our only serious mechanical failure. Just a few feet before we got back on the Transpeninsular Highway, Justin's bike lost drive power. The engine ran, but nothing made it through to the rear wheel. Justin's countershaft sprocket nut decided to take a powder.

I was devastated. We had a couple of battery problems on the trip and a couple of centerstand problems, but these were minor annoyances and relatively easily remedied. Losing the countershaft sprocket nut, though, literally in the middle of Baja, was not so straightforward. This happened right after we rode that gnarly dirt road to the cave paintings, but I really don't think the road had anything to do with it.

As you read this, you might be thinking that this was not such a big deal, but that's not the way I saw it. On every one of these trips, my feeling is that I'm basically betting the company. If we do well, we're showing people how good the RX3 is. If things go wrong, the bike's reputation will suffer. I cringed every time any of our bikes had a problem.

Justin didn't see this as a problem at all. He just walked back along his path and found the nut retainer, but we couldn't find the nut. That didn't slow Justin down at all. He put the retainer on, grabbed some baling wire he had brought with him, and he fixed the problem. To be sure, Justin's fix was a temporary one, but it got us the 70 miles back to Guerrero Negro. We had bought spare parts with us, but not the countershaft sprocket nut (I had never seen this happen before on any motorcycle, and it never occurred to me to bring a spare countershaft sprocket nut).

Justin (aka MacGyver) and his emergency countershaft sprocket fix.

I knew there was a motorcycle repair shop in Guerrero Negro, and I thought we would just buy a new countershaft sprocket nut the next day (or so I thought). Ah, if it were only that simple.

The next day we split up again. Baja John led nine of the guys to the Old Mill Hotel in San Quintin while five of us hung back in Guerrero Negro to get a countershaft sprocket nut for Justin's bike.

The old saying about the adventure beginning when things go wrong was certainly true on our Baja ride. Like I alluded to earlier, I was feeling down about Justin's bike losing that countershaft nut, but Justin and the guys who hung back in Guerrero Negro with us were enjoying the hell out of trying to find a replacement. Abe and Pete rode off from Malarrimo's Hotel (our Guerrero Negro digs) to find the motorcycle repair shop, and Pete, Justin, and I went to an automobile repair facility. No dice at the auto shop; those guys work on cars and Baja race trucks. And Abe and Pete struck out at the motorcycle shop. The guy who owned the shop had died a few days ago. I know it's cruel, but my initial thought was, gee, if only he could have hung on for a few more days.

There's a small airport outside of Guerrero Negro, and airports usually have hardware, so Abe and Pete left for it. Juddy and I rolled up the town's main drag and we found a very small auto parts place. When I say it was an auto parts place, don't get the idea that I'm talking about something like a Pep Boys or an AutoZone. This was a tiny building that looked like the Mexican version of the old TV show *Sanford and Son*. It was full of rusty parts, junk lying around, and a shop owner right out of Central Casting.

I explained what we wanted and I thought I was doing a pretty good job until I realized that my new best friend Santiago (the proprietor) spoke no English. Santiago spoke to me in Spanish. "*No habla Espanol,*" I said. Santiago was like an American. When he saw I spoke no Spanish, he spoke loudly and slowly (in Spanish, of course). It was pretty funny. "*Me Stupido,*" I told him, tapping my chest. We had a good laugh.

Hey, *no problemo*...Santiago disappeared into his inner sanctum and he brought out a large coffee can. He emptied it on the grease-encrusted floor, picking through corroded nuts and bolts for several minutes. No luck.

No problemo, said Santiago again. He took us outside and showed us a ratted out old ATV. It was under a disintegrating tarp. The thing looked old enough (and corroded enough) for Moses to have ridden it across the Red Sea. Santiago pulled the tarp back, and smiled as he pointed out the countershaft nut (the very-heavily-corroded countershaft nut).

We tried for half an hour to get the nut off that old ATV, using a socket wrench and a cheater bar that probably could have reached all the way back to the US border. It was hot and humid. We were perspiring profusely. That nut wasn't budging.

Do you remember the scene in *Animal House* when D-Day fires up a blow torch? You know, after the guys wreck Flounder's Lincoln? It's the scene in which the torch casts this weird glow on D-Day's face and he gets a wicked grin that says "all is well with the world now that I have my torch lit." Folks, picture Santiago doing the same. He put the jet of

Hell on that countershaft sprocket nut, all the old grease (and most of the crankcase paint) vaporized instantly, and Santiago got the nut to break loose! He poured water on it, unscrewed it, and….and…wrong thread size. Too coarse. Rats!

Just then, Abe and Pete rolled in on their RX3 motorcycles. They found a castellated nut at the airport that looked right, and it had the fine thread we thought we wanted. Our spirits rose again, only to sink when the thread still wouldn't allow the new nut to fit on Justin's bike. Major league bummer. It's already close to noon, it's terribly hot and humid, and I'm wondering if maybe I ought to start looking into real estate in Guerrero Negro. Maybe I could give up writing the CSC blog and sell fish tacos.

Abe, who speaks fluent Spanish and is cool as a cucumber, said not to worry. Abe is unflappable. He said that the guy at the airport has a friend at the salt factory who has a machine shop, and he could make us a new nut.

Folks, once again, I can't make up stuff like this. So we all saddled up and rode to the edge of town, where we pulled into the salt factory parking lot. Abe went up to the gate, talked to a guy there, and in a few minutes this friend-of-a-friend-who-works-at-the-salt-factory-and-has-a-machine-shop walked out of the plant, looked at Justin's bike, took a few measurements, and…you guessed it…he told us *no problemo*. But he had to go to lunch first. He'd make us a nut when he came back.

Wow. Juddy and Abe rode back up the road to get us some fish tacos from Tony (everybody loved Tony's fish tacos), and Justin, Pete, and I hung out in the parking lot in front of the salt factory. Lots of people were interested in our RX3s. I had brochures in my panniers. I was doing my full tilt sales boogie (you know, what do you need your monthly payment to be?), all the while wondering how these guys (Pete, Justin, Abe, and Juddy) are staying so relaxed about this countershaft nut business. I felt depressed, embarrassed, and guilty, and that's when it struck me. Justin said "it's not an adventure until something goes wrong." Well, folks, if that's the criteria, we were having one hell of an adventure. My embarrassment and guilt aside, these guys were loving it. They were amazing.

While all this was going on, the guys were busy snapping photos. I didn't photograph any of this stuff. I felt responsible for it, and I didn't want to take pictures of all that ensued during the countershaft sprocket nut's absence without leave. The guys were loving it, though. Maybe I'll get some of their photos later, I thought.

The friend-of-a-friend Mexican machinist came back from lunch, he measured the shaft again (always a good sign...there's an old saying in the machine shop business that goes "measure twice, cut once") and he disappeared into the factory. I wondered if he tells his wife when he goes to work each morning that he'll be spending another day in the salt mines. An hour passed, the machinist emerged, and *voilá*, we had our new countershaft sprocket nut.

That nut was a thing of incredible beauty. If Justin ever rides into a nuclear conflagration and his RX3 takes a direct hit from a nuclear intercontinental ballistic missile, that nut will still be hanging on to the countershaft sprocket. My feelings soared. I went from being depressed to being jubilant. Let's ride!

And ride we did. We left Guerrero Negro around 2:00 p.m. and pinned it all the way up to San Quintin. Gas in Catavina, gas again in El Rosario, and then the turn on the dirt road to the Old Mill Hotel. Four miles of dirt road. In the dark. 30 miles an hour on hard pack, and then pow, we hit the soft sand.

By the grace of God, I didn't crash. It wasn't due to any great riding skills on my part. I'm convinced I had a lot of help from the Almighty. My bike was sashaying around like an exotic dancer in a room full of heavy tippers, except I was most definitely not enjoying this show. I was the star, and I didn't know how the movie was going to end. We went through about a mile of this stuff. It seemed like it went on forever. I was sure I was going to drop the bike, but I didn't. It hadn't been nearly this bad the last time I rode this stretch of road.

Finally, we pulled into the Old Mill Hotel's gravel parking lot. Baja John came over and said he sure was glad to see us. Me, too, dude! I asked if everybody got in okay and if there had been any problems with the bikes. No problems with the bikes, said John, and everybody got in okay. That's good, I thought. I was really worried about the soft sand we had just ridden through and I didn't want to even think about anybody dropping their bikes.

"So everybody got through it okay?" I asked again. I don't know why I asked it again. Maybe it's because I've known Baja John for 30 years.

"Sort of," John said. "Four guys dropped their bikes. One guy has a sprained ankle. We thought he broke it, but it's just sprained."

Whoa! Four dropped bikes. One sprained ankle. Other than that, Mrs. Lincoln, how did you enjoy the play? Another emotional roller coaster. I felt terrible that this happened.

John told me everybody was over at the restaurant, and they had the fight on big screen TV. I didn't even know there was going to be a fight, and I was a little bit afraid to face the guys (especially the ones who dropped their bikes). But I was hungry.

The restaurant was jumping, and we had to wait to get a table. Folks, we're 4 miles out on this sandy dirt road, and the place was packed. Mexico is like that. You just never know what you're going to find.

I found our guys and they were having a blast, along with more than a few beers. The guys who had dropped their bikes were grinning ear to ear. They were excited to see us (we were 8 hours late getting into San Quintin due to the nut debacle in Guerrero Negro, and they had been worried about us). The restaurant was a cool place. It had this marine motif (we were, after all, right on *Bahia San Quintin*). It all came together to make for a fun evening. Beer, the big screen fight, stories about the ride over the last several days, and the knowledge that we'd be home the next night.

To my amazement, the guys were telling war stories about losing it in the soft stuff and dropping their bikes. They were enjoying it. I looked around. I listened. It was amazing.

Do you remember the scene in *Jaws* when Captain Quint (played by Robert Shaw), Chief Brody (played by Roy Scheider), and Richard Dreyfuss are comparing scars? You know, they're in this fishing boat, bobbing around on the ocean, drinking, and they're comparing war wounds? I looked around and listened to the riding and dropped bike stories in this marine-themed restaurant. I suddenly realized I was in that scene in *Jaws*. I was living it. It was yet another awesome moment in what was turning out to be a truly great adventure ride. Everyone was in high spirits.

Day 5 was a fairly uneventful ride back to the border, and then that was it. Our CSC Inaugural Baja Run was over. What a week it was: 15 riders, 15 brand new motorcycles, and a 1700-mile adventure ride through Baja. Wowee. Do the math…that was 25,500 miles in 5 days on Chinese motorcycles that were brand new to America. The RX3 motorcycles and our band of intrepid Baja blasters were awesome!

And folks, that was it for our Inaugural Baja ride. As you read this book, you might be wondering: Are we going to do this again? The answer, of course, is yes. Almost as soon as I returned from Baja, Steve wanted to know when we could do the next one. We will almost certainly head down there the third week of March in 2016. It's when the whales will be in town, and that's another adventure I want to be able to share with my RX3 riding buddies. Keep an eye on the CSC blog for more information on this upcoming ride.

Chapter 10: Another Chongqing Visit

In May, it was time for another visit to Chongqing. We had experienced a few issues on some of the bikes and it was time for someone from CSC to sit down with the folks from Zongshen to make sure the issues were being addressed to our satisfaction. Overall, we were happy with the motorcycle, but as is the case for any new endeavor, there were improvement opportunities. And there were many other things we needed to talk about:

- Some of the things were technical issues on the RX3.
- Some of our discussion would be related to a new bike (the TT Special) we were evaluating as an addition to our US line.
- We wanted to see the new Zongshen models.
- We had several things to talk about related to the upcoming Western America Adventure Ride.
- A lot of our discussion would be focused on the boring administrative things associated with running any business.

This was to be a quick 3-day visit. I didn't want to do any sightseeing, and I was hoping that if I limited my time in China to just 3 days, I wouldn't have too much difficulty with the time change when I returned to the US. Bella did her usual outstanding job in scheduling meetings with the right people. I had sent a suggested agenda to her, and she made it happen. It was an intense 3 days, with back-to-back meetings from 8:00 to 5:00 p.m. every day.

Things had been progressing well at CSC. RX3 sales were great, and Steve, Ryan, and Gerry had been developing new accessories that were similarly flying out the door. As an aside (and because I'll be mentioning these guys later), Ryan is our Sales Manager, and Gerry is our Service Department Manager. Both are great guys.

The technical discussions proceeded quickly in Chongqing, as did all of the administrative stuff. The TT Special discussions were also expeditious. We had specified what we wanted on this new bike, and they had already left Chongqing bound for California by the time I arrived in China. The shipping time from Zongshen to CSC being what it is, I didn't get to see the TT Specials until I returned home from the Western America Adventure Ride, but when I did, I sure liked them. I think those bikes are going to do well for us and for our riders.

I saw several new Zongshen models, including the new RC3 (a sports bike based on the RX3 engine) and a dynamite 150cc motorcycle called the Z-One. I rode all of the development samples of the new Zongshen models and I really fell in love with the Z-One. The Z-One engine has swirl technology, roller rocker arms, and many other features I've seen in other engines for decades, but I could feel there was something more to this new motor. What I didn't tumble to was why the engine felt so powerful. It was way more than I expected from what appeared to be yet another Honda CG-150 clone motor. I asked the Fan why it felt so much more powerful and he told me: It was the new engine's offset crank.

The concept is brilliant. The piston in an offset crank engine has better leverage when the fuel-air mixture ignites, which is achieved by its 4mm crankshaft offset from the piston's connecting rod pivot point. The design increases both torque and smoothness. This was the first I'd heard of the concept, and I can tell you from my ride on the Z-One that it works. The thing had the bottom end torque of a much larger engine, and it was unnaturally smooth.

The challenge for CSC, of course, was would it make sense to invest another $100K to take the Z-One through the CARB and EPA certification process, particularly in light of the fact that it was "only" a

150cc motorcycle. Ultimately, we decided that the market for a 150cc motorcycle in the US was not big enough to make the bike viable. It sure was a nice motorcycle, though. I'd buy one.

After the riding session around the Zongshen campus, we headed back to the main administration building. I was glad. It was well over 100 degrees in Chongqing and it was very, very humid. Bring on the air conditioning!

Our next meeting focused on the upcoming Western America Adventure Ride. Zongshen's original plan was to send several Zongshen employees and a few Chinese journalists on the ride with us, but that went south when most of the Zongshen employees were denied visas by the US Consulate near Chongqing. It may seem strange to us, but many of the people in other nations do not enjoy the freedom of movement we enjoy as US citizens.

When the Zongshen marketing people explained to me that they had been turned down for entry visas by the US government, I thought at first that they must have been mistaken and what they meant was that the Chinese government had denied them permission. I asked the question a couple of different ways and it became apparent to me that it was in fact my government (not theirs) that said they could not visit the US.

Bella explained to me that the US consulate officer asked only a couple of questions before denying her entry visa. I could not understand why this had occurred, and I did something I had never done before: I called the office of my US senator (Barbara Boxer) to find out why this had happened. The Boxer aide listened to my story, and then he told me that the US State Department has absolute authority in these things. He went on to tell me that the most likely reason Bella had been rejected was because she was a female of child-bearing age. I am assuming the rejection was driven by the current birth tourism issues in the US (people from other countries come to the US to have their babies so the babies can be US citizens). It was bizarre, but there was nothing we could do about it.

Bella told me that Zongshen was sending Hugo (his Chinese name is Ying Liu), the Zongshen in-country representative from Colombia, and five

Chinese journalists. That's interesting, I thought. We weren't going to have any Zongshen employees from China, but Bella assured me Hugo was a good guy. We went from the initial plan of having mostly Zongshen technical people and a couple of Chinese journalists to having one Zongshen representative (from Colombia, of all places) and five Chinese journalists. I wasn't too sure what to make of this, but in any event, there wasn't anything I could do about it at this point. The US government wasn't allowing the Zongshen employees from Chongqing come to the US. You can't fight city hall or the US government, I suppose.

After these discussions with Bella, the marketing managers entered the room. They were some of the same marketing people I had met on my previous visit, including one who looked a little familiar. I couldn't remember everyone I had met during earlier Zongshen visits and I wasn't sure if I had met any of these guys.

One of the marketing guys who looked a little familiar smiled at me and said "ah, You Tubby, You Tubby..."

I was surprised at how forward he was and I didn't know what to say. I looked at my belly. I guess I was a few pounds overweight. Well, okay, I'm fat. I just didn't expect anybody to be so direct about it.

"I saw you. You Tubby," he said again. "I saw you on You Tubby."

Ah, yes. YouTube. Or, as my new friend called it, YouTubby.

Don't get me wrong. I'm not making fun of how the Chinese speak English. The Chinese learn English in high school, and they speak English way better than I speak Chinese. And there is that nonsensical silent "e" on the end of YouTube (something we unnecessarily do a lot of in the English language). It's an entirely logical and phonetic pronunciation. You-Tub-e.

The Zongshen marketing exec was referring, of course, to the video I did several months ago with the blue EPA test bike. That particular YouTube video has had a ton of hits, and even though officially there's no YouTube in China, my Zongshen marketing friend had seen the video. Many people have. We did that video in one take with no script;

it was just sort of a quickie thing to explain the bike. At the time, it was the only English language video that described all of the RX3 features, and it sure made the rounds. I have had people approach me at motorcycle events because they've seen me in it, and it's still pulling hits. I'm a star. A tubby one, but a star nonetheless.

Anyway, the "me tubby" meeting at Zongshen made for a good story, and in talking about it back here in California, Steve asked me to make a new video when I returned from the Western America Adventure Ride. The original video used the blue test bike. Our production configuration motorcycle has a lot of improvements. We wanted to show the production configuration bike, two of our Special Edition models, and a few of our accessories.

And, I did lose a few pounds on the 5000-mile Western America Adventure Ride, I'm not quite so tubby anymore. Considering the weight I lost in those 5000 miles on the RX3, by my calculations I would need to ride another 38700 miles to be officially out of the tubby category. For my height, anyway. Maybe I'm not really tubby. It might be that I'm just too short. Whatever.

I talked with my good buddy Hugo after the ride (on Skype) a few evenings ago and he told me that the Chinese riders on the Western American Adventure Ride gained weight, no doubt due to our ridiculous serving sizes here in the US. But that's another story for a later chapter.

Chapter 11: Preparation

We had many things to do before departing on the Western America Adventure Ride, not the least of which was defining the route.

As you know from reading this book, the original suggestion I made to the Chinese was to duplicate the Three Flags Rally I rode several years ago. That's a ride organized by the Southern California Motorcycle Association. It starts just inside Mexico (the year I did it, we started in Tijuana, just across the border), meanders through the American West (which is the bulk of the ride), and then crosses into Canada to end in Calgary (our destination the year I rode the Three Flags). Those countries constituted the three flags (Mexico, the US, and Canada).

Although the Chinese were very excited about this route during our December meeting in Chongqing, the issues of actually crossing several international borders ruled out riding in Canada and Mexico. I already described what the Chinese encountered attempting to get US entry visas for the Zongshen employees. The intrigue associated with getting permission to cross the US border into and out of Canada and Mexico for several folks from the People's Republic of China (and, as we were about to find out, Colombia) added complexity where none was needed. The Chinese wisely opted to restrict the ride to the United States.

The next step was to plan the route. My good buddy Baja John volunteered to do that, and I told him what I thought would be a good general approach:

- I wanted to follow the general route I had several years ago when I rode the Three Flags Rally, less Canada and Mexico. Those two countries almost didn't count as part of that earlier ride, anyway, as we had started from Tijuana (literally just across the border), and the distance from the US border to Calgary was relatively small.

- I wanted to hit the big national parks on an initial northeasterly diagonal line from California all the way out to South Dakota, including Joshua Tree, the Grand Canyon, Zion, Bryce, and Mt. Rushmore.

- I wanted to head west from Mt. Rushmore, and then pick up Devil's Tower, Hell's Canyon, and the Columbia River Gorge.

- I wanted to roll up into Washington to get on the other side of the Columbia River and take the Bridge of the Gods back into Oregon. I had crossed that bridge before and it was a special place. I knew the folks who would ride with us would feel the same way.

- I wanted to spend a night in Portland and have a dinner at Kelly's Olympian Bar and Grill. It's a cool bar in downtown Portland with a dynamite antique motorcycle collection. I wrote a "Destinations" piece on Kelly's for *Motorcycle Classics* magazine (the "Destinations" pieces are a regular gig for me), and I thought the Chinese would like seeing the place. In fact, now that I think of it, most of the places I wanted to see on this ride were ones I had written about in *Motorcycle Classics* magazine. There was a lot of synergy here.

- I wanted to head southwest from Portland down to Tillamook, and then take the Oregon Coast Highway south to California.

- Somewhere in all of this, I wanted to pick up Crater Lake in Oregon.

- I wanted to pick the Redwoods National Park in northern California.

- I wanted to take the Pacific Coast Highway back down to the CSC plant in Azusa.

- I wanted to hold the daily mileage to about 300 miles.

- I wanted to be on the road for 15 days.

That was a tall order, and I knew not all of it would be possible. It was John's job to translate my wish list into an actual route, find places we could stay that wouldn't break the bank, and maximize our time on scenic roads (preferably not freeways). It was no easy task, and it would take a hell of a lot of work on John's part. John was up for it, though. He and I have been on many rides, and the guy knows how to do it right.

I suppose one of the issues I should mention is that once we had a tentative route, we had to wave it by the Chinese to get their approval. I also chatted up our plans on the CSC blog. I asked people who owned RX3s to join us for part or all of the ride. This turned out to be a double-edged sword. What I didn't ask for (but what we had a lot of) were suggestions on where we should ride. Some of it worked out fabulously well. Utah's Highway 12 is a good example; it was not part of the initial plan, it was one of the recommendations that floated in from our blog followers, and it is one of the most beautiful and dramatic roads I have ever ridden.

In general, though, the route suggestions from others were problematic. I had learned some of the issues that could emerge when guiding a large group like this from our experience on the Baja Inaugural ride, and although some of the suggestions "were only a couple of hours out of the way" or "would only add 150 miles to the ride" I knew we wouldn't have the time. We had several suggestions for dirt roads, and that wasn't going to happen, either. I had a chase truck and several riders of unknown experience to worry about. If someone crashed out in the boonies, it would be a real problem. Nope, no dirt roads on this ride (or so I thought, but more on that later).

I guess this is as good a place as any to talk about the email I sent to John after the Baja ride. I thought about the challenges we had on that ride and they resulted in this email:

John:

There are a lot of things I learned on this last Baja trip that we should incorporate on the next one:

- *We need cell phone coverage.*

- *We need to have commo from the lead guy to the guy riding at the back; maybe a helmet cell phone Bluetooth deal. There were folks selling those for motorcycle helmets at Overland Expo. J Brandon has such as setup, I believe. He can make phone calls while riding his KLR.*

- *We have to keep the mileage down. Some of us old guys ain't up to 370-400 mile days.*

- *We have to stay out of soft sand. No crashes is a good strategy. I hate soft sand. In my mind, it's just not a good thing to plan on riding in it.*

- *We need a first aid kit and we probably need someone who knows first aid. I don't remember if you brought a kit on the last trip or not; I did not. I'm not a first aid guy, either. You know, "doc says you gonna die" when the snake bites you and all that.*

- *We may need to bring a few more spare parts...maybe a countershaft sprocket nut or two (although I doubt we'll ever see another failure like that). Batteries are heavy, but we could have used a couple down there in Baja.*

- *We need to think through the meal breaks. I don't know if you heard it, but I got a lot of "when do we eat?" queries every time we stopped for any reason in Mexico.*

- *We probably need to take more photo breaks.*

- *We need to do better on designating rally points. Overall as a large group we did well. That day Justin lost his sprocket nut we got split up sending people out for help (of those that stayed to help Justin) and that was a little disconcerting. When I saw that ambulance coming back to Guerrero Negro and we still had two guys out, it really shook me up.*

- *If we bring folks on new bikes (like we did last time), we need to make sure the batteries are good in every bike before we leave.*

Joe

We would need to factor all of the above into our preparation for this trip.

We had the mileage thing down; John would factor that into his route planning. I thought that 15 days should give us enough time to get it all in. John called me a couple of days into his planning and told me we either had to cut some of the places out of our trip, or increase our daily mileage, or add a couple of days to the ride. My response was immediate: Let's tack on the extra two days.

Cell coverage wouldn't be a problem. We had cell phones, and service in the US (unlike Baja) is generally good.

On the motorcycle helmet communications thing, the guys worked that hard, but I was the long pole in the tent on that one. John researched the suppliers offering such equipment and found the best one. Ryan talked the supplier into giving us a set of helmet intercoms, and John mounted them in our helmets. When I tried my helmet on, I didn't like the way the speakers interfered with the fit. John screwed around with my helmet for an hour trying to find a way to position them so that they didn't bother me, but we just couldn't find a way to do that. I finally thought I would just live with it, but when we tried to activate the system, we couldn't get it to work. That was enough for me. Even though I was the guy who initially suggested it (and our guys put a lot of work into making that thought a reality), I had made up my mind. I wasn't going to wear the helmet intercom. I just didn't like it.

For the spare parts, the first aid kit, and all the rest, we would have a chase vehicle (unlike Baja). We had plenty of spare parts, including a couple of batteries. We didn't too well on that battery thing and I'll talk more about it later in this book. To cut to chase, we had battery problems the first few days on three of the bikes (and we only brought two batteries). We kind of dropped the ball on the bringing spare chains, too, and I'll cover that later as well.

We had two bikes with battery problems on the Baja ride. We got around it by just push starting the bikes in Mexico when we needed to. We subsequently encountered battery problems on a few of the production bikes (recall that we left for Baja right after the first shipment of production bikes arrived). Our conclusion was that the first RX3 shipment had batteries with high infant mortality (that's an engineering term that means if they're going to fail, they do so early). Zongshen has since corrected that problem with improved batteries. I would have thought that the seven bikes they sent to us for their journalists' use would have had the improved batteries, but I didn't check on that. You can guess where this story is going. The bikes Zongshen sent over for the Chinese journalists had the crummy batteries. The bottom line is that we had three battery failures in the first week of our Western America Adventure Ride, and we only brought two spares. Walmart was our salvation, but more on that later.

On the chain issue, we found out on this trip that the stock RX3 chain has a predicted life of about 7,500 miles. Three of the bikes (mine included) already had about 3,500 miles on them, so that put us squarely in the "your chain's not gonna make it" category (at least for those three bikes). We had a couple of spare chains, but they were the continuous kind (not the kind with a master link). We would have needed to remove the swingarm to replace the chain, and that's not something I was going to attempt by the side of the road. More on that later, too.

Seven of the bikes on this ride were brand new bikes, and on those (as well as the bikes that already had a few miles on their clocks) we would need to change the oil a couple of times during the ride. We brought everything we needed to do that.

Gerry Edwards, our Service Department Manager, adjusted the valves on all 10 motorcycles before we left. In our CSC RX3 Service Manual, we had initially stated that the first valve gap inspection should be at 500 miles, and subsequent valve gap inspections and (if necessary) adjustments should occur every 2500 miles. Zongshen had told us the valve inspection and adjustment interval should be something like every 1000 miles, but we felt that was a ridiculously low number. When I asked the Zongshen engineers during one of my visits if that could be extended to 2500 miles they readily agreed, but there was something in their answer that led me to believe they were just telling me what I wanted to hear. My impression was they really didn't know.

Based on all of the above (and the amount of labor that would have been involved), we made a decision not to do any valve adjustments during the ride unless the motorcycles starting exhibiting symptoms consistent with the valves being too tight. Valve gaps always tighten when the valves and valve seats wear. The symptoms can include hard starting, low power, or the engine stops running and starts making clanging sounds when things break inside. We figured we'd know if the valves were getting too tight.

It was a good call. We had no valve problems on any of the bikes during the Western America Adventure Ride. We checked the valve gaps on all the bikes when we returned to Azusa, and based on our findings we subsequently increased the valve gap inspection and adjustment interval to 5000 miles. We feel comfortable with this, especially considering the way we rode the bikes on this ride. But you already know that. We rode 5000 miles at 8000 rpm!

John finished his route planning and it was magnificent. Based on the map he prepared, Steve had a decal prepared for the ride participants. I liked it and I immediately put it on my gas tank. When our guests arrived from China, they did the same. The decal was classy, and we used it several times when people along the way asked where our ride started and where we were going.

The Western America Adventure Ride decal Steve Seidner prepared for us. The decal above it on my tank is a similar one for the CSC Inaugural Baja Run.

We had some uncertainties about the financials on this trip. I had estimated our costs and what I thought Zongshen's costs would be, but I couldn't get an answer on how Zongshen wanted to handle their expenses. I would pay for the fuel, food, and hotel expenses for our guys; Zongshen would pick up the expenses for their guys. What I didn't know until the Zongshen guys arrived in California was if they intended to transfer the funds to us (and have us pay for expenses incurred along the way), or if they would pay they own way.

When the Chinese arrived, I learned that they would pay their own way. It would be a bit messier in handling it this way when we had to pay for the hotels, the fuel, our meals, and the entrance fees at the national parks, but that's what they wanted to do. I'll tell you more about that later.

I assumed the Chinese would arrive with a company credit card. They did not. Hugo, the Zongshen rep, had been provided with a debit card that had a maximum daily withdrawal rate of $800. To compound the difficulty inherent with that approach, the debit card Hugo had was with an obscure bank I had never heard of. I wondered if we'd be able to find ATM machines that would work with his debit card in some of the more rural areas we would be visiting. This is going to be interesting, I thought.

The Chinese had shipped their bikes to us in crates (just like we receive all of the new RX3s), so we set them up. Gerry oversaw this part of the preparation effort and he road tested every bike before the Chinese arrived (just like we do on every bike we set up).

When they arrived, the Chinese and the Colombians wanted to prepare their bikes with their accessories. Two days before we left, they were all over the bikes in our Service Department area. I made a mistake here. I should have paid more attention to what they were doing.

The Colombians were golden; their only mods to the bikes Gerry had set up were the handlebar and control positions (you know, setting the angles and such to their personal preferences), and one set of cosmetic changes on the white RX3 Juan Carlos (one of the two Colombian riders) would ride. On the single white RX3 on this trip, the Colombians removed the CSC RX3 badging and decals and installed the AKT Moto items. AKT Moto is the Colombian RX3 importer. Their decals looked pretty cool, and the AKT colors really worked on the white RX3.

The Chinese riders' modifications were much more extensive and problematic. One guy removed the windshield and mounted four cameras. The others all mounted one or more cameras, their cell phones, GPS systems, and one or two other electronic gizmos I didn't recognize. This is where I dropped the ball.

I mistakenly assumed because these folks were from China, they were Zongshen people or they already owned an RX3 and they would know the bike (I found out later that was not the case). The US configuration RX3 has two underseat-mounted accessory 12-volt outlets that are controlled by a handlebar switch (I described these a few chapters ago).

When the Chinese made their modifications to the bikes for this trip, I assumed that they used these outlets to connect their accessories. They did not. They hardwired the accessories directly to the battery, and some of their accessories had a constant draw (even when turned off). If they had used the accessories outlets, the constant draw would be interrupted when the ignition was switched off. By hardwiring directly to the battery, these devices continued to draw current even after the ignition was off. This would greatly aggravate our battery problems in the coming days.

This above problem was further exacerbated by the Chinese riders' practice of routinely using the kill switch to turn off the engine, which left the headlights on for long periods without the engine running. This put a hell of a load on the battery. The US RX3 has a 300-watt alternator. It does not have a 300-watt battery. I'll get into this in more detail later, too.

After all of the above, we felt we were ready to go. One more day in Azusa, and we'd be on the road.

Chapter 12: We Want to Shoot a Gun

The Chinese and the Colombians all arrived around the same time, and they all came in through Los Angeles International Airport. Steve and I met our six Chinese guests as they arrived. I'll take a minute here to introduce everyone.

Hugo was the first to arrive. Hugo is a Zongshen employee, and he is the Zongshen representative and sales manager assigned to Colombia. Colombia is Zongshen's largest export customer, and Zongshen keeps a full time representative in that country. Hugo came to us as a result of the US government denying entry visas to the original Zongshen people who planned to accompany us on the Western America Adventure Ride. I liked Hugo the instant I met him. He's a good guy.

I should also tell you at this point that our Chinese guests' names may be a little confusing. The Chinese use their family name first, and their given name second. Hugo's real name is Ying Liu, so Ying is his family name and Liu is his given name. I read that and I called Hugo "Ying Lew." He laughed at my pronunciation and told me how to say it correctly. I tried a couple of times and then dropped any pretense of being culturally sensitive. Hugo it would be.

A lot of the Chinese adopt an English name to make it easier for big dumb Americans like me to communicate with them. It's a nice move on their part. I'm telling you all of this so you'll realize that some of the guys have Anglicized names, and some have Chinese names. You'll get the hang of it as the book progresses.

The next flight brought Lester, Tony, Tso, Kong, and Kyle to us.

Lester is a tall man who looks just like Yul Brynner in *The King and I*. He's a physical fitness instructor in a primary school in China, and he also owns a very successful motorcycle and bicycle luggage manufacturing company in China. Lester spoke English well. He is a prominent blogger in China on their premier motorcycle forum. Lester blogged about our trip extensively while we were on the road.

Tony is a celebrity photographer. He owns several motorcycles and his photos are widely published in China and other parts of Asia. He's an interesting man. You'll see him holding a small stuffed dog in my photos. That's MoMo, a mascot who has accompanied Tony to more than 20 countries.

Tso would emerge as the quiet one in our group. He stuck with his Chinese name (it's pronounced "szo" with a hard "sz" sound). Tso is another industrialist; he owns a motorcycle clothing company in China. He was wearing his company's motorcycle gear, as were several of the other Chinese riders.

When I met Kong, I immediately told him that from this point forward on our ride, he would be "King Kong." The Chinese got a big laugh out of that. They all knew the movie and they all liked Kong's new name. Kong is a prominent automotive journalist in China.

Kyle had an English name, but he didn't speak much English. He is an advertising designer and executive, and his customers include the big oil companies in China. Kyle was a lot of fun, and he sure could work wonders with a video camera.

I asked Hugo how Zongshen selected these guys for the Western America Adventure Ride. I didn't understand everything he told me, but I think it was based on their motorcycling experience and a contest of some sort Zongshen had held in China. Each of these guys has a huge media following in China. They were all what I would call high rollers. These folks owned their own companies and were well-known writers and bloggers in China.

The two Colombians also met us at the airport that night. Their participation in the ride was a last minute arrangement. I received a Skype message from Hugo about a week before the ride asking me if the Colombians could accompany us. It was a surprise to me, but I didn't have a problem with it. I thought they would be AKT employees, but they weren't.

Juan Carlos, one of the two Colombians, owns the only motorcycle magazine in Colombia. He's a tall thin guy and an excellent rider. He once rode a KLR 650 to Tierra del Fuego, the southernmost tip of South America, and he had written a hell of a story about it.

Gabriel Abad was the other Colombian. He was instrumental in helping Juan Carlos start his motorcycle magazine. Although Gabriel is a Colombian, he lives in Canada. That certainly was in keeping with the international flavor of our team.

When our good buddies from China and Colombia arrived in the USA that evening, one of their first requests was for an In-N-Out Burger. We did that on the way home from LAX. Then it was on to the hotel in Duarte (the next town over from Azusa) and a good night's sleep after their long journeys to America.

We had a spare 2 days before the ride. We rode around locally to get everybody used to their bikes on the first day, and on the morning of the second day I asked our guests what they would like to do.

Their answer was direct: **We want to shoot a gun.**

I was happy to oblige. I'm a firearms enthusiast and I've been a member of our local gun club for decades. I put my Ruger Mini 14 in the van and we were off to the West End Gun Club.

Our guests were fascinated with everything America has to offer, and the freedom guaranteed by our 2nd Amendment was obviously high on that list. After a brief lesson at the gun club on the rifle, the .223

cartridge, and firearms safety, we set up a target and took turns putting the Ruger through its paces. The guys loved it. The smiles were real, and I had brought along plenty of ammo. The Chinese and the Colombians did well. Literally every shot was on target. They told me I was a good teacher. I think they are just good shots.

Lester Peng putting the Ruger Mini 14 through its paces. Photo by Ying Liu.

Now before any of you get your shorts in a knot about guns and shooting, let me tell you that even though I am a strong 2nd Amendment supporter, I can understand why some of you might be opposed to the freedoms guaranteed by the US Constitution. When I go to a public range I sometimes see people who I wouldn't allow to have oxygen (let alone firearms).

The problem, as I see it, is that if you restrict our rights in this area, it would be a government pinhead making the call on who gets to have guns and who doesn't (and that scares me even more than some of the yahoos I see with guns). It's a tough call, but I'll come down on the side of the 2nd Amendment every time. The founding fathers knew what they were doing, and they did it before the pinheads permeated the government.

Ah, but I digress yet again. Back to the main attraction...my day at the range with our guests.

I didn't get photos of that event. I was busy teaching, watching, and explaining, and I just didn't have an opportunity. The Chinese and the Colombians did. They were having a blast (literally and figuratively), and they captured hundreds of photos. I didn't realize just how special this would be to them when we first left Azusa for the gun club, but it became apparent as soon as we arrived at the range. They all ran up to the line and were fascinated by the spent brass lying on the ground. Several of our guests took pictures. Imagine that...taking pictures of empty shell casings!

When I took the rifle out of its case and opened the ammo box, there were even more oohs and aahhhs. And more photos. I guess I'm so used to being around this stuff I didn't realize how special this day was for our guests. These guys had never held or fired a gun before. Ever. I was amazed by that. They were amazed that we have the freedom to own and shoot firearms. It was an interesting afternoon.

When we finished, all of our guests collected their targets. I had brought along enough targets to give each person their own. We had the range to ourselves that afternoon, so each of the guys would shoot a magazine full of 5.56 ammo, we made the rifle safe, we went downrange to see how each person did, and then we put up a new target for the next guy. Many of the guys repeated that cycle three or four times. It was fun. The guys were like kids in a candy store. I enjoyed being a part of it.

It was hot when we finished shooting at around 4:00 p.m. that day. We were due to meet for dinner at Pinnacle Peaks (a great barbeque place in San Dimas) at 6:00 p.m., and we had a couple of hours to kill. I asked our guests if there was anything else they wanted to do before we went for dinner. My thought was that they might want to go back to the hotel and freshen up. That's not what they had on their minds. They had another request: **Can we go to a gun store?**

That sounded like a good idea to me. We have a Bass Pro near where we were, and it's awesome. Okay, then. Our next stop would be Bass Pro.

I was already getting a sense of how much our guests liked taking pictures, so I told them when we entered the gun department at Bass Pro we should put the cameras away. Usually there are signs prohibiting photography in these kinds of places. We gun enthusiasts don't like being photographed by people we don't know when we are handling firearms (big brother, black helicopters, and all the rest of the unease that comes with a healthy case of paranoia and a deep distrust of the government). I told our guests I would ask if we could take photos, but until then, I asked them to please keep their cameras in their cases.

The guys were in awe when we entered Bass Pro, and then they were even more astounded when we reached the gun department. They were literally speechless. Open mouths. Wide eyes. Unabashed amazement. There isn't anything like Bass Pro in China or Colombia. I've been to both countries and I know that to be the case. Hell, there wasn't anything like Bass Pro in America until a few years ago. It's a combination of a museum, a theme park, a gun store, an armory, and a shopping emporium. I love the place and all that it says about America.

Now, you have to picture this. The Bass Pro gun department. Hundreds of rifles and handguns on display. Targets. Ammo. Gun cases. Reloading gear. A bunch of guys from China talking excitedly a hundred miles an hour in Chinese. The rest of the customers watching, literally with dropped jaws, wondering what was going on. We were a sight.

The Colombians were talking excitedly the same way, but in Spanish.

I was the only guy who looked like he might be from America (my YouTubby belly probably gave me away). The gun department manager looked at me with a quizzical eye. I explained to him who we were and why these guys were so excited. He smiled. "Would they like to take pictures?" he asked. Hoo boy!

The guys loved it. So did the Bass Pro staff. They were handing the Chinese these monster Smith and Wesson .500 Magnums so they could pose for photos, ala *Dirty Harry*. It was quite a moment and it made quite an impression. One of the guys had his video camera out and he was recording one of the Chinese riders holding a huge Smith and Wesson revolver. The guy with the revolver did a pretty good impersonation of Clint Eastwood (albeit with a Chinese accent):

Do you feel lucky, punk? Well, do ya?

It was pretty funny. That *Dirty Harry* movie is 40 years old and it was made before most of our guests were born, but these guys knew that line. The Chinese would surprise me a number of times with their mastery of many American things from our movies and our music. All that's coming up later in this story, folks.

The Chinese and the Colombians were absolutely fascinated with the whole guns and shooting thing and what it is like to live in America, and the Bass Pro staff were quite taken with them. I was pleased. Our guests were getting a first-hand look at American freedoms and American hospitality. It was a theme we would continue to see emerge throughout the Western America Adventure Ride.

For me, a crowning moment occurred on the way to dinner that night. One of the Chinese told me that all the time he was growing up he had been told that Americans were evil and we were their enemy. "That's just not true," he said.

Mission accomplished, I thought.

Chapter 13: The Departure

Our departure the next morning for our first day of the Western America Adventure Ride was at 5:00 a.m. Steve took the van and picked up our guests from the Days Inn. Our guests included the Colombians, the Chinese, and Joe Gresh, the columnist from *Motorcyclist* magazine who would ride the entire 5000 miles with us.

Baja John and I fired up our RX3s at my place at 4:00 a.m. (John had spent the night at my home). We arrived at the plant around 4:30 and things were already happening. It was still dark outside. The chase vehicle, a big yellow Penske truck, was parked out front and everybody loaded their gear into it.

We had a safety briefing, partly to make sure everybody stayed safe, and partly to kill time. Our chase vehicle driver (John the truck driver) wasn't there yet and that worried me. I would have thought everybody would be early for our first day's departure (and everybody was, except for the truck driver). It was not a good sign, and it was a portent of things to come.

During the safety briefing, I emphasized riding in a staggered formation and keeping a good distance between riders. I recommended 30 meters. I told everybody not to do anything nutty and not to run any red lights for fear of being left behind. If anybody was left behind at a traffic light, we'd see it and wait for them as soon as it was safe for us to pull over. I know what it is like to ride a motorcycle in a foreign country and I emphasized and then re-emphasized that we weren't going to leave anybody behind. I described our route for the day, what we would see, and our evening's destination. I hadn't thought about it much in the days before the ride, but at Baja John's urging I would continue these morning briefings every day. The guys seemed to like them.

Hugo was all over us that early morning, taking photos of everyone and everything. So were most of the other riders. I snapped a couple of photos myself. It was a significant moment.

The Western America Adventure Ride at 0:Dark:30 on Day 1.

I looked at Steve, and without me saying a word, he told me that he had called the truck driver. "He's 10 minutes out," Steve said. Okay. It was already 5:00 a.m.

John the truck driver rolled in at around 5:20 a.m. and spent the next 10 minutes leaning into the driver's window talking to whoever had brought him to the plant. All of the bikes were running, all of the riders were on their bikes, and we were being delayed by our chase vehicle driver, who seemed oblivious to it all. I started beeping my horn and several other riders did the same. The truck driver extracted himself from the front window of that car, lumbered over to the Penske truck, and finally, we were off.

The ride out that morning was nice. The sun was starting to come up, it was reasonably cool, and we rolled east on the 210 freeway for about 50 miles until the 210 intersected Interstate 10 just east of San Bernardino. I was in the lead spot (where I would spend most of the next 5000 miles), and from what I could see in my left rear view mirror, everybody was riding well. I also discovered that the yellow Penske truck was an exceptionally good idea. Even though the bikes were strung out behind me for a good distance, I could see the top of the truck. As long as that big yellow submarine was visible in my rear view mirror, I knew we had everybody.

Our first stop was Gramma's Country Kitchen, a restaurant in Yucaipa, California. The food there has always been excellent, and our breakfast this morning would be no exception. When we parked the bikes, I suddenly realized that the logistics of ordering our meals, working through the language barriers, getting our meals, eating our meals, paying for our meals, and getting on the road again would be a challenge. It's funny, I guess. I had thought about a lot of things for this ride, but something as simple as eating had not been on my radar.

The guys were all talking and having a good time in the parking lot. I went into the restaurant and found Alice, a waitress who had served breakfast to me many times before. I told her we had a dozen guys, and about half of us did not speak English (most of our guests spoke English way better than I spoke either Spanish or Chinese, but you get the point). I also explained to Alice that I would be paying for four guys, and Hugo would be paying for eight.

Alice was cool with all of it. I then looked around and realized I was the only guy from our group who was in the restaurant. I had assumed everyone would follow me in, but that's not what happened. I went back outside. The guys were still having a good time taking photos and talking.

Ordering our meals was interesting. Many of the guys, as I said, spoke

English reasonably well. Reading and ordering off a menu was a different challenge, though. Alice was going through her normal routine after each order, and each time it was an adventure. She'd ask each person how they wanted their eggs. Blank stare. What kind of toast. Blank stare. Coffee. Blank stare. Hugo and I followed Alice around the table and started making choices for each person to keep things moving.

Breakfast was good, but we were there a good 2 hours. We already had a late start because of our chase vehicle driver's delinquency. We still had 310 miles to go that day, Joshua Tree National Park to get through, a ride across the Mojave Desert in what promised to be sweltering heat, and a run into Kingman, Arizona (our first night's destination).

Paying proved to be interesting, too. Hugo, not being familiar with our customs, asked me about tipping. I surmised that they don't tip in China, which explained why the waiters and waitresses who waited on me when I visited China were always all smiles when I frequented their restaurants. I explained to Hugo that 15% was customary in the US. The challenge here was that Hugo, who had to pay cash for everything, needed a printed receipt (not a handwritten one) showing the cost of the meal and the tip. That's usually not how it works in an American restaurant (the receipt shows the amount and the customer fills in the tip). We first ran into that at Gramma's, and it came up as an issue in nearly every restaurant on the entire trip.

The other thing I discovered at Gramma's (and it would be a recurring theme every place we stopped) is that these guys were addicted to their cell phones. They would literally enter a restaurant and the first thing they would ask the first person they saw was "You have WiFi code?"

I'm not complaining; I'm just explaining. We actually got pretty good at this restaurant business after the first day. The drill was I would enter the restaurant first, I'd explain to the waitress that we had 12 guys, I would be paying for 4, Hugo would pay for 8, Hugo had to have a printed receipt showing the tip, and we needed the WiFi code. That was working pretty well the first day or two, except for the business of the guys ordering their meals. Hugo and I found an answer for that, too. I'd go in first and ask the waitress what was easy to prepare and could be served expeditiously. I would tell each waitress that we wanted to get in and get out quickly, and then Hugo and I would order the same thing for everybody before we even sat down. We ate a lot of hamburgers on this trip.

After breakfast in Yucaipa, we rolled east another 80 miles or so on Interstate 10 and then turned north for the ride into Joshua Tree National Park. I like Joshua Tree. It has a lot going for it, even though it is not nearly as well known as the other big national parks. I also liked that it had one way in at the south end, and you can ride through it to the single exit at the north end.

What I didn't like when we got to Joshua Tree National Park were the prices. I had been to Arches National Park with Susie just 3 weeks earlier, and the posted entrance fee at that park was $5 for a motorcycle. At Joshua Tree, it was several times higher. I asked the park ranger why it was so expensive, and he explained to me that all the national parks had just raised their fees. There was nothing we could do. We had to pay the higher fees.

Tso riding through Joshua Tree National Park.

Once we entered Joshua Tree, I realized there was another thing I had not considered. Do we ride as a group through the park, or do we just turn everybody loose for a couple of hours and then meet at a designated point at a designated time? I liked the idea of not having to lead the entire group through the park, but I was leery about getting everybody to show up at the rally point on time. I pulled Baja John aside and asked his opinion. He, too, liked the idea of individually exploring an area and meeting up at a designated time. We did that and it worked well. It would be the model we followed at all of the national parks. We stayed together as a group when we were on the road, but at our destinations, everyone was on their own. It worked very well.

The guys loved Joshua Tree, and we all came out with some great photo and video. It's a grand place. I hung out with Lester, and I showed him a few places I liked. I grabbed a great shot of Tso, and it's one we later used as the banner shot on the CSC blog. Tso is a physically expressive guy and because of that he was extremely photogenic.

After Joshua Tree, it was a dash through the Mojave Desert to Amboy. That was a scorching ride. It was 105 degrees that afternoon. It was like riding into a blast furnace, but it wasn't as bad as I thought it would be. We were doing our best to stay hydrated (it's very easy to get dehydrated on a motorcycle on days like this). I also used a trick I learned years ago. I drank a bottle and a half of water, and then poured the remaining half bottle inside and down the back of my riding jacket. It's a shocker when that cold water first hits you, but it would dampen my shirt and the back of my jacket. The water would slowly wick up and evaporate while I rode, and it kept me cool for about 45 minutes while riding in that heat. The Chinese guys looked at me like I was nuts the first time I did this, but after a few days, several of them were doing the same thing.

We stopped in Amboy for photos. It's a quirky little place in the Mojave Desert on Route 66, and the photo ops are impressive. Our guests were excited when they saw the Route 66 signs painted on the road. Some of the Chinese guys actually got down on the road to get their photos snapped with the Route 66 emblem. There's an old hotel there, too, that the owner of the Juan Pollo fast food chain is bringing back to life as a kitschy artists' studio.

Several other tourist groups were in Amboy that day, including a group of Germans who were renting Harley-Davidsons. Lester was immediately drawn to them, and he took a lot of photos. As I would come to learn, Lester makes friends easily and people like talking to him.

Before we left Amboy, we drank a lot of water and a lot of Gatorade (that combination works well when riding through the kind of weather we were experiencing). We rode on desert roads for another 15 miles and then hopped on Interstate 40 for the run into Arizona and Kingman, our first night's destination.

On Route 66 in Amboy, California.

Wow, was it ever hot! We saw a sign for gas at Topock, Arizona, so we pulled off the freeway. We were down to one bar on the fuel gage and some of the bikes' fuel lights were already blinking. That led to a ride of a few miles on a single lane road to a restaurant and resort. It was right on the Colorado River, which we had crossed a few miles back when entering Arizona. Topock had gas, but it was for boats only at their docks on the river.

The Topock resort also had food. It was about 5:00 p.m., and I suddenly realized we had not had lunch. Hugo asked if we were going to only eat two meals each day. "No, I was just having so much fun I forgot to eat," I said, which was exactly what had happened.

I looked long and hard at the Colorado River. I was thinking about walking down to the docks, stripping down to my jeans, and jumping in. The pretty young lady who was taking care of us read my mind. "That water's pretty funky," she said, "and the carp get pretty big. You'd do better swimming in our pool." I looked. There were families there with kids. I didn't want to jump in with my pants on. But that river sure was tempting, and it sure was hot.

After a great dinner (hamburgers of monstrous size, which impressed the Chinese mightily), we were back on the freeway. We found a gas station and filled the bikes, and we rolled into Kingman for our first night on the road.

The bikes ran flawlessly at 75 mph all day long across the scorching Mojave Desert and into Arizona. We had covered 361 miles, which would be our highest mileage day of the Western America Adventure Ride. The riding had been brutal on us. The bikes took it in stride without missing a beat. The hotel in Kingman that night had a pool and we had cold beer (John the truck driver made up for his earlier tardiness by picking up a case of beer).

Life doesn't get much better than this, I thought after our first day on the road.

Chapter 14: The Grand Canyon

I was up early the next morning, as is my habit. Juan Carlos and Gabriel (the Colombians) and I would be the only folks on this trip who consistently were up early. Everyone else liked to sleep, I guess, but on this day I was up before the sun. We were in Kingman, Arizona, and I knew it was going to be another hot day. I made a cup of coffee in my room. While it was brewing, I went out to walk around the parking and check the bikes.

What I saw that morning surprised me. You may recall that I told you the Chinese had mounted more than a few electronic gizmos on their bikes (you know, cameras, GPS devices, cell phones, etc.). Several of the Chinese riders had tank bags. To my astonishment, they had left all of these things on the bikes overnight, and two or three of the guys had even left their helmets on the bikes. I don't know what surprised me more: The fact that they had left all of these baubles out overnight, or the fact that they were still there. I knew I'd have to mention that to the guys.

All the chains were good, all the tires were good (yep, I kicked 20 tires that morning), no oil had leaked anywhere, and when I tilted the bikes to the vertical, all of the oil levels were good. That last thing was amazing all by itself...not that the oil levels were good, but that I could see the oil levels in the viewing ports on the right side of the engine.

I had learned on my last trip to Chongqing that there was a secret handshake to checking the RX3's oil level. You have to let the engine completely warm up, and then you have to let it idle for one minute, and then you have turn off the engine and wait for one minute for the oil level to settle. That's because the RX3 engine is essentially a dry sump engine with two oil compartments (the transmission and the crankcase). The bike has two oil pumps that operate at different rates (one pumps from the tranny to the crankcase and the other pumps in the opposite direction, and they do so at different rates). If you don't follow the procedure described here when checking the oil, the oil level either won't be up to the viewing port, or it will be over it. It will usually appear as if the engine oil level is too low. In fact, on our first day out, a couple of the Chinese riders and one of the Colombians told me that their bikes did not have enough oil. I had watched Gerry service these bikes, though, and I knew that wasn't the case. I told the guys not to worry about it and I explained how to check the oil level.

The Kingman Best Western served breakfast. I came to really love it when the hotels included a breakfast. The meals were mediocre at best, but they minimized the morning delays. If the hotel served breakfast, we could get in, get everybody fed, we didn't have to struggle with who wanted to order what, we didn't have to pay for breakfast, and we could get out. It's just so much easier when you have a large group if the hotel takes care of breakfast.

After breakfast, the truck was still closed and John the truck driver wasn't up yet. I asked Baja John where our truck driver was (they had shared a room the night before), and he didn't know. Hugo rode in the truck, and I asked him if he knew where the truck driver was. He did not. Everyone was standing around at the back of the truck waiting to load their luggage. Wow, this was the second day in a row. The truck driver was holding us up again. I'd have to do something about that.

While we were waiting, I figured I'd use the time for the morning talk (the briefing that became our habit each morning). I told the Chinese guys they should not leave their goodies on the bikes overnight and that if they did, someone would steal them. They looked surprised. King Kong told me that they heard America was a safe place. I explained that while that was generally true, you couldn't leave valuables on the bikes overnight. We had been very lucky that nothing had been stolen.

One of the Chinese guys asked me what they should do if we were stopped for a traffic violation. I don't know what came over me, but I saw a chance to get cute. "That most likely won't happen, because we're not going to speed," I said, "but if you do get stopped, the trick is to look the police officer directly in the eye and tell him: Don't f*ck with me. I have a gun."

The Colombians and a couple of the Chinese guys smiled at my little joke. I asked the Chinese rider who had asked the question, "You got that?"

"Don't f*ck with me. I have gun!" he parroted back with a Chinese accent.

"Okay, you got it," I said.

Thank God, on the entire trip, we were never stopped by a police officer.

John truck driver finally appeared. He opened the truck and we loaded the luggage on the truck. I told everyone to start their bikes, thinking we could get on the road. At that point, our truck driver told me he needed to get ice for the ice chest (you know, to keep our water and Gatorade cold). It dawned on me this wouldn't be from the ice maker in the hotel; he was telling me he needed to go find a store and buy a couple of bags of ice. Another delay. We waited. After another half hour, John was back with the truck and we were finally able to get underway again.

Our route was a good one. We picked up Interstate 40 and rode east at 75 mph. As we were doing so, Joe Gresh (who had been somewhere back in the pack) passed me as we were climbing a long uphill grade. He made a rotary motion with his left arm, which I recognized as an imitation of a steam locomotive. The little engine that could. I got it, but I still didn't understand why he was passing me. We're both older guys, I thought. Maybe he's trying to get to a restroom.

What my good buddy Joe was up to was getting in position further up the road so he could photograph us as we rolled by. I saw him with his camera on the side of the road several miles later, waiting for us. That's right, I thought. He's working. He needs the photos for the feature he's going to write for *Motorcyclist* magazine.

We stopped on the way to the Grand Canyon for fuel in the little town of Seligman. It was interesting, with a lot of stuff from the 1950s and earlier. We were on one of the sections of old Route 66 that paralleled the freeway, and the cameras were out again. Our guests were fascinated with everything. Hugo asked me what a sign that said "No Semis" meant. I explained to him that a semi was a tractor trailer (a semi-truck), and he explained that to the other Chinese guys.

We entered Grand Canyon Village (the little town outside the Grand Canyon) and we stopped for lunch at a McDonald's. Easy in, easy out. It was quick. I liked that.

Entering Grand Canyon National Park was crowded and chaotic. There were long lines of cars waiting ahead of us. I was the first in our group to get to the kiosk at the entrance. I was the leader of the pack, to borrow a phrase from that 1960s song. I explained to the ranger that we had ten motorcycles, one truck with two guys in it, I would be paying the entrance fee for four of the bikes and the truck (at the tail end of the pack), I personally had the lifetime senior pass, and Hugo (who was in the truck at the tail end of the pack) would be paying for the rest of the bikes. It was complicated, even to me, and I was the guy trying to explain it.

The park ranger rolled his eyes, but he was pretty savvy. He asked if we were going to be visiting several of the national parks on our trip, and when I said yes, he told us we would probably save money by purchasing an annual pass for the truck and for each pair of motorcycles. I explained all of this to Hugo. There was a long line of cars behind us and we were holding them up. It was hot out. If this was supposed to be fun, I wasn't feeling it at that moment.

Hugo was cool with the ranger's suggestion, and that's what we did. That entrance into the Grand Canyon was a big bump financially, but it saved us a lot of money on the rest of the trip.

Hugo, King Kong, Lester, and Tso on the South Rim of the Grand Canyon.

We parked the bikes and agreed that our rally point would be where we had parked the bikes. We split up again, and walked over to the visitor center area, which you have to pass through to get to the canyon. We then walked from the visitor center toward the canyon's edge a few hundred yards away. While we were walking, Hugo tapped my shoulder and asked, "What's that?"

Whoa! I hadn't even noticed it until Hugo asked me the question. A huge elk was munching grass not 10 feet away from us, oblivious to our presence. I had never been that close to an elk before. The animal was totally at ease being among people. It was almost as if it was domesticated. These creatures are huge. I didn't think it was a good thing to be that close to an elk; it could do serious damage to a person if it wanted to.

That elk was the first of many wild animals we would see on this trip. The Chinese took several photographs. They must have thought elk mixing with humans was a common event. It looked perfectly natural for it to be that close to us, but trust me on this, it is not. Try hunting elk sometime and see if you can get close to one. I kept one eye on the elk and one eye on our guests. I would stop them if they tried to get any closer to it. I didn't get a photo, probably because I was unnerved by the whole thing.

The Grand Canyon was indeed quite grand. It was crowded with tourists, but the place was magnificent. It was amazing. It was awesome. It was beautiful. I know I'm using those words a lot and I'll continue to use them throughout this book as I describe the things we saw on our journey. We were seeing the best America has to offer. I'd been to the Grand Canyon before, but seeing it again I realized just how amazing it is. I was enjoying our guests' reactions to it. We took a lot of photos.

We spent about two hours at that location before reconvening at the bikes, and then we saddled up and rode along the southern rim of the Canyon. We stopped at a couple more locations for photos. One of the Colombians had asked if there was a place where we could park the bikes at the canyon's edge and get a photo. I spotted a place where we could do that and we took more photos.

We were only a couple of days into the trip. We had seen so much already it felt as if we had been on the road longer. I was having a good time with everybody, and I was especially enjoying Joe Gresh's banter. He has a sense of humor a lot like mine and I was finding we had several things in common. Joe is a bit younger than me. We are both life-long motorcycle enthusiasts and we had both owned Harleys (a rite of passage for motorcycle guys our age, I guess). We both love old British twins. We both get the small bike thing (small bikes make sense and they are fun to ride). Joe writes a regular column for *Motorcyclist*; I write a regular piece for *Motorcycle Classics*. In short, we are both riders and writers. But don't get me wrong; I'm nowhere near the caliber of writer Joe Gresh is.

I was finding Joe to be a photogenic dude, too. At that last photo stop along the edge of the Grand Canyon, he was hamming it up for the camera and I grabbed what would become one of my favorite Western America Adventure Ride photos.

The photograph of Joe almost looks like he was Photoshopped into the picture, but it's real with no post-processing trickery. I used my 16-35mm Nikon lens with the polarizer removed and fill flash when I took it. It looks like Joe is popping out of the photo.

A grand guy at the Grand Canyon - Joe Gresh of Motorcyclist magazine.

After the Grand Canyon, we rode to Page, Arizona, for the night. It was a glorious ride along Highway 89, with magnificent red cliffs lining the road on both sides. It was still warm, but it was getting cooler as we continued to travel north. We were gaining altitude and cutting the heat as we did so.

When we checked into the hotel that evening, a nice young man took care of us in the lobby. Based on his appearance, I asked him if I could ask him a personal question. He said it would be okay.

"Are you of Navajo ancestry?" I asked.

"I am," he said.

Hugo had asked me earlier what became of the Native Americans who first inhabited these regions, and I told him many of their descendants still lived and worked in the area. Hugo found that intriguing and asked if I would point one out to him. When Hugo witnessed our exchange at the hotel lobby, he was impressed. He shook the young man's hand.

Hugo wanted to change the oil in the new motorcycles. CSC and Zongshen advised doing the first oil change at 200 miles, and we were up to about 600 miles or so already. I told Hugo and the rest of the guys we would do it in the morning. I was just too tired to do it that night.

We ordered pizza for dinner in the hotel lobby that night. It was good, and so was the conversation.

Chapter 15: Zion

The next morning we changed the oil in all of the motorcycles in the hotel parking lot in Page. Hugo had been worried about going too long before changing the oil. I was worried about it taking too long to change the oil. Everything is a question of perspective.

It seemed to me like everything was taking longer than it should on this trip. I was afraid we would get into our evening's destination this day in Panguitch, Utah, after sunset. We were going to visit Zion today, our third day on the road, and we had many miles to cover. I knew Zion would be crowded, which would slow things further.

I didn't want to get into Panguitch after sundown, and I didn't want to ride at night. It was enough of a challenge keeping everybody together in the daytime. I generally don't like riding at night, anyway. The good news was that our scheduled mileage for the day was a bit lower than the first two days, so I reckoned we would be okay even with the oil change.

The oil changes went more quickly than I thought they would. We arranged a little assembly line. Each rider wanted to change his own oil, and we developed a system that kept things moving. John the truck driver measured the 55.4 ounces each bike required, and we moved through the maintenance actions quickly. Surprisingly, we didn't spill any oil. I thought the hotel owner might object to us using his parking lot as a Jiffy Lube, but we got through it so quickly that we were finished before the hotel people realized what we were doing. After we finished, our work area was spotless. You would have never known that we changed the oil on 10 motorcycles.

All of our US national parks are beautiful, but Zion is one of my personal favorites. That might be because Zion is the first national park I ever visited. I did so on a motorcycle trip with my late buddy Dick Scott about 30 years ago when we both rode Harley-Davidsons. To me that ride with Dick epitomized everything that is right in the world. That ride had it all: Motorcycles, adventure touring, my knees in the breeze, America, great scenery, camaraderie, and all the rest. I've been to Zion several times since, and I always enjoy going back. I was proud to be bringing our guests from Colombia and China to Zion. I knew the scenery would be magnificent and they would enjoy it.

We had a great ride from Page to Zion. One of the high points was our lunch stop in a little Utah town before we got to Zion. Sometimes I see things and I don't have a camera in my hands to capture the moment, but the images are indelibly etched in my mind. What happened in Mt. Carmel Junction was just such a moment.

I stopped so I could check my map and we parked directly in front of the drive-through window at a Subway sandwich shop. Two very young Asian women opened the window, thinking we wanted to order. They were amazed when the guys started taking off their helmets and they saw Asian faces. These young ladies' obvious delight and the conversation that followed was a Kodak moment if ever there was one. The young women were Chinese exchange students working part time at Subway. To make a small world even smaller, Hugo told me he had worked at a Subway shop in China when he was a student. Fun times. I missed the photo, but I'll remember that moment forever.

A short ride later we were at the entrance of Zion National Park. Our entry there (as had been the case with the Grand Canyon) was mildly chaotic. We had our annual passes, but when we arrived at the gate we were not organized by which two motorcycles shared each annual pass. The chaos was compounded by the fact that the truck was bit further back in the line, and cars had wedged their way were between the bikes and our chase vehicle.

I arrived at the entrance first and explained who we were, the two-bikes-per-annual pass deal we had purchased at the Grand Canyon, and the chase vehicle situation. Like I said, the bikes were not organized in pairs, and the poor park ranger to whom I was speaking became confused and flustered. She waved all of us through without checking any of our passes.

After we entered the park, we stopped to designate a rally point, but something was wrong. I looked around. Our group had grown smaller.

"Where's Baja John?" I asked nobody in particular.

"I think he pulled off," Juan Carlos said. "Lester stopped, and John stopped with him."

The chase truck was behind us still waiting to get through the Zion entrance. When the truck arrived, I asked about Baja John and Lester.

"Yeah, he pulled off," John the truck driver said. "I think Lester wanted to take a few photos, so they stopped. I pulled over, but he waved me on."

Hmmm. I tried calling Baja John on my cell phone, but I had no service. I had just assumed John the truck driver, as the guy driving the chase vehicle, would know to stop and wait if anybody pulled over. Seeing that big yellow submarine bringing up the rear was my way of knowing that everybody was still in the group. I was relying on that, but I had failed to make it clear to everyone that this was my register on the group's staying together. It was my failure. I explained to John the truck driver that I wanted him to wait every time anybody pulled over for anything. He was cool with it. I just hadn't explained it to him earlier.

We waited about 30 minutes, but Baja John and Lester didn't arrive. I couldn't reach John on my cell phone. John the truck driver tried to call Baja John (his phone had service), but he couldn't connect, either.

I reasoned that Baja John and Lester would catch up with us eventually, so we designated the Zion visitor center as our rally point, and we told everyone we would convene there in 3 hours. Our group split up and set about seeing the park and taking photos.

The traffic in Zion was extremely heavy, and it was terribly hot that day. We finally made it to the famous Zion tunnels. They were not a lot of fun for me. The tunnels are narrow (they were built in a time when RVs did not exist), so the park rangers stop traffic and only let vehicles through one way at a time. We had to wait about 15 minutes before we could enter the tunnels.

We were suited up with our ATGATT stuff (all the gear, all the time) and it was sweltering. I could feel the sweat pouring off of me. People who don't ride have this vision of being cool and comfortable riding a motorcycle because you create your own breeze. That's true to an extent when you're moving, but when you're stopped, it's miserable. You're wearing a full face helmet, gloves, a jacket, jeans, motorcycle pants, and boots. Imagine dressing for a cold winter day with all of your winter clothing and then stepping out into 100-degree weather holding up a 400-lb motorcycle while stopped in the sun on a hot tarmac. That's what it's like.

Finally, the rangers motioned for us to proceed. Yippee!

It was a very bright day, but once we were in the tunnels it was darker than an executioner's smile. I had my high beams on and I still couldn't see much. There was an RV in front of me and for the first hundred yards or so I just fixated on its tail lights. When my eyes finally adjusted to the darkness, bam, we were in the sunlight again. I saw that we would be in the light for just a short distance and then we'd be in another tunnel, so I resorted to an old trick I learned in the Army. I shut one eye to preserve my night vision, and I did a lot better in that second tunnel (even though it was longer).

After making it through the tunnels, the road wound down into the Zion National Park valley. We stopped for photos, but what I was hoping for was to get a call to or from Baja John. I checked my phone, but I still had no service. I wasn't worried; I just wanted to make sure we'd regroup and keep moving so that we wouldn't have to ride at night.

We grabbed some good photos at that stop, and one of them became a banner for the CSC blog. Tso came through for me once again. Like I said before, he is a physically expressive guy. Tso is not a hugger or anything like that; he just naturally strikes these poses that make for incredible photographs. He was posing for Hugo with one of the Zion arches in the background, and the photos looked so good I grabbed a shot, too.

Tso in Zion National Park.

We rode on to what I thought was the Zion visitor center and stopped. Our guys were out exploring the park, so I just stayed in the shade and kept cool. My phone rang (I was enjoying the shade so much the phone surprised me), and it was Baja John. John the truck driver had it right (John and Lester had stopped for a photo), but when they started again Lester's bike had difficulty starting. It was running okay now, but it was tough getting it to start wherever they had stopped earlier. It sounded like it might be a battery failure; these were the same symptoms I saw on a couple of the bikes in Baja. Then, to compound the felony, Baja John and Lester missed the turn for Zion. They rode another 20 miles beyond where they should have turned before realizing they had made a mistake, and that's why it had taken them so long to rejoin the group.

Okay, everybody was accounted for, and I was feeling better. I was enjoying the shade at what I thought was the visitor center. My phone rang a second time. It was Baja John again. "Where are you?" he said.

"I'm at the visitor center," I answered.

"So am I," John said, "but I don't see you."

Well, as it turns out, I wasn't at the visitor center after all. I was at the Zion museum. The visitor center was outside the park's entrance. Okay, another mistake. But it was easily corrected, and 30 minutes later John found me. Other guys started drifting in, too.

When we were all back together again (about 45 minutes past our scheduled regrouping time), we began the ride back through the park and headed for Panguitch.

Traffic through the park was still heavy and the going was slow. It was still very hot. Heavy traffic. Heat. All the gear, all the time. Uggghh. We went back through the tunnels (with me doing my one-eye-shut routine for a couple of miles before we got there).

A mile or two after the tunnels, we came upon a car that had stopped in the middle of our lane. Traffic had stopped going the other way, too, and people were outside their cars milling about. My first thought was that there had been an accident, but that wasn't the case at all. What had caused all the excitement was a herd of 20 or so bighorn sheep slowly meandering along the side of the road. They were majestic. It was something right out of a Dodge truck commercial. Ram tough, I thought. Just like these RX3s.

Once we left Zion, the roads outside the park were wide open. We made good time to Panguitch. Baja John had arranged our lodging in three separate hotels. They were all older hotels that had seen better days, but they were fine by me. John had done an absolutely incredible job finding towns that put our daily mileage right where we wanted it to be each day, and he found us inexpensive hotels in every location. The guy was awesome. I didn't mind the lower-tier hotels, either. In fact, I kind of liked it. All I needed was a place to sleep. As long as the place is quiet and has good Internet connectivity, I'm a happy camper.

All of us asked our respective innkeepers where the best place in town was for dinner (Panguitch is a small town), and they all recommended Cowboy's Smoke House Café. Based on the recommendations' unanimity, Cowboy's Smoke House Café it was.

Waiting for dinner at Cowboy's Smoke House Café in Panguitch, Utah.

We had to wait to get into Cowboy's (that's always a good sign). We enjoyed hanging around out front and chatting before we could be seated. Hugo went off to find an ATM. We all took photos of Panguitch at night.

When we were called, I explained the billing arrangements to the young lady who seated us, and they were fine with that. The place had a good vibe and the food was outstanding.

Cowboy's was expensive, though. It's not that the prices were high, it's just that our guys (the ones for whom I was paying) seemed to have a penchant for ordering whatever was the most expensive thing on the menu. That night in Panguitch was no exception. $35 porterhouse steaks. A $35 rack of ribs (it was two racks, actually). Appetizers. Desserts. To me, it was excessive. It wasn't just the excessiveness in making every dinner a three or four course event with the most expensive things on the menu; it was also the portion sizes. They were embarrassingly large.

The Chinese and the Colombians weren't doing this; they were ordering sensibly. It was just my American guys. Steve and Maureen were paying for our meals, and what was happening made me uncomfortable. I made a mental note to talk to our guys about it in the morning and I did, but it made no difference.

As a side note, if you ever have an opportunity to run an event like this, don't simply pick up the meals for everyone. You either need to order for your group so that you can control the expense, or you need to tell people to pay for their own meals and give them a per diem amount. That way if they order the big bucks stuff, it comes out of their pockets. That would have brought the gluttony under control (in fact, it probably would have prevented it from ever emerging). Next time I'll know.

All that aside, the meal was excellent. It was one of the best dinners of the entire trip. The only downside (other than the aforementioned gluttony) was that the Cowboy's Smoke House Café owner liked to talk. We finished our meal around 10:00 p.m. and the most of the guys were eager to get back to their hotel rooms. We just couldn't seem to get the checks and the owner kept telling us more stories. Hugo asked me three times why it was taking so long to get our checks, and every time we were just about ready to leave, the owner had another story. Then the waitress made a mistake on our invoices and she had to redo them. Then Hugo needed his invoice to show the tip.

Hugo finally told me, "Joe, I've got to send reports to my bosses in

Zongshen every night and answer their emails. I've got to get back to the hotel." Incredibly, it took another hour before we had the checks and we could finally leave. Before we left Cowboy's, everyone agreed to meet in my hotel's parking lot the next morning before we headed out for breakfast.

I felt bad for Hugo. For him, just like for me, this wasn't just a motorcycle ride. We were seeing the sights and having fun like everyone else on the ride, but there's a difference between being a tourist and being responsible for a group of tourists. For Hugo and I, and for Baja John (who was handling all of the hotel arrangements), much of the work started when we returned to our hotel rooms each evening.

That night, after dinner and before we returned to our hotels, Baja John told me we needed to think about shortening the ride. He suggested eliminating Mt. Rushmore and Devil's Tower from our itinerary. They were the two easternmost points on our Western America Adventure Ride. The reasons for John's suggestion were obvious. We were struggling every morning with getting started on time, and we seemed to be arriving later and later every evening. Part of the problem was a couple of the Chinese riders who were late for everything, part of the problem was our truck driver who was similarly late, and part of the problem was that John and I were feeling the stress of herding the cats. "Herding the cats" is an old expression that describes situations in which you're having difficulty making things move in a coordinated manner. It sure seemed like an appropriate analogy.

I told John I'd think about it. The truth is I was already thinking along the same lines. I had the same concerns, but I didn't really want to cut the ride short. We had promised the Chinese managers at Zongshen a series of stops that included these two iconic American monuments (and like CSC, they were spending a ton of money on this ride). I had written about the trip extensively on the CSC blog describing all of the cool places we would see. Steve had that cool decal printed that showed all of our stops. The bottom line was I just didn't want to admit defeat. Cutting two key stops from our plan, to me, would be doing just that. But things were looking pretty bleak from the perspective of my ability to make all of this happen. I couldn't seem to get everybody started on time, be it in the morning, after a stop for gas, after lunch, or anywhere else that required us to stop and then get moving again.

Not much happened when I got back to the hotel that night. It was close to midnight and that's usually a good time to get on the Internet, but not in Panguitch. The connectivity at our hotel was terrible, so I didn't post anything on the CSC blog that evening. I crawled in bed and I think I fell asleep before my head hit the pillow. We'd been on the road only 3 days and I was already drained. 14 days to go.

There was another restaurant across the street from the Cowboy's Smoke House Café, and we had unanimous recommendations from our hoteliers that it was the "go to" spot for the best breakfast in Panguitch. That was our plan for the next day.

Chapter 16: Bryce

We were up the next morning in Panguitch to find that the weather had cooled considerably. It rained during the night. If you're on a motorcycle trip and it's going to rain, having it do so at night is a good thing. It wasn't cold, but the oppressive heat wave we had been struggling with was broken and it was much more comfortable.

Predictably, we were late getting over to the restaurant for breakfast, but it wasn't by much. My thinking had progressed from wanting to be on time to being content if we weren't late by much.

There were a three armed rustic types hanging out in front of the restaurant. Utah is an "open carry" state, and that means anyone without a criminal record can openly wear a firearm. Our three armed bears (I always get it wrong...was it keep and bear arms, or keep armed bears?) included two fellows and one woman who looked like they came straight off a movie set. All three were wearing sidearms. One of the men who had a scraggly gray beard and the lady wore Peacemaker-type six guns low on their hips (you know, the old Colt six shooters like we used to see in the cowboy movies). The third guy was wearing a .45 auto (a 1911) cocked and locked. If the invasion was coming, these three were ready.

The Chinese and the Colombian guys were astounded with this open display of firepower. They asked if they could take photos, and the Panguitchians were cool with it. Lester was in the lead here; as I've mentioned before he has this natural ability to make friends. Lester's Yul Brynner appearance adds to his charm. When he speaks English it's obvious he is choosing his words carefully with an internal translation going on in his head, and it naturally makes any listener pay attention.

Our Utah desperados recognized that Lester, Tony, Tso, Kyle, King Kong, and Hugo were definitely not from Utah and they were highly amused by it all. I suppose I was little leery about the locals' reactions to our group. You know, here we were, a bunch of people from other countries (China, Colombia, and I'm originally from New Jersey). We were dressed like teenage mutant ninja turtles with all of our motorcycle clothing, and it seemed to me that if the roles were reversed I'd be a bit on guard. We never had any problems or experienced any kind of hostility, though, and I think a lot of that was due to Lester's unnatural ability to have people like him immediately.

We went into the restaurant for breakfast and the wait staff treated us well. After the monster portions we had been served at the Cowboy's Smoke House Café the night before, everyone was looking for a small breakfast. Our Panguitch hotels had seen their best days in the 1960s (none of them served breakfast), so our visit to what we had been told was the best breakfast restaurant in Panguitch was our only option.

Hugo wanted a small breakfast and he opted for the short stack of pancakes. He told me he was eating too much. The menu said the short stack had only two pancakes, so Hugo figured it was a safe bet. It's interesting to view the world through the eyes of our Chinese and Colombian friends. These guys were blown away by everything they saw in America. In particular, they were amazed at the portion sizes in our American restaurants.

Well, Hugo got a short stack all right. Just two pancakes. They were about 14 inches in diameter and each one was maybe three-quarters of an inch thick. Maybe even thicker. The look on Hugo's face when the waitress put the plate in front of him was a classic. He displayed both surprise and terror. Hugo just shrugged his shoulders and sighed. His body language simply said, "I give up." Funny stuff. Hugo made a dent in those two monster pancakes, and then he cut up the rest and gave some to the other guys.

Hugo was kind of like a lieutenant for me, especially where the Chinese guys were concerned. Even though he was the youngest of our Chinese guests, as the Zongshen rep he was the guy paying the freight. If I needed something to happen, I could tell Hugo and he made it so. When I first heard we wouldn't have anybody from Zongshen's Chongqing plant on the ride my antenna went up, but Zongshen did very well selecting Hugo as their representative. I enjoyed my time with him enormously.

While we were having breakfast, Hugo and Lester told Joe Gresh and me that they had Chinese names for us. Because we were both named Joe, they viewed us as the older uncle (that would be me) and the younger uncle (that was Joe Gresh). As I understood it from their explanation, the Chinese word "Jiu" means uncle, and "Jiu" sort of sounds like "Joe" the way they say it. I would now be Da Jiu (older uncle) and Joe Gresh would be Ar Jiu (younger uncle). We were both flattered.

Lester was also fascinated by my fixation with being on time. "You are our Captain, just like we are in the US Army," Lester told me. Wow. I used to be in the Army, but I only made it to Lieutenant. A promotion to Captain. It was 40 years too late for me, but I made grade on only our fourth day on the road with these guys.

After the best breakfast in Panguitch, we were on the road heading to Bryce National Park. It was another place of inspiring, colorful, and majestic beauty. Bryce's claim to fame are the hoodoos and their colors. Hoodoos are earthen structures of pink, white, and orange sandstone.

As had become our pattern, we split up again once we were in the park. We agreed on the rally point and the rally time, and we were off. I rode with Baja John, Tony, John the truck driver, and Kyle. We visited one of the many vantage points and took it all in. Kyle shot some video for about 10 minutes of the clouds moving overhead, which he later sped up and used in a video about the trip. It was all great.

So far, we'd been to Joshua Tree National Park, Grand Canyon National

Park, Zion National Park, and Bryce National Park, and we had been on the road 4 days. We were seeing a lot.

Tony, MoMo, and Kyle in Bryce National Park.

These different parks are all beautiful in their different ways. Joshua Tree is mostly flat with an other-worldly stark landscape accentuated by rock formations and Joshua trees. It's dominated by brown, gray and tan colors, with a little bit of green thrown in. In Joshua Tree, you're on the ground floor. At the Grand Canyon, you are on top of things looking down into a long canyon so majestic it almost looks as if it were a painting with various shades of purple, red, and pink, all contrasting sharply with a brightly polarized blue sky. You're upstairs at the Grand Canyon, so to speak, looking down. In Zion, you're in the valley, looking up at these amazing red, orange, and cream-colored rock formations and mountains. In Zion, you're in the basement looking up. In Bryce, the format changes yet again. You're back on top looking down at kaleidoscopic red, orange, and white formations in yet another set of different shapes. I was in awe during these first 4 days, and I had already visited all of these places prior to our Western America Adventure Ride. To the Chinese and the Colombians, it must have been overwhelming.

Another thing that stuck in my mind regarding how our guests were taking all of this is was a comment from Joe Gresh. Most of our riding so far had been through very sparsely-populated areas, and we'd already covered about a thousand miles. "Do you think they're wondering where all of the people are?" Joe asked. It was a good point. The only places we saw more than a few people were in the national park visitor centers. "They have to be wondering: Where are all the people?" Joe said again.

Our planned stop for that evening was Hanksville, Utah, which was close to the Colorado border. We sure were racking up the miles. After Bryce, we pointed the bikes east. I didn't know it yet because I had never been in this part of Utah, but were we heading for two of the most dramatic and beautiful roads I had ever seen: Utah's Highway 12 and Highway 24.

Highway 12 runs northeasterly across the state and the scenery is drop dead stunning. There's no other way to describe it. To be blunt, it was the best part of America and the best motorcycle ride I've ever experienced. If you ever have a chance to ride this road, do it. It's a combination of sharply descending and climbing twisties bordered by dramatic pink and white rock formations that look as if they were made of molten plastic painted in stunning pastel colors. It was breathtakingly beautiful riding.

After the pastel panoramas, Highway 12 climbed into an area called Hell's Backbone. It's a set of twisties along a very sharply pronounced ridge. The road has shear drops of great depth on both sides that drop off right at the road's edges. It looked as if you couldn't pull off the road or you'd go over the edge. It was fantastic riding, the stuff of both dreams and nightmares. I have never experienced anything like it.

You're probably wondering if I have photos of this magnificent road. I do not. I was not taking as many photos as I normally would, mostly because I had a lot on my mind: Getting people moving on time, watching our gas to make sure we didn't run out before we got to the next gas station, looking for safe places to pull over when we needed a break (which was roughly every hour), and finding photo op spots and stops for the rest of the guys. It was intense and I didn't want to be Joe Tourist so I could take pictures. I wanted to get everybody to the next destination safely before dark so that they could take it all in and take pictures, and I wanted to find good spots along the way for us to do that.

On Highway 12, I didn't take any photographs, but it wasn't because of the reasons I just listed. It was because the road was so magnificent I just wanted to experience it without thinking about anything else. And that's what I did. The riding, like I said, was the best I've ever experienced. It was that good.

We stopped at a restaurant along Highway 12 after Hell's Backbone because I thought there was a gas station there. I screwed up again. I didn't tell anyone that's why I stopped. Once we were there, we found that it was a local motorcycle spot and there were some fairly exotic bikes in the parking lot (Ducatis, Triumphs, and even one of the modern Nortons). The guys wanted to stay and talk but we were running late and I didn't want to stay too long.

We had passed a gas station a half mile further back, so I left to fill up there. Some of the guys realized what I was doing and followed me, but some of them did not and had to scramble to get their gear back on so they could catch up. It was my fault. I was tired and I simply hadn't bothered to communicate what I was doing.

At that gas station, Baja John caught up with me and I could tell he was upset. Being the gentleman that he is, he pulled me aside privately and told me what I had done was wrong. I had to agree with him.

John suggested that any time we were going to get on the road, either he or I should beep our horn three times as the "get ready" signal. It would let the rest of the guys know we had 3 minutes to get our gear back on and then we would leave. It was simultaneously brilliant and simple (as the best ideas always are). I felt dumb and guilty for not thinking of it myself, and I really felt bad about upsetting John. John is about the easiest-going guy I've ever met, and if I had offended him, I can only imagine what the other guys must have been thinking. I went into the gas station and bought John a candy bar as a peace offering. John likes candy. It worked. We then pulled everybody together and briefed them on our "three beeps" strategy. We did it after everybody had topped off, and that worked, too.

Before we left, though, I had John the truck driver replace the battery in Tony's bike. Tony's bike had a tough time starting at the last stop, and in this case, there was no doubt it was the battery. We could see where acid had leaked out of it. John had the battery out and a new one installed in less than 5 minutes. He was good at this. Tony's bike started easily. We were good to go.

Utah's Highway 12 ended when it intersected with Highway 24. We turned right on 24 and continued east. Highway 24 was yet another magnificent road, and it carried us directly into Capitol Reef National Park.

Gabriel, Juan Carlos, and Joe Gresh on Utah Highway 12.

Capitol Reef is as magnificent as the other four parks we had already visited, and it was a special treat for me. In fact, the entire afternoon was special. I had never been on Highway 12, I had never been on Highway 24, and not only had I never been to Capitol Reef National Park, I didn't even know it was going to be on our route. Wow! Two national parks in one day! One planned, and one a surprise. I was over feeling guilty about my "no warning" early departure from the gas station a hundred miles ago. This was turning out to be a dynamite day.

We were hit with our first rain of the trip on that stretch along Highway 24, but instead of taking pleasure away from the ride, it added to it. The skies had been darkening all afternoon, and for about three minutes on Highway 24, they opened up. It was a deep, heavy rain, and then it was over. We didn't have time to put on our rain gear, and although the rain came down hard, we barely got wet. The RX3 windshield is phenomenal in that regard. That little bit of formed clear plastic not only directed the wind over and around us with no buffeting; it apparently did the same thing with the rain. Joe Gresh told me he thought it was the best windshield he had ever experienced on any motorcycle. I agree. It's one of many incredibly well engineered things on the RX3.

We stopped after the rain did. We were at a good spot to grab a few photos. Juan Carlos sent Gabriel back down Highway 24 for a return ride up so he could capture some video. Everybody was in high spirits.

Dinner with the Duke in Hanksville. What could be better?

We arrived in Hanksville about an hour later, found our hotel, and checked in. It wasn't hard; there were only maybe six buildings in Hanksville. Hanksville is not much of a town, but it had a clean hotel and a nice steakhouse. We had a great dinner. The Chinese had developed an affinity for steak and they ate heartily. The restaurant staff was efficient. The steakhouse had a full size, upright cardboard mockup of John Wayne, and we took turns posing for photos with it. Steak. John Wayne. Cold beer. It was a good way to wrap up a great day of riding.

That evening, I talked to Baja John and asked him how he was feeling about continuing our journey all the way to Mt. Rushmore, our planned spot for pointing the bikes west again. I wanted to know if he still wanted to drop South Dakota and Wyoming from our route.

"No, I think we're doing better now," John said. "I think we can take it all in."

I was glad to hear that. It was exactly the conclusion I had reached. We were still having our challenges getting moving on time, but I had made up my mind we were going to do the whole 5000 miles.

Our delays came down to the same two or three guys who were late all the time...two of the Chinese riders, and John the truck driver. One of the Chinese guys was either late in getting out for our departures or he'd invariably decide he needed to use the rest room just as we were about to leave. He had another bad habit, and that was taking 15 minutes to put on his helmet, his gloves, his man purse, and everything he connected to his bike (he ran a lot of things on this bike that required electrical connections). The other Chinese rider was just a little slow getting ready, but I was getting to know him and I knew he'd be easy to change. John the truck driver was our third wayward traveler. He was either late getting out of his hotel room, or he'd decide he needed to buy ice, fill up the truck, or do some other thing that delayed us, and he always seemed to recognize the need to do these things just as we were about to leave. If I could get these three guys squared away, we'd be good. Everybody else was pretty good about being on time.

Chapter 17: It's Okay, It's Okay

This is a chapter for which I had to struggle to pick a title: "It's Okay, It's Okay," or "Oh, Say, Can You See?" Read on, and you'll see what I mean.

Our destination this fine day was the magnificent state of Colorado, yet another notch on our Western America Adventure Ride gun barrel. We would not have any national parks to visit on our route today; we wanted to make progress across the western United States toward Mt. Rushmore. This was going to be a big traveling day of about 350 miles. It would be our second-highest mileage day.

Before I continue, let me interject a thought. You probably read that last sentence and thought to yourself "350 miles? What's the big deal?"

You'd be right, if you were riding by yourself or with one or maybe two other guys. Run the headcount up to 10 riders, though, and watch what happens. It's that herding cats thing again. The more riders you have in a group, the more delays you have. The delays go up and the miles go down. It's predictable, like gravity. As a former paratrooper and an engineer I know a thing or two about gravity. You can bitch about gravity all you want, but it's not going to change.

I had wanted to make Arches National Park in southeastern Utah when we were planning the trip, but it just wasn't in the cards. When he was planning our daily travels and the places we would stay each night, Baja John tried hard to include Arches in the plan. John called me a couple of weeks before we left and he told me we wouldn't be able to do it. Our route this day would take us within 50 miles of the entrance to Arches, but that 50 miles would become 100 miles for the roundtrip, plus the 2 or 3 hours we'd spend in the park, plus the hour it would take beyond our scheduled rally point time to actually leave. John was right, it would be too much. Arches was out.

We were up early that morning in Hanksville, the usual guys who were late were late again, and we walked over to the small restaurant next to the hotel. The hotel didn't serve breakfast, but they had an arrangement with the little restaurant next door to serve the morning meal to their guests. The restaurant was run down, but it answered the mail. Our breakfast was sufficient.

After breakfast we rolled over to the gas station a quarter of a mile down the road and everybody filled up. Let me go off course for a moment to discuss the fuel situation. I had always used 87 octane in my RX3. Zongshen recommends 89 octane, but I don't know if 89 octane in China is the same as 89 octane in the US. Like I said, I always used 87 octane and it works well (no pinging and great performance). In Utah, we found that the pumps had an option for 85 octane gas. I wasn't using the 85 octane gas, but to my surprise I found that the Chinese guys had been and their bikes ran just fine. The bottom line for me regarding the RX3's fuel requirement is this: Use what you can get. The RX3 is perfectly happy with pretty much whatever you put in it.

Okay, back to the story. All the bikes had been filled and we were ready to go, but the chase vehicle was not ready. John the truck driver still had to fill up. Then he had to buy ice. Then he had to use the bathroom. John saw my frustration and told me to go ahead. He and Hugo (Hugo rode in the truck with John) would catch up.

"Good enough," I said, and we left Hanksville, bound for Colorado.

Our route ran us north on the final leg of Highway 24, where it would intersect with and end at Interstate 70. From there, we would roll east into Colorado. I kept the speed down to about 60 mph on that 44-mile stretch of Highway 24 from Hanksville to I-70, thinking I would soon see the big yellow submarine (our Penske truck) in my rearview mirror. It never appeared.

We pulled off the road just before getting on the freeway and waited about 15 minutes. No luck and no truck. I tried calling the truck on my cell phone. Again, no luck. The day was ticking by. It was getting hot again. We had to do 350 miles that day.

It's okay, it's okay.

I knew the truck would have to catch up eventually. I couldn't imagine why it was taking so long to do so. "Let's go," I said. We'd let the truck catch up with us on the freeway.

We rolled east another 20 miles on Interstate 70 and I still didn't see the truck. I was getting nervous now, so we pulled over at a rest stop. Baja

John was able to call John the truck driver. He told me the truck was on the way.

While we waited, the guys lost no time taking their cameras out and photographing everything. There really wasn't anything to photograph out there in eastern Utah, but maybe that's what they wanted to show…the vast open spaces of the American West.

About 20 minutes later, our yellow Penske truck pulled into the rest stop. Even while he was still in the cab, I could see that Hugo had a look of abject terror on his face. It wasn't his fault they were late, but Hugo felt responsible for their tardiness. He looked so nervous about it that when he got out of the truck, I put my arm around him. "It's okay, it's okay," I said.

Everybody laughed.

At the time I said it, I wasn't sure why I said it. "It's okay, it's okay" is not an expression I had ever used before, but it sure got a laugh. Then I realized why. I had picked it up from Hugo. Hugo used that expression a thousand times every day. It was part of his personality. My picking it up and using it to reassure Hugo was actually pretty funny. It instantly became the mantra for everyone in our group, and we all started using it as a general response for everything. Good food? It's okay, it's okay. Bike won't start because the battery leaks? It's okay, it's okay. Can't find an ATM? It's okay, it's okay. Want to eat here? It's okay, it's okay.

I asked John the truck driver what happened. He had taken the wrong road after leaving the gas station in Hanksville. I would have thought he had seen us head north on Highway 24 when we left on the motorcycles, but he did not. If he had been ready to roll with us when we left, it wouldn't have happened. I wasn't upset that he took a wrong turn (that happens), but this habitual lateness had delayed us a good 45 minutes that day. That wasn't okay.

We continued to ride east on I-70 and we crossed into Colorado. This was good stuff, folks: California, Arizona, Utah, and now Colorado. All on 250cc Chinese motorcycles. It was overcast and it looked like it would rain, but it did not. The riding was comfortable.

Our plan was to stop in Rifle, Colorado, for lunch and then pick up Highway 13 north. It would get us off the freeway through some pretty country.

A nice lady named Cheryle had contacted me earlier by email. Cheryle told me that she and her husband Kim wanted to see the bikes and ride with us. I told her that would be great, but the onus was on them to pick us up along the way. We weren't going to stop and wait for anybody. She was cool with that, and when we exited the freeway, Cheryle and Kim were there waiting for us.

On the road in Rifle, Colorado, with Kim and Cheryle and the pups.

We ate at a Subway and I had a nice conversation with Cheryle and Kim. Cheryle rode a Triumph Bonneville and her husband Kim rode a Harley Sportster. Kim had a small trailer behind his bike, and their two dogs were in it. That was pretty cool. A husband and wife riding team, accompanied by their dogs in a motorcycle trailer. The Chinese were impressed. I'm guessing they didn't bump into things like this in Chongqing too often.

Our newly-enlarged group (the 10 RX3s, Cheryle's Bonneville, Kim's Harley, the two dogs, and John and Hugo in the chase truck) left Rifle on Highway 13 and headed north. It was beautiful country. We rode past a school just outside of Rifle that said Columbine in large steel letters on the side. Can't be, I thought. It wasn't. That Columbine High School was somewhere north of Denver, far from us.

We had already seen deer and elk in the Grand Canyon. Highway 13 had a couple of wildlife treats for us. A bald eagle flew directly across the road in front of me. I was at the head of our formation and I wondered if anybody else had seen it. They had; Kyle asked about it at our next stop. Then I spotted a pronghorn antelope on the right side of the road in the tall grass, watching us intently as we rode by. I pointed at it as we rolled by at about 70 mph, hoping the guys behind me would see it. I needn't have worried about that; we saw many more antelope in the coming days. Antelope always amaze me. They are an exotic species and seeing them in the wild is a treat.

Heading north on Colorado Highway 13.

We intersected Highway 40 in Craig, Colorado, and meandered through that town. There were a lot of turns and stop lights, and a couple of times we had to wait as the bikes at the rear of our formation (and the truck) were caught at the lights. After one of these delays involving both a turn and a traffic light, I and four of the guys waited several minutes before the rest of the group rejoined us.

"Lester's bike died and we had a tough time starting it," Baja John told me when they caught up with us. I looked at Lester's exhaust pipe and it was stained by battery acid. We had no choice, we had to take the 5 minutes it would take for John the truck driver to throw a new battery in it, and that's what we would do. John could change a battery in less time than I could change my socks.

I didn't know if the Lester's battery problem was the result of the accessories he had mounted on his bike (which were pulling a draw on the battery even when they and the motorcycle were turned off), or if we were seeing the same thing on Lester's bike we had seen in Baja (i.e., defective batteries). I suspect it was more due to the battery than the additional load Lester had put on it. Once John installed the new battery, Lester's starting problems were no more.

Lester's bike was fine after the battery swap, but now we had no more spare batteries in the truck. We had only bought two spares with us. I had hoped we wouldn't need either of them, but now we had none. I was thinking about that as we continued, and then a short distance later I spotted a Walmart.

We pulled into a McDonald's next to the Walmart. I asked John the truck driver to go to the Walmart with Hugo and buy two more motorcycle batteries. Walmart sells motorcycle batteries. They're expensive, but I didn't want to be caught without spares and I wasn't about to shop around. I did not want to get caught without a battery.

That little stop took another 1-hour bite out of our schedule. I thought we might be there 15 minutes, but the minutes were ticking by. After 30 minutes, I called John to find out what was taking so long. "I'm in line paying for it now," he said. Okay, I thought, it wouldn't be too much longer. Cheryle and Kim had gone out of their way to meet us and ride with us. There were interested in buying an RX3. We were making a hell of an impression with this battery issue, I thought.

I thought about how we could possibly be having battery issues again after the problems we had with two batteries on the Baja ride. Zongshen had specifically shipped these bikes to us for use by their riders on a ride that was being more closely watched than the second coming of Christ. John and Hugo seemed to have fallen into a black hole in that Walmart. I was not a happy camper, but I kept my thoughts to myself.

While all this was going on, the Chinese riders were up to something in the McDonald's parking lot. The RX3 is available in 2015 in four colors: Orange, red, white, and blue. We had bikes in all four colors on this ride. Kyle, King Kong, and Tso were aligning the red, white, and blue RX3s in one area of the parking lot. Lester told me they wanted to duplicate the colors of the American flag. Hmmm, I thought. That's interesting.

As soon as they had the red, white, and blue RX3s organized, the Chinese riders stood behind the bikes and started singing *The Star Spangled Banner*. They sang in English, and they did a good job. It was another one of those moments that will remain forever etched in my mind. I choked up a bit. It was powerful. It happened quickly. Joe Gresh commented that he wished he had caught it on video.

John the truck driver and Hugo rejoined the group after spending an hour in Walmart. The guys were joking about John and Hugo taking too long. When John and Hugo finally returned, I asked what happened. John told me he had bought the wrong size batteries and didn't realize it until they were back in the truck. Then they had to go back for the right batteries.

"We are sorry, Da Jiu," Hugo said.

"It's okay, it's okay," I said.

Well, I thought, at least we now have a couple of spare batteries again. And the Chinese guys had done a pretty good job with *The Star Spangled Banner*. That was a memorable moment, and it wouldn't have occurred without that Walmart stop.

I was pleasantly surprised when we arrived in Steamboat Springs. It's a small resort town and the place had a nice downtown area. Baja John had worked his travel planning magic once again and he had booked us into the Nordic Lodge, a nice little place in the center of the downtown area. The owner went out of his way to show us the rooms and he found a way to rearrange our reservations to save us money. He made a recommendation for dinner in a Mexican restaurant just up the street and that made for a stellar evening. The Nordic Lodge had a nice breakfast (included in the price of the room) waiting for us the next morning). I liked the place.

When we arrived at the Nordic Lodge (and before we checked in), I pulled Baja John, Hugo, and John the truck driver aside. It was time to read the riot act, or to have a "come to Jesus" meeting, or whatever you want to call me venting. I had a few things I wanted to communicate. I didn't have anything to be critical about with Baja John, but I wanted him there because he was helping me manage the ride. Joe Gresh approached our group just as I was getting started and I told him we were having a meeting. He said okay, thinking he was included.

"I'm about to kick some butt, Joe, and I don't want you to hear it," I said. The guys (including Joe) laughed, and he left.

I told Hugo he was responsible for the Chinese riders, and he had to get them up and out of their rooms on time. Three of the Chinese guys and the Colombians were okay (in fact, they were always early). Two of the Chinese guys were always late. "You need to tell that one guy to start putting on his gear an hour before we're ready to leave," I said, "and you need to start knocking on hotel doors early enough so that all of your guys are ready to go when the rest of us are."

"I will do so, Da Jiu," Hugo said. He was mortified, but he got it.

John the truck driver was laughing; he found my climbing all over Hugo entertaining. It was, for him, like watching a rerun of that old Jack Webb movie, *The DI*, and John thought his role was that of a mere spectator.

I turned to John and let him have both barrels: "John, the truck is a major problem on this trip."

John was genuinely surprised. "It is?' he asked softly. He wasn't being cute. He didn't recognize the burden he had been putting on the group.

"It is," I said. "Big time. We have to wait for you every morning. Look, the chase vehicle and you are here to support the guys riding the motorcycles," I said. "It's not the other way around. We're not here to support you. You're here to support us. You cost us 45 minutes this morning by not being ready on time and by not being ready to go when we were gassed up. I was stupid for leaving with the bikes and counting on you to catch up. I've thought about this and I'm not going to be stupid any more. You're going to help me with that. I'm not going to leave without the truck and the truck is not going to keep us waiting. I want you to do whatever you need to do the night before or early in the morning before we're ready to roll. Gas up, take a dump, buy ice, whatever. But do it before everybody is up or do it the night before. You're not going to keep us waiting again."

"Okay," John said.

In that instant, I realized that John wanted to do a good job. He just didn't know what his job entailed. I had not explained it to him.

Damn, I thought. I had screwed up again. I think I can read people pretty well. John the truck driver wanted to do well. He didn't know what he was supposed to do. That was my fault, not his. This was John's first time doing something like this and I had failed to make sure he knew what it involved. I hadn't explained to him what the expectations were.

You know, W. Edwards Deming (the father of modern quality management in the manufacturing and service industries) wrote that 80 percent of all quality lapses were due to management failures. On his deathbed, he is reputed to have said he had it wrong; it was really more like 95 percent. I believe he was right.

The next morning, I was up early just like I always am. When I left my room, Hugo was out there knocking on doors. The truck was parked in front of our rooms with its rollup door open, and it was fully fueled. The ice chest had ice. John had already had breakfast and was helping our riders load the truck.

Deming. I knew all that stuff; I just hadn't used it. Things got a lot better after that day in Steamboat Springs.

Chapter 19: Medicine Bow

This chapter is not entirely about Medicine Bow, Wyoming, but it's where we had our lunch that day and I fell in love with the place. That's a bit weird on my part because there's not much in Medicine Bow, but I fell in love with it nonetheless. I think maybe it's because the name has popped up in a few stories about our westward expansion and I greatly admire the people and places who formed that part of our history. I knew I had heard of the town before, either in a western movie, or a novel, or a history book. I just love the sound of it. Medicine Bow, Wyoming. Wow.

After having a great breakfast at the Nordic Lodge, we left Steamboat Springs right on time thanks to Drill Sergeant Hugo and John having the truck ready to roll. We left town on Highway 40. It was a comfortable, brisk, beautiful day.

We stopped for fuel as we left Steamboat Springs and I noticed that the gas station, which was a thoroughly modern facility, had two antique motorcycles parked in front. They were old and unrestored motorcycles, and they were there as display pieces. I don't think they ran, and I was surprised nobody in our group had noticed them. I knew Lester would want to photograph both bikes. I tapped his shoulder and pointed to the antique motors, and he was over there in a heartbeat.

Fully fueled, we continued on Highway 40 and climbed further into Colorado's Rocky Mountains. The road was magnificent. It had four lanes without too much traffic, but what little traffic there was smoking right along.

I looked to my left and saw a sign designating the Continental Divide. It said we were at 8,722 feet. It wasn't safe to pull over, but I sure would have liked to grab of photo of that sign. The road was twisty, there was no shoulder, we were moving at about 70 mph, there were cars around us, and we were getting bunched up. If I tried to stop suddenly I might cause an accident. Nope, no photo this time.

The Continental Divide. Crossing it on the RX3 was quite an accomplishment. It's the line through the continental United States that denotes which way the water goes. To the east of the Continental Divide, runoff flows toward the Atlantic. To the west of the Continental Divide, it flows toward the Pacific. And we were up here crossing it on our RX3 motorcycles. At nearly 9,000 feet!

I didn't realize we were that high up, and I had not noticed on the map that we would be crossing the Continental Divide (if I had, I would have been looking for it so we could stop for photos). But here we were. The RX3s were running great. Our U.S. RX3s are fuel injected, and they handled the altitude with ease. No coughing, sputtering, or missing. There was none of the stuff you would have to contend with on a carbureted bike.

Like I said, I wanted to grab a photo when I saw that sign, but we had momentum on our side. Not just physical momentum, but emotional momentum, too. We had a lot of miles to cover, and I reasoned we would have to cross the Continental Divide again to get home. I would look for it on the map and get the photo the next time. I wanted that photo. I had something in mind.

We picked up Highway 14 right after the Continental Divide and then rolled north through more beautiful Colorado country. We rode through green grassy flatlands with the odd cow and plenty of antelope keeping an eye on us. A golden eagle flew across our path. It was much cooler than it had been, and I was enjoying the ride and the climate immensely.

We continued rolling across Colorado for another hour. A coyote ran across the road directly in front of me as we approached Walden, Colorado. When we entered Walden, it was time for a break. I had never been here before, but it looked like the kind of little American town people from China or Colombia (and maybe New Jersey) would want to walk around and photograph. And that's what we did. It was simply magnificent and everyone was having a grand time. I took my Nikon out and grabbed several photos.

Hugo, King Kong, and Kyle in Walden, Colorado.

Around the same time we were on the road, BMW was having a rally somewhere in Wyoming or Montana, and we saw more than a few riders on those motorcycles. Two or three had stopped in Walden and they were doing the same thing we were. The BMW riders were fascinated by our bikes. They couldn't imagine us doing the same kind of huge miles they were doing. They had motorcycles of 1200cc or greater displacement. We had 250cc motorcycles. Yet, here we were doing the same thing they were doing on motorcycles that cost maybe an eighth of what their bikes cost. You could see the gears turning as the Beemer boys tried to process that.

Lester, true to form, struck up a conversation with a couple of GS riders and he took several photos. Hugo and the guys were wandering around town taking pictures. Somebody had a big fake moose (in blue, no less) on his front lawn. I grabbed a photo. Joe Gresh somehow got somebody to take a picture of him kissing that moose. It was on his Facebook page within an hour. It was cool little town and it was fun.

After leaving Walden, we pointed the bikes north and rolled into Wyoming.

Wyoming.

I keep typing Wyoming here because I like the way the word looks on my screen and how I know it will look on this page.

Wyoming. On 250cc motorcycles. This was cool stuff, folks!

We were bound for Medicine Bow, Wyoming.

Medicine Bow. That has a nice ring to it, too.

I didn't know what to expect in Medicine Bow. I was thinking maybe they had a McDonalds and we could have lunch there. Wow, was I ever surprised!

Medicine Bow has maybe six buildings spread out along maybe half a mile, and one of them dominates the others. That's the Virginian Hotel. It's a three-story structure that's old. Really old. We pulled into the gravel parking lot and looked at it. I didn't know if they served lunch, or if they served anything at all. I was hoping they did, because there was nothing else there.

I walked in the front door and there was a bar and a restaurant. It was a scene from a *Gunsmoke* episode. When I walked in the people inside stopped talking and looked at me. They were all wearing cowboy boots and western wear. I was wearing combat boots and my hi-viz Olympia motorcycle jacket, with my motorcycle helmet under my arm. If there had been a piano player banging out *Buffalo Gal* it would have been perfect. The hotel, the bar, and the restaurant weren't just decorated in an Old West theme...this was the Old West. I had walked into the Long Branch saloon. I thought I might see Milburn Stone having a whiskey with Miss Kitty and Festus. This was good stuff. I knew the Chinese would love it.

The Virginian Hotel in Medicine Bow, Wyoming.

I asked the young lady behind the cash register if she could whip up some chow for 12 hungry riders (yeah, I was going with the flow...I actually said "whip up some chow"). I wanted something quick so we could get in and out, and there were 12 of us. We would effectively triple the number of people in the restaurant when all of our guys entered. She told me it would be no problem.

Hugo and the guys came in, and Hugo and I decided everybody wanted hamburgers and French fries for lunch. The burgers were outstanding, and as was proving to be the usual case with this team, so was the conversation. The burgers weren't made from store-bought frozen paper-thin patties. They were real burgers, made from real ground beef, and the patties were formed by hand. That young lady and her young helpers put four tables together for us, and it was one of the best meals we had on the entire trip.

I could say the same about the conversation. We had real riders here from all over the world sharing an experience that few might ever enjoy...a 5000-mile ride across the greatest land that ever existed. This wasn't just a motorcycle ride. We were making a point, and that point was that this little 250cc motorcycle was as good as or better than any other bike out there, at any price.

Art in the Virginian Hotel. Does the lady on the left look like Miss Kitty?

The inside of the Victorian's restaurant, the hotel, the sitting rooms, and the bar were all a step back in time. The décor looked like it might have lifted right out of the 1870s. All of us wandered around. And all of this wasn't all for show; people passing through Medicine Bow actually stayed in this hotel. The maids were cleaning the rooms as we wandered about taking pictures. Our cameras were getting a workout.

The lunches were huge. The topic turned to our portion sizes and our personal sizes here in America. Lester had completely abandoned his vegetarian eating preferences by this time and he, too, was going with the flow. He said he was going to be Baja John's size when he returned to China. It was all good-natured ribbing. John was loving it.

John and Lester sharing an intimate moment.

I liked the bar in the Virginian Hotel, even though I'm not much of a drinker. While I was peering into it, the fellow who ran the place (an old timer who looked like he, too, belonged on the *Gunsmoke* set) saw my interest in photography and showed me a photograph he said I might enjoy. He told me only six or seven copies of it exist. Spend a minute reading the signatures if you can make them out...Theodore Roosevelt, Butch Cassidy, Judge Roy Bean, and many more. The manager told me the photo was taken at the train station (presumably the one in Medicine Bow), and everyone in the photo was on a hunting trip. I don't know if the photo was genuine. I decided I didn't need to know.

I would have loved to have stayed at the Virginian Hotel, but our schedule didn't allow it. It would have been grand fun to have dinner there, move over to the bar and have a few too many whiskeys, and then sleep it off in one of those old rooms. Some day.

After lunch, the guys were putting around Medicine Bow taking pictures. I didn't think there was that much to photograph, but hey, what do I know? Like a lot of small western towns, there was a tiny museum across the street. It was about the size of a two-car garage, and it had a few old things in it (a telephone, an old typewriter, the kind of stuff you might see on *American Pickers*). The Chinese were impressed by it.

One of the Chinese guys told me the small towns in China are disappearing. I already knew that from my many trips to China and from my following the events in that country. The largest human migration in the history of mankind is occurring right now as China moves its rural population into the cities. Their government's thinking, as I understand it, is that this will stimulate their economy. Maybe they're right. Maybe not. I don't pretend to be smart enough to know.

An impressive photo. Genuine or not, I enjoyed the accompanying story.

We talked about this a bit. My Chinese friend said China does not preserve the history of its small towns, and there are no small museums. He felt that one of the reasons America is a great nation is that we hold on to our history with these small museums. Maybe he was right.

Anyway, after our discussion on the benefits of maintaining rural areas and small town museums, we were back on the road headed north. Our destination that evening was Casper.

The Wyoming countryside was stunning. It was a wonderful afternoon. As we rode across the Wyoming prairies at 75 mph toward Casper, I thought about riding into South Dakota the next day and all we had seen and done so far. We had ridden from California to Wyoming on our RX3 motorcycles, and we would soon be at our turnaround point, Mt. Rushmore. I went through a mental checklist:

- Joshua Tree National Park: Check
- Grand Canyon National Park: Check
- Zion National Park: Check
- Bryce National Park: Check
- Capitol Reef National Park: Check
- California: Check
- Arizona: Check
- Utah: Check
- Colorado: Check
- Wyoming: Check
- Deer: Check
- Elk: Check
- Bighorn Sheep: Check
- Coyote: Check
- Antelope: Check
- Bald Eagle: Check
- Golden Eagle: Check

We would see bison in South Dakota. I wanted to add those creatures to the list, too.

I was having fun. We had another high-mileage day in front of us the next day to get to Mt. Rushmore, but I was feeling pretty good about the RX3 motorcycles and our team taking it all in stride. These motorcycles are mile-munching monsters, and they were performing magnificently. So was the team.

Chapter 20: The Run to Rushmore

The day we left Casper was a big day for us. We would ride across Wyoming, enter South Dakota, and in the late afternoon take in our sixth national park, Mt. Rushmore. I was excited. Mt. Rushmore is in South Dakota's Black Hills, and I believe that area to be one of the most beautiful in the United States.

Mt. Rushmore, of course, is the incredible monument that has 60-foot busts of Washington, Jefferson, Teddy Roosevelt, and Lincoln carved into the side of a granite mountain. It should be on everyone's bucket list.

I had been to Mt. Rushmore and the Black Hills about 8 years ago. My wife, Susie, had talked about it for years before that. I resisted going all those years because I thought it was the kind of the place where we'd fly out, see the thing, and then wonder what to do before we boarded the airplane for the flight home. I was sure wrong about that. That trip to Mt. Rushmore with Susie was the best vacation I ever had.

I fell in love with the Black Hills area and I wanted to show it to our friends from China and Colombia. Had it not been for that earlier trip with Susie, Mt. Rushmore would not have been our turnaround point. We would have probably just picked up the parks in California, Arizona,

Utah, and Oregon. You may recall that I mentioned our Western American Adventure Ride was loosely based on an earlier Three Flags Rally I had ridden (except that on this trip we were not going to include Mexico and Canada). We had not gone as far east on the Three Flags Rally, but now that I had been to Mt. Rushmore on the trip with Susie, I wanted to include it.

Four very presidential Mt. Rushmore guys – King Kong, Lester, Hugo, and Tso.

Adding Mt. Rushmore to the Western America Adventure Ride would put our total mileage at 5000 miles, and that had a nice ring to it. One of the reasons we were doing the ride was to show the world that the RX3 is a bike that can go the distance. The Western America Adventure Ride would be one more thing we could mention in response to unfounded Internet accusations aimed at the RX3's reliability. I realize that the folks who post most of the Internet venom are not, by nature, logical or informed creatures and they are probably not worthy of attention, but I still wanted to be able to say we had made the ride in response to any future Internet forum silliness.

While I am on that topic, let me mention another observation. The anti-China Internet rants directed at this motorcycle have subsided greatly. Part of it, I believe, is due to the Baja run and the Western America Adventure Ride. Another big part of it is due to the fact that there are now thousands of RX3s running around all over the world and when the uninformed post unfounded things about the bike, there are knowledgeable people to refute those comments. And maybe, just maybe, part of it is that some of the people who used to post the negative comments now realize they were wrong.

Anyway, to get back to the story, our day leaving Casper was another beautiful, clear, and crisp one. We rolled north at 75 mph on Interstate 25 out of Casper. There were signs warning of deer and we saw a pickup truck that had hit a deer. The deer carcass was still on the side of the road and the pickup was in the median. I couldn't believe how much damage the deer had caused to that truck. It was totaled. Tangling with a deer on a bike would not be a good idea.

After about 35 miles, we turned east on Highway 387. It was nice run across the Wyoming plains. We stopped to fill up in Wright, another small town, and continued east on Highway 450 toward Newcastle. Newcastle is in east Wyoming, near the South Dakota border.

That ride along Highway 450 was an interesting one. We passed an immense coal mining complex. It was absolutely enormous. It looked like something out of a science fiction movie. The buildings, conveyors, and processing equipment seemed to go on for miles. We never saw any coal, and I don't know if they used strip mining or deep earth mining in this part of the country. All we could see were the buildings, conveyors, and other industrial stuff. There was a sign on the landscaped front lawn (a lawn that was bigger than an 18-hole course) identifying the company as the Thunder Basin Corporation.

All the industrial stuff was on the right side of Highway 450. On the other side of the highway there were massive rail yards, rail cars (hoppers, for the coal, I suppose), and scores of diesel locomotives. What impressed me about all of this was how clean everything was.

There was no smog in the air, the fields were a brilliant green, and the sky was that big blue Wyoming sky with bright white clouds suspended low in the sky. The whole area looked like it was a photo taken with a polarizer on the lens, and then run through PhotoShop with the vibrance cranked all the way up. This part of the world has always looked that way to me. I love it.

After another hour, we rolled into Newcastle, Wyoming. There was a big "Welcome to Newcastle" sign at its edge, and then I wondered. Hmmm. The big coal mine. Newcastle. Coals to Newcastle? Nah, that saying had to come from England. I later researched it on that bastion of academic integrity, Wikipedia, and the old saying about taking coals to Newcastle is, in fact, of British origin. Now I'm wondering…did the good forefathers of Newcastle, Wyoming, name their town based on its proximity to the Thunder Basin Corporation and that old English saying?

As we entered Newcastle, I was struck by how photogenic the town is. The guys are going to love the photo ops here, I thought as we rolled into town. I was looking for a McDonalds, but I didn't see one. Instead, I spotted a restaurant called Isabelle's, and the sign out front said "pizza." That sounded good to me. I pulled into their gravel parking lot and asked the rest of the guys if pizza would work for them. They were already off their bikes, ready to walk around Newcastle with their cameras.

Pizza is a good thing to do with a large group. It may not be the best food from a cholesterol perspective, but it is relatively quick and you don't have to order individually for everybody. It speeds up the ordering and paying. Hugo and Baja John were good with pizza, and that was good enough for me.

That lunch at Isabelle's in Newcastle, Wyoming, turned out to be another one of the best lunches of our entire trip. We ordered five large pizzas of various configurations, and there might have been two slices left when we finished. The pizza was exceptional, as was the service. I'm not going to ride 2500 miles again just for a slice at Isabelle's, but if I was ever within 100 miles of that place, you can bet that's where I would eat.

The Chinese riders were making fun of our American portion sizes and our American girth again (let's not be politically correct here...we're fat, folks). They were slowly coming around, though. You read about the lunch in Medicine Bow. Lester might have come over here as a vegetarian, but he went home as a steak and potatoes man. He had four very large slices that afternoon (some with chicken, some with sausage, and some with ground beef). Even Hugo was getting with the program. I told him it looked like he was getting a pot belly and he could probably pass for an American pretty soon. His response was, "It's okay, it's okay, Da Jiu."

After leaving Newcastle, we were in South Dakota before I realized it. I was hoping for a "Welcome to South Dakota" sign (I wanted to get a photo of that for the CSC blog), but if there was one I missed it.

Kyle's bike was acting up a bit. It didn't have any visible evidence of battery leakage, but when we had pulled over for gas in South Dakota, I asked John the truck driver to install another battery in it. The old battery didn't show any evidence of leakage once John pulled it, but I figured we were better safe than sorry. This was the third battery we had changed on the Western America Adventure Ride, and it would be our last.

We had changed two other batteries earlier (Tony's and Lester's), and their bikes had no problems after we changed them. I'll cut to the chase on Kyle's bike here by telling you that two days later in Yellowstone National Park it stalled. After checking the bike and finding nothing wrong with it, I had Kyle ride directly behind me in our formation. I didn't think I emitted any kind of an aura that would prevent Kyle's bike from stalling again; I just wanted to be able to see right away if he was stopping. Having said that, maybe I was giving off a vibe. Once I had Kyle stick close to me, his bike never gave us another problem, and when we got it back to the plant, we could neither duplicate the problem nor could we find anything wrong with his motorcycle.

On Tony's bike and Lester's bike, the batteries definitely were bad. I'm not sure if they were defective or if we did something wrong when we prepared them. We had a lot going on in the plant in the weeks before we left on the Western America Adventure Ride, so it's possible somebody made a mistake at CSC (such as overfilling the batteries). As I mentioned before, the batteries in the seven bikes Zongshen sent for the ride were the same type as we had used on the Baja bikes, and we had a couple of battery problems on that ride. Zongshen is putting better batteries in our next shipment of RX3 motorcycles.

Okay, so, back to the main attraction, which on this day was Mt. Rushmore. After refueling and changing Kyle's battery, we rode directly to Mt. Rushmore National Park.

Getting into Mt. Rushmore was as chaotic as we had experienced elsewhere, but for different reasons. It was also disappointing, because I thought we had left all of the drama behind with our purchase of the annual national park passes. Our government is running a special kind of scam at Mt. Rushmore. When we got to the gates (there were four or five lanes leading up to the entrance and many cars behind us), I told the young lady in the booth that we had 10 motorcycles and one truck, and we had national park annual passes for everyone.

"We don't accept those here," she said.

I was dumbfounded and I just stared blankly at her.

"Admission to Mt. Rushmore is free," she continued, "but you have to pay for parking because that's handled by a private concession."

Okay, another instance of something being different than what it used to be. Ah, the trials and tribulations of growing old…new and creative ways to be taken advantage of.

"How much for us?" I asked. People in cars waiting behind our group were growing impatient.

I don't remember the exact amounts she told me, but they were high. By that time, Hugo and one of the other Chinese riders were standing there with me. The young lady in the glass booth went on to explain that they charged by the vehicle, and she told me what each motorcycle and the truck would cost.

I was okay with that and so was Hugo, but for reasons I still don't understand, the other Chinese rider who was with us at that payment window was not. He started to explain something to me that I could not understand, and then Hugo looked at him and said, "No, no, no." That didn't slow our guy down, though. He started arguing with Hugo in Chinese, growing louder and more animated with each sentence. There was an argument going on, but I had no idea what it was about.

"What does he want?" I asked Hugo.

"He wants us to ride two on each motorcycle, so we only have to pay for one motorcycle," Hugo said.

I looked at Hugo and then at our rider. Cars were backing up in a longer line behind us. We were all tired.

"Hugo, CSC and Zongshen are paying for all of this," I said. "Why does he even care? And where would he have us leave the other bikes? There's no place to park out here."

"I know, I know," said Hugo.

Our rider wasn't taking no for an answer, however. He continued to talk rapidly to Hugo in Chinese, with the volume climbing. It was bizarre.

Hugo lost it. He kicked up his volume a couple of notches (in Chinese, of course) and the hand gestures started flying. The other Chinese rider went back to his bike. I asked Hugo what it was all about. "It's okay, it's okay," he said, but he was clearly annoyed. To this day, I still don't know what really happened there.

It was nice inside the park. It's arranged in a viewing pavilion and you have this great view of the Presidents on the mountain. As you might imagine, our cameras were out and the photos were flying.

I was hanging with five of the Chinese guys (Hugo, Lester, King Kong, Kyle, and Tso), and I asked them to stand in the pavilion so I could get a photograph of them with Mt. Rushmore in the background. They started to comply, and then Kyle stepped away from the group and started issuing instructions in Chinese. I didn't realize what was happening at first, but then I did: Kyle he was posing King Kong, Lester,

Hugo, and Tso to match the presidents on Mt. Rushmore. It was pretty cool. Kyle has an eye for things like that. It's the photo you saw at the beginning of this chapter.

The Rushmore photo instantly became (and remained) one of my favorites of the thousand or so photos I took on the Western America Adventure Ride. These were great guys and there's just something about that picture that, for me, captured the essence of our adventure. I had the photo framed and it now hangs in my office.

We stayed in Mt. Rushmore National Park a couple of hours. Let's see, we had now hit Joshua Tree National Park, Grand Canyon National Park, Zion National Park, Bryce National Park, Capitol Reef National Park, and with our visit that day, Mt. Rushmore National Park. We were only staying an hour or so in each place. Lester had commented to me a few days ago that you could easily spend several days at each location. Without question, he was right. We were covering a lot of territory. The idea was to get a feel for America with our quick national park visits and the extensive riding we were doing across the western United States. We were speed dating America.

Baja John outdid himself when arranging our lodging in South Dakota. We stayed in the small town of Keystone, nestled in the Black Hills just below Mt. Rushmore. It's a touristy, kitschy, wild west, souvenir-shop-laden place, which was just I needed that evening. Our hotel was right on the main drag (the town's only drag, as a matter of fact), in among all the shops and restaurants, and it was surprisingly reasonably priced. We had a good time walking through the tourist beat in Keystone and taking photos, and we had a good Mexican seafood dinner that night. It's pretty funny when you think about; we weren't close to either Mexico or the ocean, but that dinner sure was good.

We were in good spirits. We had completed about half of our Western American Adventure Ride, and we had made it all the way to Mt. Rushmore. Tomorrow we would point the bikes west to start our long ride home.

Chapter 21: Deadwood, Sturgis, and Devil's Tower

Tonight's destination would be Gillette, Wyoming, about 200 miles down the road. We had several places to visit along the way: The Black Hills, Deadwood, Sturgis, and Devil's Tower National Park. It was to be a busy day.

The hotel in Keystone served the so-called continental breakfast many of our hotels had. I have always wondered on what continents you find these breakfasts (other than the North American continent, that is). I've been on "the Continent" many times (assuming they mean Europe with that description) and I have yet to see a similar breakfast offering at any hotel. Here in the United States, it's amazing how much variability there is from hotel to hotel. Some have a great morning meal; others, not so much. The breakfasts have ranged from stale cold cereal with no milk to outstanding bacon-and-eggs, toast, and fresh fruit offerings. One of the best breakfasts so far had been the Best Western in Kingman (after our first night on the road); another great one was at the Nordic Lodge in Steamboat Springs (those guys had delicious bagels and cream cheese, and coffee that would have done Juan Valdez proud).

We rode north on Highway 385 through South Dakota's Black Hills that morning. It was a great ride and I was familiar with the area from my previous visit to this area with Susie. I kept an eye out for the bighorn sheep; Susie and I had seen those along this route during our prior visit. When we saw them a few years ago, cars were stopped right on the highway, and I could understand why as we approached. I remember that the sheep were amazing. They were standing on nearly vertical sheer rock walls just a few feet above us, secure in the knowledge that we could not match their climbing ability. That was then, though, and this was now. We had no such luck this on this trip, but that was okay. Our intrepid RX3 adventurers had seen a magnificent group of bighorn sheep in Zion on the third day of the Western America Adventure Ride. That was a first for me; I had never seen bighorn sheep in Zion on any of my prior visits.

We were riding toward Deadwood, South Dakota, a famous Old West town that today is a famous Old West tourist trap. Deadwood is famous because it's where Wild Bill Hickok was shot to death in a poker game. Hickok took one in the back, reportedly holding aces and eights (forever after known as the dead man's hand). Deadwood also gained some notoriety due to the HBO television series of the same name a few years ago.

I'd been through Deadwood on my previous visit to the area and I thought it was nothing special. Nothing on this visit changed my mind, but it is a well-known spot and we had to pass through it on our way to Sturgis. We encountered a construction roadblock on the way into Deadwood that held us up for about 45 minutes. Joe Gresh text messaged several of his friends on their way to the famous Sturgis rally, which was to start the following week. If that construction was still underway when the rally started (and it looked like it would be), the backup would be terrible.

Baja John and I settled in for a cup of coffee in front of a rundown casino in Deadwood (and folks, take it from me, the expression "rundown casino" is redundant for any casino in this town). Lester sized the place up pretty quickly, and he joined us for a coffee while the other guys scattered to the four winds. Nothing special here, folks. Move along. We hung out for an hour in Deadwood and then we continued on to Sturgis.

For those of you who have never heard of Sturgis, here's the *Reader's Digest* version: There are three big motorcycle rallies in the United

States. These are Daytona's Bike Week, the Laughlin River Run, and Sturgis. These events are dominated by Harleys and Harley riders. That should give you a sense of the crowd these events attract. If big-inch bikes with terrible handling, open pipes (c'mon, folks...do loud pipes really save lives?), high temperatures, mind-numbing crowds, tattoos, public drunkenness, beer bellies, obesity, and body odor are your thing, you'll love all of these events. Me, not so much.

The guys were excited about going to Sturgis. As I mentioned earlier, the Sturgis rally was going to start the following week. That was a good thing for a couple of reasons:

- Many of the vendors and booths were already set up (or in the process of setting up), so our Western America Adventure Ride team would get a feel for what was going to be on display.

- The hordes of Harley riders that would clog every road in South Dakota's Black Hills had not arrived yet. There were a few of the "loud pipes save lives" folks who had arrived early and were busily converting gasoline into noise, but we did not have to contend with the great unwashed masses that are the Sturgis event. I had read in the morning newspaper that the organizers were expecting over a million motorcycles to converge on Sturgis this year. It was going to be crowded. We had done well in planning to be someplace else when that happened.

I'm not a big Sturgis fan. It is a motorcycle touchstone, though, so I knew that if we were going to do Mt. Rushmore, Sturgis had to be on the itinerary. I wanted our guests to see it and to be able to tell their friends in China and Colombia that they had been to Sturgis. Everybody needs to see Sturgis once in their lifetime (but preferably not during the event).

We rode completely through the town to let our guys get the lay of the land and to get to the sign that says "Sturgis" at the east end of town. It would make for a good photograph. We pulled our RX3's right up to the sign, parked on the sidewalk at the base of the sign, and took a bunch of photos. After that, everybody scattered to get their lunch (some of the guys wanted to eat at the Buffalo Chip, a famous Sturgis center of sophistication that features such things as wet T-shirt contests).

Sturgis, South Dakota, best seen before the hordes descend.

I was tempted to go, but I've never placed in the Top 10 in any wet T-shirt contest I've ever entered.

Baja John, John the truck driver, and I went across the street to a restaurant for lunch. The meal was a bust, but it was hot out and the place was air conditioned. Both Johns left after they finished eating to explore Sturgis. I hung back to enjoy the air conditioning. I needed to adjust the chain on my motorcycle (a 5-minute job) and I had about an hour to kill.

About 10 minutes before the guys were due to converge, I went outside and attended to my chain. I was at about the 6000-mile mark on that chain, and it was the first time it needed an adjustment. I really like the chain adjustors on the RX3. Unlike most motorcycles, the adjustment locknuts straddle a plate at the end of swingarm. That allows using one of the nuts to drive the rear wheel forward, and the other to drive the rear wheel rearward. Most motorcycles have both nuts on the same side of the swingarm adjustment stop. On those other motorcycles, it's easy to drive the rear wheel to the rear to tighten the chain, but a royal pain to push the wheel forward if you overtighten it initially (which is something that frequently occurs when adjusting a chain). The RX3's arrangement makes it easy to drive the wheel in either direction. It's a nice touch.

Anyway, while I was wrapping up the chain adjustment, two fellows on BMW GS 1200 motorcycles rolled up to me. I'm pretty sure they weren't in town for the Sturgis event; they were most likely just passing through on their way to that BMW event I mentioned earlier.

"How you doing?" one said.

"Good," I answered. "How are you doing?"

"We're good, too," he answered. "How's this restaurant? I saw you're on a GS, and I know a fellow GS rider won't steer me wrong."

I smiled. "It's okay. If you could find a Denny's you'd probably do better."

I smiled because of his thinking the RX3 was a GS. That happens a lot. Not only do a lot of people think the RX3 is a BMW, but BMW riders are also often convinced it is a BMW. One time on the ride to the Overland Expo in Flagstaff, I had a guy riding a BMW come up to me while I was filling up my RX3's fuel tank and tell me, "I know it's a BMW, but I don't recognize the model." That sort of thing happens a lot.

You know, I work for CSC, so if you were to assume I am biased in favor of the bike, I'd understand. I'd feel the same way if I was reading stuff about a bike by a guy who works for the company that sells it. But it's not just me saying this stuff. People who see the RX3 (and its fit and finish) assume it is a BMW.

On that subject, the bikes were holding up amazingly well on this trip. We'd had three batteries conk out (a known issue already being addressed by Zongshen) and one exhaust pipe heat shield screw fall out. That was it.

Don't get me wrong. I was worried about the bikes' ability to get us through this trip. I had no indications they wouldn't be reliable and a lot of indications that they would be, but we had a lot riding on the outcome of this adventure. If everything held together, it would be a feather in our cap. If it didn't, there was no hiding it. The information would be on the Internet immediately and the keyboard commandos looking for any opportunity to criticize us, the bike, Zongshen, China, me, and anything else associated with CSC would crawl out from under their keyboards and hammer us.

Staying on the topic of reliability for minute, we were having more issues with our camera gear than with the motorcycles. One guy lost a camera (it fell off the bike), another guy had his helmet's camera mount break, another guy broke the LCD screen on the back of his camera, and another guy's camera just gave up the ghost. As I said, the bikes were doing well. Regarding the cameras….well, that was someone else's problem to fix.

We left Sturgis bound for the Wyoming border and Devil's Tower National Park. Like I said at the beginning of this chapter, this was to be a busy day for us. We rode Interstate 90 and made good time. It was getting warmer, but it was bearable. After our Mojave Desert baptism on the first day of the Western America Adventure Ride, the kind of heat we felt as we rolled toward Devil's tower was nothing.

We soon saw the exit for Devil's Tower, and as we approached it, there was a school-bus-yellow airplane mounted high on a pole on the right side of the freeway. It was a real airplane (a Beechcraft, I think), up on this pole about 90 feet in the air. I have no idea what kind of business it was advertising, but it was an attention-getting thing. You couldn't miss it. Keep that in mind as this chapter progresses.

The ride through the gently-rolling Wyoming plains out to Devil's Tower was great. We rode along Highway 14 to Highway 24 (a different Highway 24 than the one we had ridden in Utah). The guys were making videos, taking photos, and generally enjoying more of our epic adventure.

If you've ever seen the movie, *Close Encounters of the Third Kind*, you've seen Devil's Tower. It's a stark rock formation that juts up abruptly from the earth with these precise serrations on its walls. The serrations make it look like the whole thing was machined on a CNC mill. In a way, I guess it was. I'm no geologist, but my understanding is that the serrations were formed by other rocks etching the structure as molten rock emerged from the earth. It's very dramatic.

A close encounter of the RX3 kind - Devil's Tower, Wyoming.

We arrived, spent a couple of hours in the park, talked to a few other people on motorcycles, and just kicked back. The Colombians and the Chinese were humming the tune from *Close Encounters of the Third Kind*. Devil's Tower. Wow. It was yet another notch on our guns.

Our destination that evening was Gillette, Wyoming. After we left Devil's Tower, the plan was to retrace our route on Highway 24, and then instead of turning left on Highway 14, we would need to turn right. Highway 14 makes a big loop that runs parallel to Interstate 90, and turning right on Highway 14 would have hooked us up with Interstate 90 down the road closer to Gillette.

That's' what I wanted to do, but I missed the right turn on Highway 14. There's a small town along Highway 24, I was rubbernecking along with the rest of the guys, and somehow I ended up traveling east on Highway 14 again. After riding about 10 miles I was pretty sure I was going the wrong way (the sun was directly behind me and it was late in the afternoon; I should have been driving into the sun, not away from it). I'm not a gadget guy and I don't have a GPS on my bike. I think some of the guys riding behind me knew we were going the wrong way, but that ride through the Wyoming countryside sure was nice. We had gentle green hills, mild twisties, fantastic scenery, and clear skies. It was awesome. Perfect motorcycle weather.

On this unplanned leg of our trip, we passed a historical marker indicating we were riding past the site of the Custer Expedition. It wasn't the Little Big Horn (although that was not too far way), which was the site of the famed Custer massacre. The Custer Expedition was an earlier military excursion led by the man himself (George Armstrong Custer) seeking the best location to build a military fort.

I wondered what it must have been like for Custer and the men he led. I was lost on a motorcycle ride, having missed the road to the freeway, and I was mildly nervous about it. The worst thing that could happen to us, though, is that we might run out of fuel. In Custer's day there were no roads, and the consequences of losing one's way were substantially more severe. Those poor souls had a lot more to worry about (like a buzz cut that didn't stop at the hairline). Me? I was out for a motorcycle ride with my friends. I was having a good time.

We were riding east and I knew the road we were on would ultimately intersect with I-90 at Sundance. I was backtracking, and we'd have to cover some of the same freeway again on our journey to Gillette. Sure enough, 15 minutes later Interstate 90 appeared and we turned west on it again. A few miles further down the road, there was that yellow

Beechcraft up on the pole. It was impossible to miss. I knew the guys would realize it was the second time that afternoon we were seeing it.

At the next exit, we left the freeway to refuel. Joe Gresh, whose sense of humor is stellar, sidled up to me and softly asked "What are the chances of seeing <u>two</u> yellow airplanes on a pole in Wyoming?" It was pretty funny.

When we arrived in Gillette, it looked like a storm was rolling in and it felt like it was going to rain. It grew colder that night, but the rain never materialized. So far, the little rain we had in Capitol Reef National Park was our only brush with bad weather.

Juan Carlos had fantastic video of the ride to Devil's Tower National Park that he had filmed from the side of the road. He showed it to us that evening at dinner. Juan Carlos is a much better photographer than I am, and when I saw his video, I asked if I could get a copy. Juan Carlos was willing to share anything and he gave a copy to me later that night.

While we were still in Gillette, I downloaded the music from *Close Encounters of the Third Kind* and dubbed it over the video. It turned out well and I uploaded it to YouTube.

MeTubby, in action again!

Chapter 22: Cody, Beijing, and Orange Motorcycles

The trek from Gillette to Cody was to be an easy one. There were no mid-route destinations planned for the day (no national parks or anything else). It was just a day to rack up the miles as we rolled on toward Yellowstone National Park (our next day's destination). We were at higher elevations so it was cooler, we had a 250-mile day in front of us, and the ride ahead was part freeway, part winding mountain road, and part country road through rural Wyoming. It was going to be a good day.

Our day started out interestingly enough. There were a couple of Harleys in the hotel parking lot and a group of three BMW GS motorcycles near where we had parked our RX3s. The Harley guys weren't out yet, but the GS riders were and one of their bikes wouldn't start. It cranked okay, but it wasn't catching. The rider cranked it so long I thought it would run the battery down (it did not), but that thing wasn't about to start. The other two GS riders were watching their *compadre* helplessly. So were our guys.

I gathered the RX3 group, took out the map, and reviewed our route for the day. While I was doing so, I wondered if I should offer to help the BMW guys, but they had their own tools and the guy whose bike wouldn't start already had his two friends watching him. The bike was cranking, so the problem wasn't as simple as a bad battery. The BMW is a complex motorcycle, and I wouldn't know what to do to help him. And if I made the offer, he'd have more than just his two guys watching him futilely holding the starter button down; he'd have all of our guys watching and taking pictures. The last thing you need when your bike won't start is more guys watching and photographing you try to start it.

Chain adjusted, bugs spattered, and ready to roll in Cody, Wyoming.

One of the things I discovered right away with our group is that whenever we had to do anything on the bikes (e.g., swap a battery, change the oil, or tighten a chain) everybody tended to crowd in and around whoever was doing the work (usually, that would be me or John). And the cameras would be out. I'm sure our guys who were shooting the photos were having a good time and didn't intend their actions to be distracting, but it made it more difficult to concentrate for whoever was doing the work. I didn't want our guys to do that to the BMW storm trooper.

When we left the hotel, that BMW guy was still trying to start his motorcycle, probably hoping for divine intervention or at least a hand from the Valkyries. He and his two friends studiously avoided looking at us while all of this was going on. I felt bad for them. Their three BMW motorcycles, with their vaunted reputation for adventure touring and high reliability, would sell for more than twice what all ten of our motorcycles cost. Yet we were rolling away, departing on the next leg of our journey, and they were not. All of our Chinese bikes started as soon as we tapped the starter buttons. Their Teutonic *über*-twin was deader than the Third Reich. I'm sure the irony wasn't lost on them.

The same three BMW guys caught up with us about 40 miles later on Interstate 90. We were putting along at 75 mph (which had become our standard freeway pace). With their 1200cc engines and Horst Wessel horsepower, the Beemers easily passed us. They didn't give us so much as a wave or a nod. They had to be going 100 mph. They sure showed us, I guess.

We exited the freeway in Ranchester, Wyoming, and picked up Highway 14 as we continued west. Ranchester is a cool name for a western town. It sounds like Winchester. I like the name. We didn't get to see the town, but it sounded like a good place to have a beer.

Highway 14 took us up and over Wyoming's Bighorn National Wilderness area and the Bighorn Mountains. The country and the views were something out of movie or maybe a Charlie Russell or Frederic Remington painting. It was majestic. Cold, but majestic. We were enjoying beautiful weather and incredible scenery. The bikes were running fabulously. Yet again, I was proud of my country and happy to see the Chinese and Colombian riders enjoying it. I knew I was enjoying it.

Highway 14 is designated as a scenic highway on the Auto Club map, and they sure got that right. Baja John commented that he had been through this area once before, and he thought it was every bit as beautiful as Yellowstone. I had not been to Yellowstone yet (I would fix that flaw in my character the next day), so I didn't know. Now I do. John was right.

The descent out of the Bighorn Mountains was dramatic and scenic. It reminded me a bit of Utah's Highway 12. The road and the riding were great. I was struggling with the classic dilemma I had on the entire Western America Adventure Ride. Do I stop to grab photos, or do I continue to ride and enjoy the road? We did both, of course.

We rolled into Greybull, Wyoming, around noon. It was time for lunch. Greybull (population 1885) is a small town, I suppose, as far was Wyoming towns go. I didn't see a Subway or any fast food joints, but I did see a Chinese restaurant. The Beijing Garden. Chinese restaurants are ubiquitous in America, but we had not stopped in one yet on this trip. Here we were, in Greybull, Wyoming, and there was the Beijing Garden. This might be interesting, I thought...bringing a group of Chinese visitors to a Chinese restaurant in a small Wyoming town. The Beijing Garden it would be, then. We'll see what the boys from Beijing (and Chongqing and Shanghai) think about our Chinese food.

Chinese food in Greybull, Wyoming. It was great.

Lunch that day was interesting for a couple of reasons. The food was superb. That's not only the opinion of Jewish kid from New Jersey (that would be me); the Chinese guys gave it a thumbs up, too. The other thing I found interesting was that the Chinese lady running the restaurant didn't speak Chinese. Our guests tried to speak to her in several of their native tongues (there are several distinct languages in China), but it wasn't working. Everyone spoke English, and that was good enough.

The rest of the ride to Cody was nice. We thought it would be an easy run, and it was.

Checking in to the hotel in Cody was not so easy, although it was entertaining. There was an elderly woman in the lobby who wasn't too sure how to work the credit card machine. Baja John had made the room reservations on his credit card at all of our hotels, and then when we checked in every night we would switch the charges to my card for the US guys, to Juan Carlos' card for the Colombians, and Hugo would pay cash from his daily ATM visits for the Chinese guys.

The poor lady in the Cody hotel was confused by the need to take the charges off of John's card. She didn't know how to do it, or maybe she didn't want to go through the effort of doing it and she was just playing dumb. I watched her for a while, and it was a pretty convincing act. John tried to explain what we wanted to do for about 15 minutes. I had to go outside to keep from laughing. It was a classic Abbott and Costello "Who's on first?" routine. John has the patience of a saint. I don't, but sometimes it's fun to watch these things.

We were all tired. We'd been rolling for more than a week at this point without a single day of rest. We were ticking off about 300 miles every day, and they were full days. We were having fun, but it was wearing us down.

Hugo wanted us to adjust the chains on each bike, so he and I started doing that. Baja John was still struggling in the lobby, trying to teach high finance to our octogenarian receptionist. He took a short break, stuck his head out the lobby door, and told me he wanted to do his bike himself. That's cool; it would be one less bike Hugo and I had to do.

John finally left the lobby shaking his head. "I guess all of the rooms are staying on my card," he said. He had surrendered. She wore him down.

"It's no big deal," I said. "Just expense it, John. We're good for it, and Hugo and Juan Carlos will give you the cash for their rooms."

John nodded his head and asked if he could borrow my tools. They were already out because Hugo and I had been using them to adjust the chains on the other bikes (which we had finished). That was fine with me; John and I have traveled together on motorcycle trips a lot and we regularly used each other's tools. *Mi casa es su casa*, and all that.

John started loosening the rear axle when I realized what was happening. He was working on an orange RX3 (the color of his bike), but it wasn't his motorcycle. About half the bikes on our ride were orange (it's our most popular color). I guess it was an easy thing to do. We had a bunch of orange bikes in our group and it was an easy mistake to make. I watched John work for a minute before I told him he had the wrong bike. It made for a good laugh and another good story.

Cody is a fair-sized town. It's touristy. They do a good job capitalizing on their name and their association with Buffalo Bill. The town is modern but it has a distinctive Old West feel to it, and they sure sell a lot of Old West trinkets. Who knows, maybe there are people who really need a Cody, Wyoming refrigerator magnet. And, there's the Buffalo Bill museum, formally designated as the Buffalo Bill Center of the West. John had been talking about going to the museum for several days, and in particular, he was excited about their world-renown firearms museum.

We rode to the Buffalo Bill Center of the West after the hotel check-in and chain adjustment debacle, but it was already late in the day. The museum would be closing in less than an hour, and it cost something like $25 per person to get in. It was probably worth it, but not for the short time we had. Once again, I realized we were speed dating our way through America. I wanted to see the Buffalo Bill museum's gun collection, but it was not meant to be. Not on this trip. Maybe next time.

There was a Subway near the hotel. We had dinner there and turned in early. We knew we would leave very early for Yellowstone in the morning, and we wanted to get a good night's sleep.

Chapter 23: Yellowstone and the Grand Tetons

Our ride through Yellowstone National Park and the Grand Tetons would be a big day for us, and it required another one of our 0:Dark:30 departures. We were on the road at 5:00 a.m. at Baja John's suggestion. I was a Yellowstone virgin (I had never been there before), but John had and he was concerned about the crowds. John knew that the roads through the park would become a parking lot full of rubber necking tourists in cars and motorhomes, and we wanted to get through the park before it became too crowded.

5:00 a.m. it was, then, and we rolled out of Cody while it was still dark. And cold. Cody is up about 5000 feet and it is pretty far north. The ride out that early in the morning was nice. I like the cold weather and I was dressed for it. If you read the CSC blog, you know that I've complained about my Olympia motorcycle jacket (the one I took on this trip). The first two times I washed it, it basically fell apart at the seams and Olympia's advice to me was to take it to a tailor (on my dime). I didn't like their customer service, but I like the jacket. It's all fluorescent yellow (not a mix of fluorescent yellow and large black sections, like most other high visibility jackets these days). I also like the liner. The jacket itself has a lot of mesh, and the liner keeps you warm and dry. And after those first two washings (and the follow-on requisite visits to the tailor, whom I got to know on a first-name basis) the jacket has held together well.

For the ride to Yellowstone, I wore my Olympia jacket, the Olympia jacket liner, a Cal Poly sweatshirt, a CSC T-shirt, my Gore-Tex combat boots, my jeans, my motorcycle pants, and my BMW cold weather gloves. I was dressed for the weather, I was nice and toasty, and I was enjoying the ride.

Following Baja John in Yellowstone National Park. It was cold!

We arrived at Yellowstone National Park just as the sun was coming up. We were so early the park wasn't open. The entrance was, though, even though there were no park rangers there yet. We sailed right through. We had already bought annual passes that covered all of the US parks, but if we had not, we could have entered Yellowstone for free.

I asked Baja John to lead us through the park. Unlike Joshua Tree, there were different routes through Yellowstone, I had never been there before, and I didn't want to get us lost. John hopped in front and I was enjoying not being the lead dog. It was nice watching the other bikes in front of me for a change.

Yellowstone's elevation is way up there. We were between 8,000 and

9,000 feet and it was really cold, colder even than it had been on the ride in from Cody. I felt it was about time to take a break, so we stopped by a lake. That's when I realized just how cold it was. The temperature was 35 degrees! That's cold, folks. It was three degrees above freezing! Steam was rising off the lake when we stopped, and the Chinese immediately hopped off their bikes and held their gloved hands near their motorcycles' engines. They were trying to warm up. Lester starting laughing at this even though he was one of the guys doing it. Lester popped his Nikon out and captured it.

This would be the coldest riding we experienced on the entire Western America Adventure Ride. It had been as hot as 105 degrees on our first day when we rode through the Mojave Desert, and now we were exactly 70 degrees colder. Wowee!

The ride through Yellowstone that early morning was surreal. There's a lot of geologic activity under Yellowstone, and we saw (and smelled) sulfur-laden steam spewing from the ground and up into the air all over the park. In many ways, it was like riding across the set of a very scenic science fiction movie.

We were running low on fuel when we entered Yellowstone. John knew there were gas stations in Yellowstone, but I was nervous about finding one. When I saw a Sinclair station ahead on the right, I guess I fixated on it without noticing what was on the side of the road.

Just before we pulled into the Sinclair station, we had a close encounter of the RX3 kind with a bison. We were cruising along at about 30 mph through a wooded area on that freezing morning, and all of a sudden I noticed this large-as-a-locomotive huge dark shape in the woods next to me. I didn't realize what it was until I was alongside, and then I was shocked. It was huge, alone, and right on the edge of the road. I passed within 10 feet of this monster buffalo. The locomotive analogy is a good one. The big buff exhaled as I rolled by, and huge clouds of steam escaped from his nostrils. It was like the steam escaping from the drive cylinders on an old locomotive.

Speaking about the gas situation for a moment, I had checked my fuel consumption two days before Yellowstone and I was sure I had somehow made a mistake. My RX3 typically returns about 70 mpg in normal (i.e., non-freeway) riding. If I am cranking it hard on the freeway, my fuel economy will drop into the mid-60-mpg range. My calculation a few days earlier said my bike had attained 81 mpg (that's when I thought I had made a mistake, but I couldn't find it). On the ride out of Yellowstone, I calculated 81 mpg again. I know that the ride out of Yellowstone was mostly downhill, but still, that was impressive fuel economy.

Old Faithful. It was all I hoped it would be.

Our next stop in Yellowstone was Old Faithful. I always wanted to see Old Faithful, but until this trip, I never had. We followed the signs and arrived in the Old Faithful area around 9:30 in the morning. It's a cool area, comprising a large flat field of maybe 2 acres with steam spouting up all over. It's surrounded by seats, and because we arrived right after the most recent eruption of Old Faithful, the viewing area was nearly empty. We were able to grab seats right up front.

The waiting was fun. We had a chance to chat, we were off the bikes for a while, and we were all giddy with anticipation. Lester, who has a great sense of humor, gave his Nikon camera to Hugo and started speaking to him in Chinese. I didn't realize what he was asking Hugo to do until he showed me the photo on the camera's screen. Lester had staged the shot so it looked like the steam was coming out of the top of his head. Then he leaned sideways and had Hugo take another one; this time it looked like the steam was coming out of his ear. One of the other Chinese guys said something, Lester laughed and said, "No, no, no," and then he and Hugo grabbed another shot. Lester stuck his butt out and it looked like the steam was coming out of his…well, you get the idea. We were having a grand time.

All during this trip, we observed many Chinese tourists in all of the national parks, and Yellowstone was no exception. There was an elderly Asian woman seated behind me. I didn't know if she was Chinese, but I looked at her and said, "Ni hao?" That's Chinese for, "How are you?" She smiled and started speaking to me in Chinese, and I laughed. She had just heard all of the Chinese I knew. Our Chinese riders picked up on it, though, and a lively conversation ensued.

Then an exceptionally attractive young woman sat down behind me. She looked Hispanic, so I said, "Buenos Dias." (I know…I'm an international man of mystery and I'm very smooth with the ladies.) She started speaking in Spanish, and Juan Carlos recognized what must have been a Colombian accent. She was from Colombia, and another lively conversation followed.

Then Old Faithful burst forth. It was everything I thought it would be, and it was magnificent. We were all in awe. It lasted about a minute. It was amazing. I caught it in several still photos and on video, which I later posted on YouTube.

When Old Faithful finished, we all got up and drifted toward the visitor center.

Well, maybe "drifted" is too lax a word. We were hustling to get to the visitor center. I thought it was just me, but it was obvious the men in the crowd (especially us older guys) were making a beeline for the latrine. Old Faithful had that effect. Juan Carlos commented about it and we had a good laugh.

After the obligatory 30 minutes trying to gather everybody together, we left to continue on our journey. I saw a Continental Divide sign and made a stop. As you will recall, I had seen a Continental Divide sign just after we left Steamboat Springs but I had been unable to grab a photograph. That wouldn't be the case this morning. I grabbed the shot I wanted. After grabbing my photo, several of the guys took similar pictures.

The Continental Divide, of course, is the line that divides the lower 48 United States. As I mentioned earlier, east of the Continental Divide all water drains toward the Atlantic Ocean. West of the Continental Divide all water drains to the Pacific. It's an approximation by people who know about these things. I always wondered if they were right.

The Continental Divide. It was really here. I proved it.

It was time to check the concept, and I guess psychologically I was still feeling the effects of Old Faithful. I stepped behind the sign in the woods and, you know. I watched. My puddle just lay there, without moving, and then part of it moved to the east, and part of it moved to the west. Yep, this was it. I was straddling the Continental Divide.

Baja John knew the way out of Yellowstone National Park toward the Grand Tetons (where we were headed next), so I asked him to lead us out. I took up a spot in the rear of the pack and I thought I was looking forward to just tagging along.

What I saw terrified me. All of our admonitions about keeping 30 meters between riders and riding in a staggered formation had been for naught. I hadn't picked up on it before because I couldn't see it in my rear view mirror when I was at the front of the pack. The guys were riding dangerously. They were two or three abreast, they were passing each other on the right, and they were generally right on top of each other. We were not safe.

This sudden brazen display of careless riding scared the hell out of me. We had repeatedly emphasized not doing this in our safety briefings for many reasons. The problem on a ride like ours is that the scenery can be distracting, and I wanted all of the riders to have room to react in case anybody did something stupid. Scenery attracts attention and riders have a tendency to slow when a new scene emerges. You want a lot of room around each rider so people don't crash into each other.

Part of the reason for wanting 30 meters between riders is because it makes sense, and part of is because I had a guy crash into me on a motorcycle trip 25 years earlier. On that earlier trip, we rode into an area with volcanos in Mexico. The scenery was breathtaking and my riding buddy was probably looking at the volcanos when he rode into me at 60 mph (I was doing about 40). He died right there. I didn't want to have that sort of thing happen again, not on this trip or any other.

I guess I should mention that some of this bunching up was also due to the videos. Several of the guys had video cameras and they wanted to record the other riders. The problem with that is these cameras (the Go Pro and others like it) typically have very wide angle lenses. That makes a bike that is only 20 or 30 feet in front of you look like it is a quarter of a mile down the road. Unless you are right on top of the next motorcycle, the bike in front of you disappears into the horizon.

I sympathized with the need to get good video, but my mission was to get everybody back in one piece. That was far more important to me than getting something that looks good on YouTube.

After watching how unsafe our riding had become, I started to get up front to slow the group, but I wasn't making much progress. The group was going way too fast for the conditions, and everybody was bunched up. When I had guys simultaneously pass me on the left and the right (the guy who passed me on the right missed me by millimeters), I had enough. I pulled over and everyone else did, too.

As soon as we had pulled over and before I could say anything, one of the guys did the stretch-out-on-the-bike-and-fall-asleep routine. While he was trying to get into position, he dropped his bike. It was a real Keystone Cops moment and I lost it. I told everybody to gather around and I basically read them the riot act. I was pretty upset and it showed.

I guess my emotions got the best of me. I felt bad about it. But it worked. I rode at the back of the pack and we were back to keeping 30 meters between bikes.

On the way out of Yellowstone, we stopped for lunch and I had elk chili. It was amazing. It was still cold out, and I had a cup of coffee, too. Good chili and hot coffee. It was a grand lunch in a grand place.

I felt bad about what had happened earlier (me losing my temper) and I blamed myself for not doing a good enough job explaining the 30 meters between bikes and riding in a staggered formation. I suddenly had an idea. I asked the waitress if she had any paper. She told me all she had was cash register paper, and that was perfect. She gave me a strip of paper about 12 inches long and 3 inches wide. I drew a road on it showing the centerline, and I drew the bikes in a staggered formation. I noted 30 meters between bikes by using my engineering dimensioning symbols. Ah, this will do, I thought. I explained it to Hugo, satisfied myself that he understood it, and I asked him to explain it to the Chinese riders (in Chinese).

Hugo did so. They nodded their understanding. Hugo passed my drawing around the table and each rider examined it. When I saw this happen, I remember thinking to myself that I'm a pretty clever guy. I dug into my chili thinking all is well with the world.

A few minutes later, my drawing had made the rounds at our table. It came back to me fully annotated. The Chinese riders had added a rider to each bike, complete with their names in Chinese. They showed Tony's bike with its four cameras. They added the Penske truck bringing up the rear. They drew a picture of a guy standing by the side of the road relieving himself (that was probably me). I laughed, and so did the rest of the guys.

After that meal and before we left the restaurant parking lot, Lester approached me. "Da Jiu," he began, "we will ride more safely. We know you are our general and we will do as you say."

Wow. A few days ago I was a captain. Lester had just promoted me to general. My rank was rising rapidly. I was on the moto tour promotion fast track, no doubt about it.

After that, we rolled through the Grand Tetons. It, too, was an amazing place. The scenery was magnificent, and we stopped in several places for photos.

We dropped down in altitude as we continued to our evening's destination in Idaho, and as we did so, the temperatures climbed again. It became uncomfortably hot again. We pressed on.

One of the things I had done prior to the ride was publicize the tour on the CSC blog and in several press releases. I made what was (in retrospect) a mistake. I told folks they could meet us at the hotels each evening and get test rides on the RX3. We even brought along two bikes in the chase vehicle for that purpose. The test ride thing felt like a grand idea at the time, but it ended up being more trouble than it was worth.

We always arrived at each evening's destination later than we wanted to due to the problems we had getting everybody moving again every time we stopped. Squeezing test rides into our evenings was just not convenient. We were tired, we had to check into the hotels, we had to get our stuff off the truck, we had to grab dinner, sometimes we had to do laundry, and we had to check the bikes every night (we never found anything wrong, but we still checked oil, tires, etc.). In short, we were busy.

Truth be told, I don't think we sold any bikes as a result of the test rides. We did sell bikes as a result of the trip, but that occurred because people saw us, they found us on the Internet, they researched the bike, and then they bought RX3s. Or they heard about the Western America Adventure Ride and realized the bikes had to be good to do what we were doing. The folks who showed up for test rides were mostly people who just wanted to ride (but not buy) one of the most talked-about bikes in America.

The other part of the problem was that, predictably, some of the people who wanted a ride didn't want to meet us at the hotels. They wanted us to stop along the way and give them test rides. One guy actually sent an email to me asking that we divert our route 150 miles so he could get a test ride. It was good to see the interest, but it was an incredibly selfish request. I wasn't going to add 150 miles to our trip and make 10 riders stand around wearing all of their gear in hot weather so someone could get a test ride.

We made a stop for someone who wanted to see the bike during our ride to Idaho Falls that afternoon. Predictably, we stood around in the sun in our gear while this happened. It was hot. We were running late. It took 15 minutes when we were done to get everyone rounded up and moving again. After that, I put the word out. We weren't going to be stopping for test rides along the way. If someone was serious about buying a bike, they could meet us at the hotel.

After the Grand Tetons, we rode for another couple of hours and then we crossed into Idaho. When we crossed the state border from Wyoming into Idaho, I was feeling pretty good. I ran through the list of states we had covered so far: California. Arizona. Utah. Colorado. Wyoming. South Dakota. Back into Wyoming. And now, Idaho. We were doing serious road work here. Major league traveling. Certainly more than most folks ever do. Didn't anyone ever tell my little RX3 it's "just" a 250?

I had a nice surprise when we got to the hotel in Idaho Falls. Arizona George (that's his screen name on the Internet forums) was waiting for us at the hotel on his RX3. It was nice. Arizona George is from (you guessed it) Arizona. He, too, was on an epic ride on his beautiful red RX3. George reads the CSC blog faithfully, so he knew all about the ride and where we would be. He changed his plans so he could meet us in Idaho and ride with us for a couple of days before continuing home to Arizona. The man is a serious rider, and that's my kind of guy. George is a Brit with an accent that everyone mistakes for Australian. I liked him the instant I met him and I thoroughly enjoyed his company.

Chapter 24: Boise, Baby!

The ride from Idaho Falls to Boise was outstanding. It was fun. Parts of it were like being Peter Fonda or Dennis Hopper in *EasyRiders*. Read on, and you'll see what I mean.

We rolled out of Idaho Falls at 8:00 a.m., we picked up Highway 20, and we rode it west across Idaho. The weather was cooperating. It was a clear and sunny day, and the road was great. It was gently rolling desert, and although it reminded me of the Mojave Desert, it was not nearly as hot.

Our first stop was at the Craters of the Moon National Monument. It's a volcanic field in the middle of southern Idaho's gently rolling hills, and it's definitely other-worldly.

We stayed at the Craters of the Moon for an hour. The group split up and we scattered to explore the place. It was like the Amboy Crater in the Mojave Desert. We had ridden by the Amboy Crater on the first day of our Western America Adventure Tour.

I believe I think more clearly when I ride a motorcycle. Like any hobby or sport, riding a motorcycle requires extreme concentration, and it's that extreme concentration that crowds other extraneous things out of my mind. I forget about things that are annoying or that make me worry. I forget about the distractions. You have to be in the here and now when you ride. You have to watch the road surface, what other drivers and riders around you are doing, and what your bike is telling you. There's no Facebook, or cell phones, or any of the distractions and intellectual debris that modern technology shoves down our throats. I don't have a GPS, or an intercom, or anything else of that nature on my bike. Even when I'm riding in a group, I like the solitude. I'm old and I find that feeling (a preference for solitude) is more prevalent among older riders.

I sometimes like having a GPS in my car, but only sometimes. To me, using it is like looking at a map through a straw. I like the big picture and I like having a paper map. When I first starting taking big rides on motorcycles, we used real maps. That's what I was doing on the Western America Adventure Ride. I didn't do it on the Baja ride because I knew the area so well I didn't need a map. On this ride, I had maps for every state on the Western America Adventure Ride except Idaho. Somehow I had either forgotten to pick up an Idaho map or I lost it if I ever had it. Whatever. I planned to pick one up at the next gas stop.

The guys were riding much better on our trek across Idaho. The Yellowstone event and my yelling at everybody about safety had an effect. I was glad we were riding more safely, but I felt bad about letting my emotions show. I thought about that as we rode across Idaho. I concluded that maybe part of it is cultural. In other countries riders ride closer together. You see YouTube videos pop up regularly about masses of scooters barely missing each other at intersections in foreign cities. Maybe that had played a role here, because that's the kind of riding some of the guys probably did in their country. They probably didn't have places where you can ride at 75 mph or where you can ride great distances. I learned how to ride in America and I like big distances with lots of space between bikes. It gives you more time to react. Maybe these guys didn't have that in their backgrounds.

Anyway, the ride through Idaho was a breeze.

I think my new Chinese name is *Sesher Me*, which the guys tell me means 30 meters in Chinese. I'm always telling the guys to keep 30 meters between bikes. At every stop I'd say it again before we rolled out: *Sesher Me*. I'd look at somebody and he'd say "I know, *Sesher Me*."

Most of the guys from China on this ride had never been to the US before, and it was sometimes hard for me to remember that the things I see all the time and don't take much notice of were new and exciting for our guests. My focus had been on getting everybody moving at the same time and minimizing the time at our fuel stops, because I wanted to get to the next spot before dark and still have enough time to take in the sightseeing stops we had scheduled. The Chinese guys wanted to see it all and get photos of everything. I was the same way when I was in China. I had to keep reminding myself of that.

Our ride across Idaho was interesting for many reasons, but what happened in Carey, Idaho, will stay with me forever.

We had left the Craters of the Moon and ridden another 50 miles or so (with literally nothing in between except open plains, rolling hills, and beautiful scenery) when we approached Carey. Carey is basically a wide spot in the road with maybe 40 or 50 structures along the way. I was focused on getting into town, filling the bikes, and getting back on the road. Gotta keep moving. You know the drill.

As we entered the outskirts of Carey, it was like my home town early in the afternoon on the 4th of July. People were sitting in lawn chairs right at the edge of the street, most were holding little American flags, and everybody was smiling. It was obvious something was about to happen. They were waiting for a parade.

Wait a minute, I thought. It's not the 4th of July. What's going on?

The good citizens of Carey were indeed waiting for a parade. It was Pioneer Day in Idaho. I imagine everybody in town was out there as we rolled into town. I'd never heard of Pioneer Day, but it obviously was a very big deal in Carey, Idaho.

We rode into the middle of this. All 11 of us (now that Arizona George had joined the party) and our chase vehicle. You can guess where this story is going. The good people of Carey thought we were the start of the parade, especially since some of the Chinese riders had large

American and Chinese flag decals on their windshields. What are you supposed to do when people are waiting for a parade and they think you are it? Is there an etiquette for this? Are you supposed to stop and tell them you're not the main attraction?

The Pioneer Day Parade in Carey, Idaho.

The Carey people waved their flags at us and cheered. What the Chinese guys were thinking I can only guess. I decided to go with the flow. Keeping my right hand on the throttle, for the next half mile I lifted my left hand and gave them my best Miss America wave. I looked in my rear view mirror and the guys behind me were doing the same.

I'm going to guess that you've seen the movie *EasyRiders*. If you're like me, you've probably seen it several times, and I'll guess further that every time it's on TV you watch it again. You'll remember there's a scene in that movie in which Dennis Hopper and Peter Fonda similarly find themselves in a parade, on their motorcycles, in a small town somewhere in America. Well, here we were. Two Colombians, a Brit, five Chinese, and three Americans riding their US-and-Chinese-flag-festooned RX3s as the advance guard in the Pioneer Day parade in Carey, Idaho. As I've said before, I can't make up stuff this good.

I spotted a Shell station on the right and we rode into it. My good buddy and kindred-sense-of-humor riding partner Joe Gresh (who was turning out to be a really great guy to be around) pulled off his helmet and said "Boy, a lot of folks are following the blog." It was pretty funny.

I wanted to get gas and get going. The Chinese guys and the Colombians wanted to stay and watch the parade. Arizona George told me if we didn't leave we'd get stuck behind the parade and we would be in Carey for an hour. I was torn. The devil on my right shoulder was telling me to get going. The angel on my left shoulder was telling me to stay.

You can guess which way that decision went. It was made for me when the crowd started cheering and whooping as I stood in the Shell station considering my options. The parade had arrived. I'm glad it went that way. It was a high point of the trip for me, and I'm sure it was for our guests, too.

People in the pickup trucks, the fire engines, the tractors, the floats, and all the parade vehicles tossed candy to the spectators. Our riders were capturing it all with their cameras. A lady in a horse-drawn carriage stopped and invited Hugo to climb up and sit next to her. Hugo radiated a smile rivaling the LED spotlights we sell for the RX3. The guys were having a hell of a time. This was a story for the ages.

Another funny moment occurred when one of the horses pulling that cart decided to pee like, well, a race horse. The horse left a large puddle. I guess the Chinese guys, having grown up in cities in modern China, had never before seen the garden-hose-like stream of a horse that's had too much beer. They started laughing and shooting photos. All of them, except Tony. Tony was off taking photos somewhere else.

The horses and that carriage moved on, and when Tony returned to our group, he chose that very spot in which to stand and start taking pictures of the parade. He was smack in the middle of the pee puddle. Hugo said something to him in Chinese and Tony answered in Chinese. I don't speak Chinese, but Tony's lack of excitement and failure to move indicated to me he didn't catch the drift of what Hugo told him. Hugo then spoke again, much more excitedly. No mistaking that, I thought. Tony jumped straight up and his feet were a study in blurred motion before he hit the ground. He looked like a character in a *Roadrunner* cartoon. Funny stuff, and it was good for another laugh.

We enjoyed that day. Our visitors had an opportunity to see a good old-fashioned American parade. You can imagine the stories they brought home to China and Colombia. I toyed with the idea of telling our guests we had scheduled it this way, but I didn't.

After the parade, we turned right on Highway 20 and rode another 50 miles or so to another tiny town with two small restaurants. It was time for lunch and we picked one. Hugo and I entered first, we reviewed the menu, and we decided on bacon cheeseburgers. I explained to the waitress what was about to happen before everyone entered.

The cheeseburgers were awesome. I was enjoying my lunch and thinking about the parade when Joe Gresh said something that I had seen but not really thought about. Joe is a student of human behavior. He observes things that others miss.

"Look at the other people," Joe said, referring to the restaurant's other customers. "Can you imagine what they are thinking?"

Like most of the places we stopped to eat, this was a very small restaurant. There were a couple of people sitting at the counter, and families at two tables a short distance away from us. They were locals. We weren't on the freeways, and these folks weren't traveling like we were. They were having lunch in their hometown. I looked at these folks and saw the same things I had observed elsewhere. I had not really thought about it until Joe Gresh made the point. The other patrons were fascinated by our guests and their excited conversations in Chinese.

I thought about it for a few seconds and then I walked over to the other tables. I told them what was happening (you know, new motorcycle in America, visitors from China and Colombia, the Western America Adventure Ride, etc.). They loved it. They had lots of questions and it was a very enjoyable exchange. Some of the towns we were going through were extremely small (for example, the town of Emblem had a sign proudly proclaiming its population to be 10). For us, it was a big deal to be on this trip. For the other people in the places we stopped, it was a big deal for them to see us.

The crew in Idaho around good buddy Justin, who had just joined the group. From L to R: Hugo, Juan Carlos, Tso, Lester, Justin, Gabriel, Kyle, and Kong.

At our lunch stop on Highway 20 in the middle of nowhere (well, okay, the middle of Idaho), I had another nice surprise. My good buddy Justin from the Baja ride (I had nicknamed him "McGuyver" during that adventure) hooked up with us. Justin, you will remember, is the guy who lost his countershaft sprocket nut in the Vizcaino Desert and calmly engineered a fix out of baling wire and a zip tie. I respect the guy enormously, and I was very happy to have him join us on the Western America Adventure Ride. It was another photo op. Grand fun, all the way around, for everybody.

From there, it was another quick 50 miles (although in much more severe heat) to the junction of Highway 20 and Interstate 84 near

Mountain Home, Idaho. We stopped for gas and on the way into that town, several of us noticed an Idaho National Guard M1 Abrams tank on display. Joe Gresh wanted to take a few minutes to photograph it. So did our guests. It was a hoot. We played around there for a good 45 minutes. The Chinese all struck a Tienanmen Square pose, holding up their hands as if they were telling the tank to stop. My good buddy Tso, whose photogenicity is off the charts (oops, the spell checker is telling me that's not a word, but you know what I mean), stood on his footpegs and held his arm parallel the M-1's main gun. It made for another great photo. Good times, folks.

The Idaho National Guard M1 Abrams.

When we arrived at the hotel in Boise, we had yet another nice surprise. My old Triumph buddy Brenden and his brother, Shelby, were waiting for us. They were there to join us for the ride the next day to Hell's Canyon. I've known Brenden for about 10 years, and I met his brother Shelby for the first time that evening in Idaho Falls. I met Brenden through Douglas Motorcycles, the Triumph dealer in San Bernardino, California, when we both rode Speed Triples. Brenden purchased his RX3 without seeing the motorcycle based on my recommendation, and Shelby did the same.

Wow, we now had four additional RX3 riders in our group (Brenden, Shelby, Justin, and George). It was impressive.

We had dinner at an Applebee's near our hotel, and when we returned we changed the oil in all of the motorcycles. Hugo and John the truck driver had group oil changes down to a science. We did the 10 CSC motorcycles in about an hour (we didn't do Brenden's, Shelby's, Justin's, or George's bikes).

It was a fun night. We had a case of beer in the ice chest, there was a lot of joking going on, and it was enjoyable. It was especially fun watching the interaction between Hugo and John the truck driver. Hugo is a young guy and he was the Zongshen rep. In his mind, he was the man in charge. John the truck driver similarly thought he was running the oil change show. John had been teaching Hugo some classic American insults and curse words during their long hours together in the chase vehicle cab, and the two of them were trading barbs good naturedly and freely. It was funny watching Hugo holding a funnel while John measured the oil. Hugo pointed to his wrist and told John "quickly, quickly." What made it especially funny was that Hugo doesn't wear a wristwatch.

Hugo had learned that point-to-your-watch, "quickly, quickly" thing from me.

Chapter 25: Hell's Canyon

Our Boise departure occurred at a sensible 8:00 a.m. The hotel had a decent breakfast, we had our daily briefing, and we were on the road. I was excited because today we would see Hell's Canyon in Oregon. We would be adding our eighth state to the Western America Adventure Ride. We'd had been in California, Arizona, Utah, Colorado, Wyoming, South Dakota, Idaho, and in another hundred miles we would be in Oregon. Heady stuff.

I remember thinking it would be hot that day. It was anything but. In fact, later in the day it would be downright cold. I'll get to that later.

I washed my clothes in the sink the night before and hung them up to dry over the bathtub. The hotel had a coin-operated washer and dryer, but I was too tired to keep going back to the machine to check on my clothes. I remember being surprised at how much dirt came out of my jeans as I wrung them out by hand in the bathroom sink. I didn't realize just how much grime accumulates in a few days of motorcycle riding.

The upshot of all this is that my clothes were still damp when we pulled out of Boise. I wasn't worried. They'd be dry soon enough, and on a hot day (which I was expecting) still-damp clothes keep you cool.

We left Boise on Interstate 84 and took it north to Highway 95 in Fruitland. We were still in Idaho, but not by much (we were just east of the Oregon border). Highway 95 was a nice two-lane road that followed the border between Oregon and Idaho. I thought to myself it was a good road, but not nearly as nice as some of the other roads we had traveled on this adventure. In any other setting, this would have been a great motorcycle ride, but by this time we had been spoiled. We had traveled some of the best motorcycle roads in the country. By that standard, this was a good road, but it wasn't exceptional.

Our first objective that morning was Cambridge, Idaho, and it took about an hour and a half to get there. Baja John had coordinated with Rob, yet another RX3 owner, who would meet us in Cambridge and ride with us for the day.

I had not met Rob yet, but I already knew him from the ChinaRiders.net forum. I knew Rob was an intelligent man from his postings and I had been looking forward to meeting him in person. Rob is a machinist. He seemed like a good guy to know from his forum comments and the accessories he had fabricated for his RX3 and posted about on that board.

When I first saw Rob that morning, we were rolling north on Highway 95 heading into Cambridge. Rob had parked his motorcycle on the edge of the road and he was seated in a lawn chair he borrowed from the motel. He was fully suited up except for his helmet, and he stood up when he saw us approaching. The message was immediately clear: You guys won't have to wait on me. I liked that

Rob had some nice touches on his RX3, including custom footpegs, a throttle lock, and a little plastic donkey mounted on his front fender. One of the guys asked Rob if his donkey had a name and he said it did not. I suggested Hoty. Joe Gresh groaned. He and Rob both got it. Donkey Hoty. As in Don Quixote.

Rob, Brenden, Shelby, and Don Quixote in Cambridge, Idaho.

Cambridge was a very small town at the intersection of Highway 71 and Highway 95. We had entered town on Highway 95 and we would be turning left on Highway 71 to head for Oregon. There was a Sinclair station on the southwest corner of that intersection and we stopped there to refuel. Everyone was in good spirits. It had been a good morning ride. We hung around in the parking lot chatting.

Justin (who lives in Washington) and Brenden and his brother Shelby (who both live in Idaho) were with us. They knew this area well. Justin told us the next 150 miles or so (and maybe 4 or 5 hours or traveling time) were scenic but extremely desolate. Justin said it would be a good idea to eat in the Sinclair station. I didn't see any restaurants in Cambridge (that's how small the town is), but the gas station had a convenience store with sandwiches and other food items. I mentioned Justin's thoughts to Brenden and Shelby and they agreed, so we all went back into the gas station and bought our lunches. We sat in front of the gas station eating gas station food and enjoying each other's company. It was a fine day.

Justin is an accomplished photographer, as are Brenden, Shelby, and Rob. They all use Canon equipment and they were extolling the virtues of that manufacturer. I'm a Nikon guy (so is Lester, by the way), so I kept my mouth shut. The Canon versus Nikon argument is an old one (it's a Ford versus Chevy thing). No sense letting politics ruin a perfectly good morning.

After sampling the culinary delights of a rural Idaho Sinclair station, we were on the road on Idaho 71. As I said above, Highway 95 was just okay. Highway 71 was another story altogether. It's one of the world's great roads. It climbed and descended and twisted and turned as we made our way to the Brownlee Dam. We arrived and it was beautiful. The Brownlee Dam creates a reservoir on its northern side. It's on the Snake River, which forms the border between Idaho and Oregon. It was stunning.

We rode across the Brownlee Dam and stopped on the other side. We had entered Oregon. Yippee! We spent another hour at that spot and we took many photographs. A sign said welcome to Oregon. Two posts held it up. Tso, Mr. Photogenic, seized the opportunity and he pulled himself up on the sign posts. That photo became another instant favorite. If a picture is worth a thousand words, my shot of Tso was easily worth a dictionary. I like it that much.

Three deer were across the road from us. We watched as they picked their way through the trees and bushes. Juan Carlos, Gabriel, and Tony saw a dirt road climbing up a hill and they immediately tore off, raising rooster tails as they raced to a hilltop photo vantage point. To me, it represented everything adventure touring is all about. I enjoyed that stop on the Snake River immensely.

I savored the moment, thinking about where we were, what we had accomplished, what we had seen, and the riding we were enjoying. We had been on so many amazing roads I was losing track of them all. I wasn't taking any notes during the trip (unlike Lester, who kept a detailed journal he updated whenever we stopped). I wondered if I would be able to remember it all. I was making entries in the CSC blog when we had good connectivity, but that wasn't every day. As I write this, I am surprised at how many details I can remember.

Tso strikes a pose at the Brownlee Dam along the Snake River.

On that day in Oregon I had no thoughts about writing a book. That idea would come to me later. During the ride, I was too busy concentrating on the details of keeping everyone moving in the same direction and keeping everyone safe. My greatest fear was that someone would crash. My second greatest fear was that one or more of the bikes would break down. Fortunately, neither concern materialized.

Anyway, that moment along the Snake River in Oregon was a memorable one. I let the realization sink in: We were in Oregon.

Oregon.

Let me say that again.

Oregon.

Oregon, by way of California, Arizona, Utah, Colorado, South Dakota, Wyoming, and Idaho. On 250cc motorcycles.

Oregon.

Okay, you get the point.

I rode my RX3 from Azusa to Oregon along with nine other guys.

I'll say it again.

Oregon.

I was feeling good. We still had a lot of miles to go that day, though, and the roads were twisty (which meant it would take a lot of time). I beeped my horn three long times and the guys converged, ready to continue our adventure.

We left that magical spot and continued along the Snake River to another dam at Oxbow, where we turned left and headed deeper into the Hell's Canyon Recreation Area. We turned right on Highway 39, climbing into the Wallowa Mountains.

Let me back up a bit to tell you about a conversation Baja John and I had about which route to take through the Wallowa Mountains. During his pre-ride research John had discovered what he described as a fairly gnarly dirt road. John wanted to do part of the ride on it. I didn't want to for several reasons:

- We had the chase vehicle to worry about. If we were going to ride a challenging dirt road through the mountains, there was no way the big Penske truck would make it. John's thought was that the truck could stick to the paved road and we would meet up later. I didn't like that based on our earlier separation from the truck and the difficulty we had reconnecting. Plus, the truck was carrying all of our spare parts. If any of the bikes had a problem out in the boonies, we wouldn't have access to our parts.

- If anyone crashed and was injured out in the boonies, we'd really be in a bad situation.

- After watching all of the riders in our group for the previous 10 days or so, I knew that some of the riders would be okay riding in the dirt. I also knew that some of them would not be. A couple of the guys made me nervous on the street; I didn't want to see what would happen in the dirt.

I explained all of this to John, and his feeling was that he could take a few of the guys on the dirt road, and I could take the rest on the paved roads. I told John that was a nonstarter for me, too. Even for the guys on the paved portion, we'd be hard pressed to get to our next town (La Grande, Oregon) by nightfall. Riding in the dirt slows things down enormously. I did not want to split the group.

John's next argument was that including a segment in the dirt would be good publicity for the bikes. That's when I knew I definitely did not want to play in the dirt. We already had plenty of publicity riding the RX3 offroad during the Mexico ride. Many other RX3 riders had been posting on Internet forums about riding their RX3s offroad. The RX3 has made its bones in the dirt. To me, to get a tiny bit more Internet coverage for riding 30 miles or so in the dirt on this ride had minimal upside. If anything went wrong, the downside was enormous. Nope, we had 5000 miles to do on this ride, and none of it was going to be in the dirt.

Or so I thought.

When we made that right turn onto Highway 39, the asphalt disappeared. It didn't look completely like a dirt road. There were construction trucks and construction stuff along the road, but I couldn't tell if they were about to pave it for the first time, or if they were repaving it. In any event, what was passing below my tires was not a paved road.

About a quarter of a mile into this stuff, I vaguely recalled seeing a different line style on the map for this road when I studied our route the night before. As I thought about that while clattering along on dirt and gravel washboard, I was pretty sure I remembered that line style represented an unimproved road.

My next thought, seeing the sporadically spaced construction equipment, was that maybe it was just a short section of the road that was undergoing repairs. That happens sometimes. Other than that one stretch riding into Deadwood, we had not experienced any road construction on the Western America Adventure Ride. We were probably due for some, I thought.

The unimproved road went on and on and on. It was maybe a 30-mile stretch. It seemed to go on forever. I remember wondering if John just said screw it and he had decided to take us on the dirt road anyway. He had planned the route. Nah, John wouldn't do that, I thought. Then I'd start to wonder again if that's what he did. Then I'd convince myself he didn't. I knew this stretch of road would go on for a while, but I didn't know how much of it would be in bad shape. I started to wonder: Should I stop and turn around? I couldn't see much behind me. I was kicking up a lot of dust and I'd catch a glimpse of a bike behind me in the dust only occasionally. I worried about what would happen if I stopped. The dust I was generating was thick. Would the guys ride right into me?

We finally reached pavement. I rode another mile and stopped. So did everyone else.

Baja John got off his bike and said, "Wow, that was rough."

"It was," I said. "I thought a couple of times about turning around."

"I'll bet you were probably thinking I ignored what you said and took us on the dirt road anyway," John said, looking almost apologetic, and maybe a little bit worried.

"That's exactly what I was thinking, Amigo, but I figured you wouldn't do that."

John just smiled.

Whatever had just happened, we were through it. I did spend a lot of time that night studying the Oregon map, though, looking for another unimproved road through the Wallowa Mountains. I couldn't find one.

Hell's Canyon lay directly ahead. It was going to be another first for me. I had never been there before, and I always wanted to see it.

Hell's Canyon, Oregon. The Snake River is down there somewhere.

The road climbed through the pine forests and then we were there. Justin knew all about this place and he gave the lesson that day. Hell's Canyon is deeper than the Grand Canyon, he told us, and the Snake River was down there somewhere. We couldn't see it. Just as the Grand Canyon had been eroded into existence by the Colorado River, Hell's Canyon owed its existence to the Snake River. It was a deep canyon. We saw hawks circling below us as we looked out over it.

Unlike the Grand Canyon, the Hell's Canyon's walls are not vertical and they don't have the signature southwestern red and orange rock colorations. Hell's Canyon was basically a valley, with forested and grassy inclines leading down to the river below.

Okay. Hell's Canyon. Been there, done that. Like I said, I always wanted to visit Hell's Canyon, and now I had. It's another place I can cross off my bucket list.

From left to right, rear to front, it's Baja John, Lester, Joe, Rob, Shelby, Tony, and Brenden, all seen through a 16mm lens.

I was having a ton of fun taking in the views and taking photos. Like always, though, the best photos are the ones of people. I asked a few of the guys who were nearby to gather around as I jumped up onto a cement cube. I had the superwide 16-35mm lens on my Nikon and I cranked it all the way over to 16mm. A cool trick with a wide angle lens is to shoot down at a slight angle, and that's what I was about to do here. That gave me a marvelous photograph showing Rob, Shelby, Tony, Brenden, John, Lester, and Joe Gresh. Another photo, another favorite.

I looked at my watch. We needed to get going. We still had another 120 miles to La Grande, and it would be a very long 120 miles. The ride west out of Hell's Canyon seemed to take forever. It was series of unending switchbacks and unmarked lanes extending for 80 miles in what became very cold riding conditions.

I was glad when we reached the small town of Joseph at the end of the switchbacks. The town is named for Chief Joseph of the Nez Perce Indians. We stopped for dinner and I told the Colombians and the Chinese it was named for me. I think one or two of them believed me.

We had a great (but late) Mexican lunch in Joseph, and then we rode another 71 miles to La Grande, Oregon, our destination for that evening. It had been a long day.

When we arrived at the hotel in La Grande, we were in for another nice surprise. Our good buddy Mark (who owns a red RX3) was waiting for us in the parking lot. We met yet another RX3 rider.

We were very tired when we pulled into the hotel, but listening to Mark talk about how much fun he was having with his RX3 was invigorating. Joe Gresh was amazed at Mark's unbridled enthusiasm about his RX3, and he was further amazed when Mark told us he also owned a BMW GS. Joe turned to me and said, "You're paying him to say this, right?"

I could tell Joe was impressed. Joe loved the RX3 he rode on the Western America Adventure Ride. He has to remain impartial to do his journalism thing for *Motorcyclist* magazine, but I could tell. He was drinking the Kool Aid. Joe was becoming a member of the Cult of the Zong.

Chapter 26: The Columbia River, Spit, and a Spat

The ride today would put us in Beaverton, Oregon. I wanted to stay in Portland, but our schedule and the traffic would not permit it. Getting in and out of Portland during rush hour on a weekday (which is when we would have arrived) made it impossible for us to stay in this pearl of a city.

All that aside, I need to tell you that Portland is one of my favorite cities, and if you ever have a chance to visit it, you should. I've been there several times and I love the place. Portland has a cool downtown area. There's a bar called Kelly's Olympian that two guys started because they wanted a place to display their antique motorcycle collection. You know that's my kind of spot (and yes, I wrote a "Destinations" piece on Kelly's for *Motorcycle Classics* a few years ago).

Baja John worked his US Air Force navigation magic (he's a retired colonel) and Beaverton, a small suburb in the right spot just southwest of Portland, got the nod for this evening's destination. It would be a good place for our launch the next day, during which we would run through Oregon's northern coastal mountains to the Pacific Ocean. I was looking forward to seeing those cold blue waters that signified it was time to turn left and head home.

Hugo, a man with a lot on his mind, on the banks of the Columbia River.

It was sunny when we left La Grande that morning, but that wouldn't last long. We picked up Interstate 84 and again headed west, climbing into the Wilderness National Forest toward Pendleton. The weather looked ominous. It was cold and the temperature was dropping rapidly.

I left La Grande without wearing my Olympia jacket liner or my motorcycle pants, and I was starting to feel the chill. I knew if I was cold, the rest of the guys were, too. The skies grew darker and then it started to rain. It was a weird rain. The drops were big, but they had lots of space between them. It was not enough to get us wet, but it looked like the start of something big.

I took the next exit, which went nowhere. There was a highway repair crew working at the bottom of the exit and the road ended there. I pulled my motorcycle pants out of my right pannier and my jacket liner out of the left. Hugo had my Cal Poly sweatshirt in the truck cab and I pulled it on, too. The other guys similarly donned their raingear and added layers under their jackets. It looked like it was going to be bad.

We had a long uphill freeway stretch after that. The skies were dark and the crest of the mountain range we were about to top was maybe two miles ahead. The rain continued with those fat, lazy, weirdly-spaced drops. Maybe they knew it was me and they were keeping the requisite 30-meter spacing. *Sesher Me* and all that.

Then a funny thing happened. We crested that mountain range, the rain stopped (it never did get heavy enough to make us wet), and the sun emerged. It was as if we were passing from one room to another, with one room dark and the other fully lit. I looked in my rear view mirror and it was dark behind me. It was strange.

We enjoyed another 75-mph stretch of perhaps 80 miles along Interstate 84. I knew the Columbia River was ahead of us and we were approaching it at a northwesterly angle.

I'd been through the Colombia River Gorge on the Three Flags Rally several years ago, and as we entered it, the region was every bit as stunning as I remembered it. The air was clear, the skies were blue, and the riding was great. You can't put a price on these kinds of moments.

We had been on the road about two weeks. I missed Susie and my daughters and I wanted to get home, but when you do long distance adventure touring you live for the kind of moment we were experiencing that crisp morning in Oregon. Those of you who ride know. Those of you who do not, well, no amount of crafty wordsmithing on my part can communicate what I was feeling that morning. I was alive and out in the world. If you want to experience it firsthand (and you should), when you are finished reading this book go out and buy a motorcycle. Trust me on this.

Ah, there it was. Just up ahead to our right. The Columbia River, forming the border between Oregon and Washington. It was a dark greenish blue, contrasting starkly with the brown hills on both sides and the powder blue sky above. There wasn't much out there except the Columbia River, the sky, the mountains, the road, and us. It was glorious.

We rode for perhaps another 40 miles until I saw a sign for a viewpoint. It was time for a break and we pulled over. Predictably, the cameras came out. This was yet another magnificent panorama on our amazing journey, a journey that was a continuing series of magnificent scenes, playing out in real time all around us.

King Kong told me the river was beautiful. I told him it was the major river in America's Pacific Northwest, and that he had now seen two of America's most famous rivers. The Colorado River (which we had crossed several times starting with the first day of our ride) provided drainage for the American Southwest. The Columbia River provided drainage for the Pacific Northwest.

Kong asked me if there were similar rivers in the eastern United States.

"There are," I said. "The Mississippi River is our major river in the southeastern United States."

"That's the Southwest, the Northwest, and the Southeast," Kong said. "Do you have a comparable river in the northeastern United States?"

"We do," I said. "That would be the Hudson River, which flows south from several tributaries and empties into the Atlantic Ocean by New York City."

"Ah," Kong answered. "Such a magnificent country."

Indeed we are, I thought. I realized I was extremely blessed in that I had seen and traveled extensively along all four rivers, mostly by motorcycle. Most Americans never get to do that. I am a lucky man and I have enjoyed some wonderful motorcycle rides.

I had the Bridge of the Gods on my mind as we continued west on Interstate 84. I first rode across that iconic crossing point on the Three Flags Rally without knowing anything about it. The Bridge of the Gods made a strong imprint on my mind all those years ago. My friend Marty and I were coming down from Canada along the Columbia River Gorge during the Three Flags Rally and we followed the river on the Washington side. I had no idea what the Bridge of the Gods was back then; we just wanted to get across the Columbia River and into Oregon. Our destination back then was Portland, and I knew I had to cross somewhere when I saw the sign for Oregon and it pointed left.

That crossing made a powerful impression on me. The Bridge of the Gods' road surface is about 300 feet above the water. It's an old fashioned iron truss bridge, a classic design that excites civil and mechanical engineers. I'm a mechanical engineer, and when I first saw the bridge's silhouette several miles away from the Washington side, I thought it was awesome. It looked like something you would see in a 1930's science fiction story. It is a classic structure and it is art to me.

The bridge's structural design is not what made the biggest impression that day on the Three Flags Rally. That honor goes to the bridge's road surface. It's an iron mesh design with 1-inch grids. Other than the metal grid, there's nothing there. You look down and you see the river surface 300 feet below. Do it on a motorcycle in motion and that's all you see. The metal grid disappears as you fly over it, and flying is the appropriate word. It actually appears as if you are flying 300 feet above the water. It's simultaneously exhilarating, terrifying, and vertigo inducing. I wanted to share this with our Western America Adventure Riders. I told John that it was one of the things we absolutely could not take out of the trip (miles-per-day and schedule limitations be damned).

We stopped for lunch (another Subway, which had become one of our favorite places to eat on this ride) in Biggs, Oregon, and crossed the mighty Columbia River there. We had to get on the Washington side so we could cross back into Oregon on the Bridge of the Gods. Biggs was a good spot to stop. It was time to eat, we needed fuel, and there was a bridge there to take us across the Columbia.

The bridge in Biggs is not famous like the Bridge of the Gods, but it was a sporty proposition getting across it. The wind was blowing fiercely as we rolled over the Columbia River into Washington. I'll admit it; it was scary riding a motorcycle on a bridge in that crosswind high up over the river. But it would be nothing compared to the Bridge of the Gods, which is where my thoughts were.

As I type this, I realize it might sound silly to cross a river just so you can cross back over it again on a favorite bridge, but I had ulterior motives. I wanted to add a ninth state to our tally, and that state was Washington. So that makes two motivations, one to add another notch to our guns (Washington) and another to ride across the Bridge of the Gods.

There was to be a third benefit I had not recognized when we planned the ride, and that was the ride along Highway 14 paralleling the

Columbia River on the Washington side. Highway 14 was stunning. Joe Gresh told me that he thought it was the best road we had ridden so far. High praise indeed, especially coming from motorcycle royalty like Joe, and especially considering the roads we had already ridden. If a guy like Joe Gresh was praising the route, I took it as an extreme compliment. We picked a good one.

The scenes along Highway 14 were incredible. It's a twisty two-lane road with small towns every few miles. We had a clear view of the Columbia River, including many spots where people were wind surfing and parasailing. It was windy along this river, and the people who live in the Pacific Northwest know how to put that wind to good use. At one point, a freight train barreled out of a tunnel on railroad tracks between us and the river. I had a simultaneous Lionel and Kodak moment…a clear view of the train appearing to come straight at us, the tunnel it was exiting, the pine forests all around, the twisting asphalt ahead, the Columbia River below, the windsurfers and parasailers, and nine RX3 riders in my rear view mirror. Heady stuff, my friends. A photograph wouldn't do it justice, nor do these words. You'll just have to get out there and experience it for yourself.

The Bridge of the Gods was everything I had hoped it would be. Much as I wanted to, I did not look down when we rode across. I didn't want to get dizzy. I thought the other guys, our younger Chinese and Colombian friends, could look down. In that instant, crossing the bridge and not wanting to look down, I knew I was getting older. But not too old to be still be doing this kind of stuff. I could ask, "Ain't life grand," but it would be a rhetorical question. You and I already know the answer.

We stopped after crossing the Bridge of the Gods in a little parking lot underneath and just enjoyed being there. I don't know why, but that spot is one of my favorite places on Earth. I know it's weird. I can't explain everything I do or every feeling I have. I knew I was sure feeling good, though.

It was very obvious that our guests were enjoying the experience and the place as much as I was. Lester was off talking to a couple of guys on Harleys. Tony, Hugo, Kyle, and Kong were snapping photos. John the truck driver had his iPhone out on the selfie-stick and he was doing his thing. Joe Gresh was shooting video with his iPhone. Seeing this, I felt good. It was a moment I am still savoring.

Tony and Joe dueling with digital cameras beneath the Bridge of the Gods.

We jumped back on Interstate 84 for the banzai run to Beaverton. The ride into Portland went quickly. It was about 4:00 p.m. and all the traffic was leaving Portland and headed east (opposite us). We flew along the freeway. Beaverton lies to the southwest of Portland, and once we were in the greater Portland area, the freeway slowed dramatically and then turned into a parking lot. We inched along, and it took us a good 45 minutes to cover the remaining few miles below Portland to Beaverton.

When we arrived at our hotel, we had a new problem. I was paying for our rooms (I had been covering the two Johns, Joe Gresh, and myself), and usually Hugo would be right there next to me to pay for the Chinese guys. He wasn't there this time, though. Ah, he'll show up in a minute, I thought.

Hugo appeared a few minutes later, but I could tell something was wrong. He had an expression of deep worry, something I had not seen before. I could see that whatever it was, it was not okay, not okay.

"We have problem," Hugo said, pulling me aside. He wanted privacy, which was another bad sign. "Two of the Chinese riders are fighting."

"As in a physical fight?" I said.

"Almost, Da Jiu," Hugo softly answered, looking at the floor.

Whoa, this was serious. Hugo explained to me that one of the Chinese riders had accused another of riding in an unsafe manner. That in itself was a surprise to me, as I thought all of these guys liked to ride a little too close together. If one of them thought it was unsafe, it must have been bad.

We had just come through some nasty traffic around Portland, so I could understand that we had bunched up again. We hadn't been able to hold our 30 meters between riders, but there was evidently a lot more to whatever had transpired out there on the freeway. Hugo was a person who maintained a calm and happy demeanor all the time, even when I was giving him a hard time the first few days about some of the Chinese riders being late in the morning. This was different, though. My young friend was clearly unsettled.

"Can you talk to him?" Hugo asked, mentioning one of the riders. I would have guessed that it would be the guy Hugo mentioned. This fellow had been a problem in a few other instances, and he was the only rider others complained about as unsafe. Now, it seems, he was accusing one of his countrymen of the same thing. My guess is he was trying to make it seem that he was not the unsafe guy in the group. Whatever, I thought.

"Sure, I'll talk to him," I told Hugo.

Hugo took me outside and I could see immediately that his guy was seething. He was borderline irrational and highly agitated. I took him and Hugo aside and we sat down on the curb.

According to my agitated Chinese friend, the other Chinese rider had done something unsafe (I never did find out exactly what), and then cursed (in Chinese) at him. I didn't even know these guys had curse words. Apparently they do, and the other guy had used some choice ones.

I told my friend to take a deep breath, to calm down, and to think about where we were and what we had accomplished.

"Look," I said, "we've spent the last two weeks riding 300 miles every day without a break. We've been in 100 degree weather and we've been in 30-degree weather. We've been at sea level and we've been at 10,000 feet. We're all tired. You're in another country. Our day is your night. You're eating food your body isn't used to. I'm surprised we haven't had more conflicts. You guys are doing great. Just let this argument go, man. It will be better in the morning."

I thought I was doing pretty well. I was using my best conflict resolution and calming skills. Hugo was nodding his head at everything I was saying. I was even making sense to myself. The only problem was I was having no effect on my agitated friend.

"I must beat him, Da Jiu," he said.

"Excuse me?" I answered.

"I must beat him," he repeated. "He cursed at me in Chinese and if I do not beat him my friends in China will find out and know I am weak."

Damn, I was giving it all I had and this guy was still permanently safety-wired to the pissed off position.

"Well," I said after thinking for a minute, "there's some truth in what you say. The only problem is that if you do beat him, whatever your friends think about it now they'll probably have forgotten when you return to China. And that will be in 5 years, after you get out of a US prison. The upside is that you'll get to meet new people in jail, you'll learn how to make license plates, and I'm guessing your cellmate will think you're cute."

That caught my *friendus agitatus* off guard. He looked like he was seriously weighing his options when he finally decompressed. I could see it. He exhaled and the tension left his face. Then he surprised me.

"I demand a written apology," he said.

"That ain't gonna happen," I said. "Just let it go. I don't want to get in the middle of a pissing contest and make demands about written apologies. We're all tired. Let it go and we'll all feel better in the morning."

"You speak wise words, Da Jiu," he said. "You are our lord, and I will listen to what you say."

Whoa. Our lord. At the beginning of this trip one of the Chinese guys told me I was their captain. After the Come to Jesus safety briefing in Yellowstone Lester told me I was their general. Now this fellow was telling me I was their lord. My rapid rise through the tour guide ranks had me up there with Darth Vader, or maybe even God. What could the next promotion possibly be? Does anyone outrank Lord Vader or the Deity?

I thought that was the end of it, but it wasn't. An hour later Hugo came to my room and said the fight had flared up again. As he was telling me this, the guy I had calmed down an hour ago came in and showed me his camera.

"He spit on my lens," he said. "He is terrorist." (That missing "a" is not a typo; that's the way he said it.)

I almost laughed, but I wisely choked it down. I didn't know what to say. He showed his camera to me. What looked like saliva coated the lens. I thought it would be funny to ask if he was sure it was spit, but I held my tongue on that one, too.

"This is evidence!" he said.

"Well," I said, "I will talk to him," referring to the other guy in what was emerging as a battle royale.

Hugo found me 20 minutes later and told me our Chinese spitting cobra (the other guy) had apologized. Okay, I thought. Crisis averted.

Not so fast, I soon learned. Joe Gresh and I were sitting by the pool having a beer a little later when the argument flared up yet again. The two of them were screaming at each other in Chinese on the second story walkway. It only lasted a minute, but clearly things were still not settled.

While all of the above was going on, we had another RX3 rider, Dave, from the Portland area join us at the hotel that evening. Dave has a red RX3 with every accessory CSC offers, and he stopped to visit and to join us for dinner. Dave had been following our adventures on the blog.

Joe Gresh, Dave, and I had dinner in a Chinese restaurant that night. It was good to get away from the family spat, and the meal was outstanding. It was made even better by the very attractive young Chinese lady who waited on us. She spoke fluent Chinese and English. I told her about the names our Chinese friends had given to Joe and me (Ar Jiu and Da Jiu) and I asked her if it really meant younger uncle and older uncle. She didn't know.

I saw Hugo later that night and I asked him where we were on the family feud.

"It's okay, it's okay," was the predictable answer.

"No, it's not okay, Hugo," I said. "If these two guys are at each other's throats, I don't want them to be riding motorcycles around the other guys. They're going to cause an accident."

"It's okay, it's okay," Hugo repeated. "I called China, and they told me if they don't stop fighting they will both be on an airplane back to China tomorrow morning. I told them and they both say it's okay. It's okay, it's okay. We just put them in different positions when we ride tomorrow. It's okay."

Well, how about that? Hugo had put his foot down and drawn a line in the sand. He had spoken to these guys in a universal language that every motorcycle rider understands. I knew from personal experience that telling someone they can't ride their motorcycle unless they behave is a powerful motivator. It had worked for my Dad with me when I was growing up. I guess Hugo was right. It was okay.

Chapter 27: Tillamook and the Oregon Coast Highway

The next morning saw us getting ready to leave Beaverton and head to the Oregon Coast Highway via Tillamook. Our destination that evening would be Port Orford, Oregon, about 270 miles down the road on the Pacific Coast.

I was looking forward to the day's ride. I'd been on the Oregon Coast Highway before (it was another story I had written for *Motorcycle Classics* magazine). It's one of my all-time favorite rides. If you've never ridden the Oregon Coast Highway, you owe it to yourself to do so. It's that good.

The guys were tense from the night before, though, and I could sense their tension as we loaded the chase vehicle with our bags. The two guys who had been at each other's throats were studiously avoiding eye contact. Everyone knew what had happened and I think all of the Chinese guys were embarrassed by it.

I was about to give my morning pre-ride briefing and I thought about mentioning last night's spat, how we had to put it behind us, and how we had to concentrate on our riding, our safety, and not letting anything from last night take us away from focusing on the ride. I was ready to say that right up until the moment I started speaking, and then I changed my mind. What all of us needed, I thought, was a good laugh.

"So before I talk about our route today," I said, "I want to talk about last night."

Everybody stared at the ground. No one wanted to hear about the fight.

"Ar Jiu (that was Joe Gresh, and I pointed to him just to make sure everybody knew who I was talking about) and I had dinner in a Chinese restaurant last night," I began. "And we had this killer Chinese waitress take care of us. She was beautiful, but more to the point, she spoke both Chinese and English fluently."

Hey, who doesn't like a story about a pretty girl?

"I asked her about this 'Da Jiu' business," I said. I had everyone's attention. My story was working like I hoped it would. "And I asked her what it meant." All eyes were on me now. They knew I was about to share with them what she had told me. Some were smiling already. They knew it would be good.

"Big Asshole!" I said. "So you guys ain't fooling me anymore."

The guys roared. Things were drifting back to normal. The tense mood had been broken.

I reviewed our planned route on the map and told the guys we'd be seeing more amazing things today. I told them we'd be on Highway 101, and they all knew what that meant. It was one of my favorite rides in the US, and it would be a ride they would never forget. Route 101 in Oregon is effectively the Oregon Coast Highway (unlike California, in which Highway 101 turns inland for much of its length and it's Highway 1 instead that hugs the Pacific Ocean).

The ride out of Beaverton was easy. We picked up Highway 26 west (a four lane road that was almost a freeway and didn't have much traffic), and after 20 or so miles we picked up Highway 6 and headed southwest.

Highway 6 is a wonderful two-lane road that snakes through the Tillamook State Forest's pine-tree-blanketed mountains. This was the third time I had ridden it, and each time has been a treat. We enjoyed 50 miles of twisties through pine-scented cold air, low-hanging mist, and dark forests. My imagination always runs wild on this road. I half expected Sasquatch to step out in front of us. It's that kind of place.

We entered the small town of Tillamook and turned left on Highway 101. That was a milestone for us. We would effectively follow 101 almost all the way down to Azusa. We still had at least a thousand miles in front of us.

If you're wondering if Tillamook is where the cheese of the same name comes from, the answer is yes. It's a quaint little place and it looks like it might be fun to spend a few days poking around there. I had other things in mind, though, and we didn't have a few days to devote to Tillamook. Next time.

We continued through Tillamook and rolled further south until I spotted the Naval Air Museum on the left just a few miles south of town. I had wanted to stop there on my previous rides through this area, but I never had. It was part of the plan for today, and I knew our guests would enjoy it.

I was right. The place was great. The Tillamook Naval Air Museum is housed in the last remaining wooden dirigible hangar in the US. You younger guys who are reading this may not know a dirigible is. Think Hindenburg or the Goodyear blimp. Dirigibles are giant cigar-shaped, lighter-than-air ships that the Navy used mostly as observation platforms. They are huge. A dirigible shouldn't be confused with a blimp, though, even though I just used the two terms synonymously. Blimps are inflated (like balloons) and the skin becomes the structure. A dirigible has a metal frame and has lighter-than-air containers holding helium inside the structure. I know all this from my elementary school adventures, but I'll get to that in a second.

The US Navy started flying dirigibles around 1906, and continued using them at least into the 1960s. When I was kid we lived near an operational US Navy dirigible air base (Lakehurst Naval Air Station in New Jersey). We had several class trips and at least one Cub Scout trip there when I was a wee one, and the Navy was still flying around in these things for a few years after that. We saw a lot of them in the New Jersey skies when I was growing up.

A North Korean MIG inside the Tillamook Naval Air Museum.

Okay, back to the present. When we paid for our tickets at the Tillamook Naval Air Museum entrance, the nice lady at the ticket counter told us we were entering the largest free-standing, man-made wooden structure in the world. It's 192 feet tall.

Once we were inside, the place was cavernous. That was good and it made for some cool photo opportunities. What was not so good was that the place was not terribly well lit. It was dim inside. My Nikon D810 camera is renowned for its low light level performance, so I cranked up the ISO to something around 5000. It worked. I took several photos of the guys inside the structure, without flash, and they turned out well.

Another disadvantage of the hangar's cavernous size was that even though the Tillamook Naval Air Museum had several aircraft inside, they looked lost in that cavernous building. The hangar's size made it look mostly empty (which it was). I don't think that took away any of the appeal for our guests, though. They were getting a firsthand look at several US military aircraft (even though they all were obsolete) and they loved it. As you might imagine, the shutters were clicking.

Joe Gresh and I finished taking pictures before the other guys did and we drifted into the gift shop. There was a small cafeteria. I bought coffee for Joe and myself. We were having a nice conversation when we saw our Chinese and Colombian friends enter the gift shop. We could see they were having difficulty selecting souvenirs. They would carefully examine everything they picked up, only to put each item down again. I thought they were put off by the prices. Nope, that wasn't it at all. Joe tumbled to what was going on before I did.

"They want a souvenir from the US, but everything they're looking at says 'Made in China'," Joe told me. We had a good laugh about that. Chinese guys looking for a US souvenir in a former US Navy military facility, and all they could find was stuff made in China.

A scene along the Oregon Coast Highway. Almost home, I thought.

After our stop at Naval Air Museum we continued along Highway 101 for another half hour or so and there it was: The Pacific Ocean.

Wow. The Pacific Ocean. It felt like we were almost home.

There was a view point right there and we stopped. They guys were all feeling good. The air was crisp. It had the fragrance of the ocean and we were all enjoying it. Lester put one arm around me and pointed out over the ocean.

"Do you see it?" he asked. "That is my home." It was good for another laugh from the group. We were having a good time.

We grabbed great photos at that stop, and we made several more stops as we continued along 101. We would be riding alongside the Pacific Ocean for the next 500 miles or so before Highway 101 turned inland in California.

The ride along the Oregon Coast Highway was simultaneously wonderful and uneventful, although I was slipping into my normal worrisome state. I had the ride, the guys, and the bikes on my mind. In particular, a couple of things were emerging on three of the bikes (my bike, Baja John's, and Joe Gresh's) that had my attention. I was worried about the rear tires and the chains.

The three of us (Joe, John, and I) had around 7000 miles on our bikes at that point. The other guys' bikes had about 4000 miles (they were brand new when we began the Western America Adventure Ride). On the three bikes of concern, the tires were showing wear and our chains needed to be tightened nearly every day.

I was impressed with the miles we were getting out of the rear tires and I was pretty sure I could get home on mine, but my antenna was up. We had brought extra tires, but I didn't want to expend the effort to change the tire on my bike. I was being lazy, I guess. I thought my tire would go the distance, but I wasn't sure. On other motorcycles I had owned, when the rear tire started to show wear the remaining tread went very quickly (the tires would finish their lives wearing at a much more rapid rate). That proved not to be the case with the RX3. My rear tire went 8700 miles before I replaced it. I made it all the way home on it, and I probably could have made it to 10,000 miles on that rear tire. Those original equipment CST tires are good.

The chains, on the other hand, were not lasting as long as I would have liked. I was surprised at how much the chains were stretching once our three bikes reached 6000 miles. I had sent an email to Zongshen the night before asking how long the chains on these bikes should last. The answer from the factory was 12000 kilometers, which is about 7500 miles. In the next sentence, though, they told me that chain life would be shortened on our ride by the continuous high-speed driving we were doing every day.

That surprised me. I always thought a chain should last about 15000 miles. The RX3 has a fairly healthy 520 chain (it's a big chain for a 250cc motorcycle), but like the saying goes, it is what it is. I knew I'd have to keep an eye on the chains on my bike, Joe's bike, and John's bike. Joe and John knew it, too. We had been talking about having to adjust the chains every day.

We had a couple of extra chains on the chase vehicle, so when I first started watching the chains a day or two earlier, I figured if we needed to throw another chain on one or more of the bikes it wouldn't be a big deal. Another thing that I kept remembering was that when Hugo arrived from China, he handed me a new chain in a plastic bag. He told me had bought a spare chain in case we needed it. I thought that was a bit odd as we had spare chains. Why would he show up with a chain and no other parts? There are a lot of different parts on that motorcycle.

What I didn't know at the time we left was that the chain life was 7500 miles under ideal conditions. Someone in China had recognized we might need to change a chain, but other than Hugo arriving with a chain in his hand, nobody said anything about it. Ah, experience. To jump ahead a bit, when I got back to California I had our Service Department put a higher quality chain on my bike. I'm confident that one will go at least 15000 miles.

Some of you may be wondering why I'm making such a big deal out of this. You're probably thinking changing a chain is nothing unusual and the chain is basically a wear item, so why all the fuss?

Think back to my earlier chapter on the Baja ride. I wasn't doing this trip just to get out and go for a motorcycle ride. Even though I was a consultant to CSC and not an employee, I was the CSC representative on this ride. If anything broke or didn't perform as expected on any part of the RX3 motorcycle, it would feel like a personal failure to me. I know all that stuff about the adventure not starting until something goes wrong, but I really didn't want that kind of an adventure. I wanted to run the entire 5000 miles with all 10 motorcycles, and have absolutely no problems.

Joe Gresh understood all of this. He was there to write a story about the RX3 and the Western America Adventure Ride for *Motorcyclist* magazine. I, on the other hand, wanted everything to be perfect. Joe was expecting things to go wrong, and in fact, he had commented several times already that he was amazed at how well the bikes were doing. We were running 8000 rpm all day long, day after day, and the bikes didn't burp once. Still, I worried. It's what I do.

"Your problem," Joe told me, "is you don't know how to handle success." Joe was getting to know me. He was right on the money with that assessment.

All right, enough soul searching. Back to the ride.

One of the best parts about the Oregon Coast Highway is the magnificent art deco bridges. These were built as part of the effort to lift the US out of the Great Depression and to develop the Oregon coast. The bridges are beautiful. You don't have to be an engineer to enjoy them. The Oregon Coast Highway bridges are stylish and appealing, and it's a special treat to ride across them. I can't imagine a bridge being built today with the style and panache of these beautiful old structures. I shot a video or two that I later posted on YouTube as we crossed a couple of the bridges. It's not something you read or hear about much when folks describe the Oregon Coast Highway, but it's one of the best parts of the ride.

As I said earlier, the ride south on the Oregon Coast Highway was both beautiful and uneventful. We stopped several times for photos, we stopped for ice cream, and finally, we made our last fuel stop before riding on to Port Orford, our destination for the evening. That gas stop in Port Orford shall forever more be known as the Site of the Burnout That Changed the World.

We had filled all of the bikes and we were waiting for the same guy who always decided he needed to use the restroom just as everyone was ready to leave. After these last-minute restroom emergencies, that fellow always needed 15 minutes to put on his gear and connect his gizmos to the bike. We were in the middle of watching this drill, waiting for this fellow to get ready, when Joe Gresh moved his bike out in front of everyone.

Joe stopped his bike, revved the engine, applied the front brake, and proceeded to execute a world-class burnout. Smoking tire. Rear wheel rotating furiously while the front end compressed the suspension. Engine screaming. Joe laughing maniacally. Me thinking two things:

- Please don't break my motorcycle, and...

- Is there a baseball bat handy so I can clobber this guy?

I couldn't believe he had done that. Some of the other guys were cheering. I shook my head. Our always-late errant rider finished dressing. We continued on to Port Orford.

A burnout. On a 250. Go figure.

The funniest parts of the burnout story became the resulting burnout banter between Joe and me on the rest of ride (keep reading; you'll see), and Steve Seidner's only question when I told him about it.

Steve's response was, "Did anyone get it on video?"

Chapter 28: Willits

Before I forget, let me mention Oregon Jim, one of our RX3 riders who hooked up with us for the Western America Adventure Ride in Port Orford. Jim had been a rider earlier in his life, and when he first learned of the RX3, he made the decision to start riding again. Jim met us in Port Orford and he rode with us the next day when we re-entered California. Having folks who owned RX3s connect with us for the ride was one of the best parts of the trip for me. I enjoyed meeting and riding with all of them. Trust me on this…you actually meet the nicest people on an RX3.

I was looking forward to getting back on the RX3 and resuming the run south. It's a strange but natural thing, the feeling you develop for your motorcycle. You folks who ride great distances will understand immediately what I am about to say. You connect with your bike on a ride like this. It becomes part of you. Yeah, you're tired, you want to get home, and you know you've got several hundred miles in front of you that day, but getting in the saddle at the start of a new day feels like the most natural thing in the world. You want to do it. You know you are where you belong. This is what I felt that morning when I strolled out into the hotel's parking lot.

I was out there, but it was mighty lonely. Apart from John the truck driver, Hugo, and Oregon Jim, I was it. The other bikes sat there, waiting for their riders.

Oregon Jim, who rode with us from Port Orford to Eureka.

The departure from Port Orford occurred on time, but it was not pretty. My patience evaporated that morning. If that waitress in the Chinese restaurant had been right about the translation of Da Jiu, I sure demonstrated it that morning (more on that a little further down).

The Port Orford hotel we stayed in was at the lower end of the spectrum. It was okay and it was relatively inexpensive. It didn't have air conditioning, but it wasn't hot. For me, hotels on a motorcycle trip are a place to flop. As I've said before, all I'm interested in is a quiet place to sleep, hot water, a coffeemaker, and good connectivity.

Our Port Orford hotel, though, pretty much struck out on every count. The coffeemaker didn't work and there was effectively no Internet connectivity (nor was there a desk to work at with my computer). After 10 minutes of letting the shower run the water only got up to "not quite so cold" (and that happened only after I won the contest with a cockroach who thought he owned the shower). All this was accompanied by a syncopated thumping that went on for about 45 minutes before I could fall asleep. I had no idea what was causing that noise. It kept me up. I finally fell asleep when it ended.

I was up with the sun and puttered around the room and the hotel for a while, thinking through what we were going to be doing that day. It should be an easy run, I remember thinking. We would stay on Highway 101 all the way down to Willits, California. In Port Orford, we were only a few miles north of the California border, and it would be good to get back into my home state.

I remember thinking about our leaving Port Orford, too, and I wondered if we'd be able to leave on time. Our group was heading south as we continued our journey home, and so was our ability to leave on time. We had been hitting the road later and later. As you have read, I am a stickler for schedules. Maybe it's my manufacturing background. Maybe it's something else.

During one of our conversations on the Western American Adventure Ride (and we had many), Baja John, Joe Gresh, and I were talking about what kind of trouble we had been in during our younger days. One of my accomplishments was getting suspended for several days when I was in high school. I was dumb enough to mutter something not very nice to a Spanish teacher (it involved suggesting an anatomically impossible act), and I was out for three days. Joe Gresh asked me what prompted me to say what I had said to her.

"She yelled at me," I said.

"What for?" Joe asked.

"I was late to class."

"Ah, that explains a lot," Joe said.

I had never thought about that. Maybe it did explain a lot. Whatever. I hate being late, and I feel the same way about others being late. It's a character flaw that I have.

Okay, so back to Port Orford and our departure that morning. John the truck driver had been doing well but our US riders and the Chinese were getting out later and later in the morning. John had the truck open when I was in the hotel parking lot at 7:30. Oregon Jim and Hugo were out there, too. The problem was that John, Hugo, Oregon Jim, and I were the only four people there. We had half an hour to go before our scheduled departure. I realized that there was still time for everybody to show up so we could leave on time. The guys will get out here, I thought.

Ah, wishful thinking. At 7:58, the Colombians were putting their stuff on the truck and Lester was just leaving his room. Everyone else was missing in action.

I told John to fire the truck up. We're leaving, I told him. Hugo's eyes got wide, and he split for the rooms and started pounding on doors.

We actually left the hotel at 8:00 a.m., right on time, and everybody was there. A lot sure happened in those last two minutes, though. Everybody was scrambling. The train was pulling out of the station and nobody wanted to miss it.

Rolling out on time with a group this size is always a minor miracle. Every big ride with multiple riders I've ever been on has experienced this challenge. I heard once that there's actually a formula somewhere that allots a certain number of additional minutes you should add for each rider. I didn't want to do that. It would feel like I was surrendering to an inability to make things happen on schedule. It's that being late thing that I hate.

I learned a few years ago on another ride that you just announce a departure time and then leave at that time whether folks are ready or not. People kind of figure it out after that. That's what we did that morning, and it worked.

We continued along the Oregon Coast Highway and I spotted a McDonalds on the right 30 minutes later. It was a good place to stop for breakfast.

I had actually been in that very same McDonalds several years earlier when Susie and I were on a road trip in the Subaru. I remember it well because it was the first time I realized I was a senior citizen. Sue wanted a diet coke and a cookie that day. I pulled into the parking lot, entered the McDonalds, and asked the teenage girl behind the counter for a diet coke, a chocolate chip cookie, and a coffee (the coffee was for me). It was our standard afternoon snack, and I had ordered this precise combination many times before in many other McDonalds.

The young lady did as I asked and then told me the amount. It was too low, and I told her that I thought she might have made a mistake. I didn't want her to get in trouble for coming up short on her register.

"No, it's correct. I gave you the senior discount."

I guess my look said it all. She blushed and then told me I really didn't look that old, but it was too late. When I told Sue about it a few minutes later, she thought it was funny. In retrospect, I guess it was.

Anyway, back to the present and our motorcycle ride. The breakfast was good. The place was crowded, but McDonalds has it down to a science, and our food was ready quickly.

The guys were laughing about the hotel the night before, and Joe Gresh and John the truck driver were particularly giggly. That syncopated thumping that had kept me up? It was their ceiling fan. They were in the room next to mine. Whoever installed the fan in their room had put it too close to the wall. Instead of relocating the fan, the installer shortened all of the fan's blades so they wouldn't hit the wall. The guy who performed the Casa Blanca multi-blade amputations apparently missed the class in surgery school on dynamic balancing. What Joe and John were giggling about during breakfast were the fan's blades. They were so short they didn't move any air but they thumped like a drummer on methamphetamines. I guess it's the thought that counts.

While we were eating, I saw an older fellow (even older than me) with his wife and a young girl who I suppose was his granddaughter. The guy was wearing an EOD T-shirt with the EOD emblem (that's EOD as in Explosive Ordnance Disposal). I had worked with EOD teams when I was in the Army and when I was an engineer on the cluster bomb programs at Aerojet. I nodded at the guy and asked, "Retired?"

"Yep," he said.

"Thanks for your service," I told him. I always do that when I meet a veteran, and I always mean it.

"Thank you for yours," he said. That caught me off guard. I didn't know how he knew I was in the Army, and then I realized I was wearing my Airborne hat. We shook hands and I noticed he was missing two fingers. Yes, he was most definitely an EOD guy. More than a few of the guys I had worked with in the munitions business were missing fingers. It goes with the territory.

We rolled out of the parking lot and continued to head south on 101 toward California. I was enjoying the ride, and I was a lot more alert after my discounted senior citizen coffee in McDonalds. They have the best coffee.

You know, I spoke about that solitude thing when riding a motorcycle earlier in this book. I like it. Even when riding in a group, there's time to think. I did a lot of that on this trip.

We had ridden the routes of and crossed over many famous western US trails on this ride...the Texas trail, the Bozeman trail, the Oregon trail, the El Camino Real trail (that was the one we were riding now), the Lewis and Clark trail, the Nez Perce trail, the California trail, the Butterfield trail, the Great Western Cattle trail, and more. The Western American Adventure Ride was impressive on many levels. One aspect of it that I thought was particularly impressive was that we were riding the routes of America's westward expansion. Even with the beautiful scenery of the Oregon Coast Highway before me, I thought that morning about what things must have been like in those early days for our pioneering forefathers.

Are you old enough to remember who Ward Bond was? He played the wagon master in the old '50s TV series *Wagon Train*. Crossing all of the historic trails I mentioned above kept driving my thoughts to Ward Bond and wagon trains for some reason. We were making the ride on motorcycles. Our ancestors made the trek in horse-drawn Conestoga wagons before there were McDonalds, Subways, or even roads. They just got up and did it. They must have been incredible people.

I found myself thinking about what it must have been like going these kinds of distances 150 years ago and more. I wondered if guys like Ward Bond struggled to get everybody moving in the morning on time. I decided it was probably easier for him. If you weren't ready to roll with the wagon train when it was time to go you risked being left behind, and there were real consequences if that happened. You could get scalped.

Okay, back to the story. We crossed the border into California and continued to follow Highway 101 south. We were back in California! We still had hundreds of miles to go to get home, but there was something special about crossing the northern California border and re-entering my home state. It was immensely satisfying.

Amongst the Redwoods, back in California!

Highway 101 was originally called El Camino Real (the Royal Road), and in California there are these bell stands (a big shepherd's crook sort of thing holding a bell) every mile along this road. It's the trail Father Juniper Serra followed in establishing the Jesuit missions extending from Baja to points north. It's one of the key parts of California's history.

California is a magnificent state with a rich heritage.

We soon found ourselves in the Redwood National Forest. It's another awesome thing to see, and we all had been looking forward to it. The cameras were out. There was a lot of traffic that day, but the guys were having a good time with all there was to see.

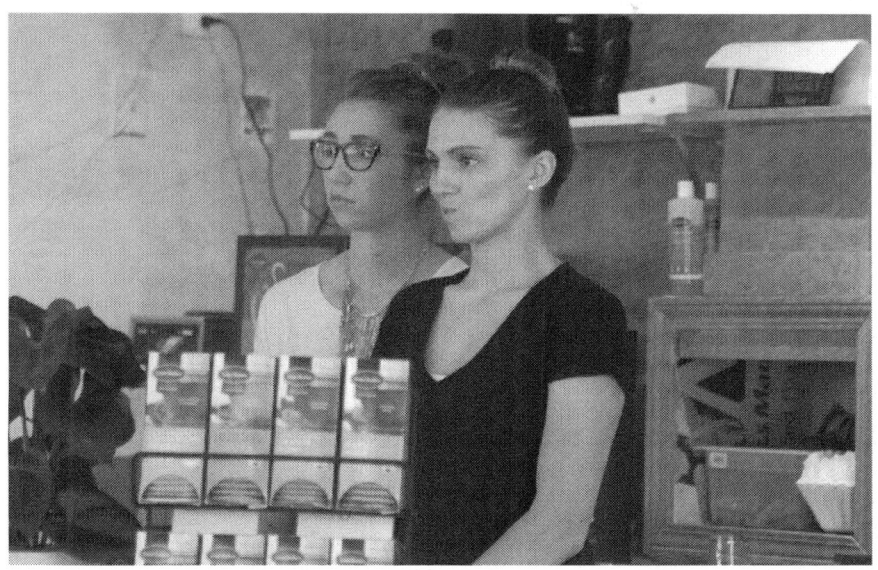

Waitresses checking out the mutant teenage ninja turtles.
Photo by Lester Peng.

When we stopped for lunch in Fortuna, Lester grabbed a photo that I liked immediately. Lester had been doing a much better job than me in capturing things with his camera, and he would do so again in that Fortuna restaurant. I mentioned earlier in this tale that to the other folks in these restaurants, our arrivals were very much out of the ordinary. Don't get me wrong. America is a land of immigrants, and that's particularly true in California. But it's one thing to have a melting pot society like we do; it's an altogether different thing to have 10 or 12 folks from three different countries speaking three different languages arrive in their motorcycle gear at your restaurant for lunch. Lester was doing a great job capturing the reactions of those upon whom we descended, and the photo he grabbed that afternoon seemed to say it all.

It was growing warmer as we continued south. Our initial plan was to stay in Willits that night, and then do a banzai run home through San Francisco and ride the Pacific Coast Highway all the way home. That would have been a very high mileage day (around 500 miles) through very heavy traffic.

Baja John and I spoke about it and decided it just wasn't a smart thing to do. While the Pacific Coast Highway is pretty, it would play second fiddle to many of the roads we had already ridden on the Western America Adventure Ride. And, the Pacific Coast Highway traffic would be oppressive on the stretch south of San Francisco. The other problem we had was that if we stuck with the original plan, we would be rolling back into the Los Angeles area late on a Friday. The traffic would be terrible.

We considered going inland to shoot down Interstate 5 and then Highway 58 over to Highway 395. That would bring us into Azusa from the east, which would avoid the Los Angeles traffic. But there was another problem with that, and that was the heat. We would be running through the central California desert, and we knew from previous rides the heat would be brutal. In fact, as soon as Highway 101 turned inland for a little bit on our ride to Willits, the heat was upon us. It would be significantly worse if we took Interstate 5.

You may recall that on the first day of our grand adventure, we rode through 105 degree temperatures in the Mojave Desert. On that first day more than two weeks ago, we were fresh. Since that day, we had been on the road riding hundreds of miles every day. The guys were tired. There's a difference between riding in that kind of heat on Day 1, and doing it after you've been on the road for 15 or 16 days without a break. The guys I rode with on the Western America Adventure Ride were troopers and no one complained about anything, but we just weren't up for big mileage days in that kind of heat as we neared home.

The decision was made. We'd be taking the 101 south out of San Francisco, and we would take two days to get home from San Francisco instead of one.

The guys back at Zongshen in China gave Hugo some grief on my decision to extend the trip by a day. They weren't on the ride and they didn't know what it was like. I reasoned that we weren't really taking an extra day. The guys would still make their flights. The only difference would be that we'd spend an extra day on the road instead of their guys spending that extra day hanging around the hotel in Azusa. To Zongshen, it would probably be less expensive to do it the way I was going to do it, anyway. Things would cost less on the road than they would in the Los Angeles area. In any event, I had made my decision.

Interestingly, this part of our route prompted another one of those inane keyboard commando comments that pop up from time to time on the forums. One guy posted his first ever comment on the ChinaRiders.net forum roundly criticizing us for taking the 101 home instead of the Pacific Coast Highway. This guy doesn't own an RX3, he had never ridden one, he certainly didn't join us on this ride, and he's not one of our customers. All that notwithstanding, he felt compelled to criticize us. When I read his comment, I wondered how empty his life must be if this was all he could offer. What could possibly motivate such a comment? Jealousy? A need to be heard? A need to criticize? A need to feel superior? Opinions are like buttholes, I guess. Everybody has one. Some people go a step beyond and become one.

The ride into Willits on the 101 was nice. We had a few spots where it was very hot, but for the most part it was comfortable.

We enjoyed Willits for several reasons. The hotel had a pool and it sure felt good after the heat we had ridden through that day. We had another nice surprise, too. Our good buddy Don drove to the hotel that evening to see us. Don owns both a CSC 150 and an RX3, and he told me he reads the blog every day. I enjoyed meeting Don that night and I was complimented that he made the trek to Willits just to meet us and say hello. Another great thing about Willits was our dinner that night. The food was nothing special, but the conversation made dinner fun. It was the first time in several days that we all had dinner together and I enjoyed it.

Chapter 29: San Francisco

Like always, I was up and out in the parking lot early in the morning before we left Willits. Our destination today would be San Francisco, and we were excited about that. San Francisco is one of those cities that define America. Its uniqueness and distinctive architecture, the Golden Gate Bridge, Alcatraz, and more are known around the world. It's a city that has been the locale for countless movies, and that's what I believe most people outside the United States use to form their opinions of what it's like to live in America.

I thought it would be an easy 130-mile ride south into San Francisco and I was looking forward to riding my RX3 across the Golden Gate Bridge. With only 130 miles in front of us I thought we would be there by 11:00 a.m. The guys could get in some sightseeing and shopping. I knew the Chinese guys wanted to do that. It would be a good day and we would be able to get off the bikes for a while.

That early morning in Willits I looked at my chain in the hotel parking lot. Once again, it was sagging. I had 8000 miles on my RX3 and I now needed to adjust the chain every day. Baja John and Joe Gresh were finding the same on their bikes. They had nearly the same mileage on their bikes as I did on mine. Everyone else's bike was newer (they all had about 4500 miles on their motorcycles), and they didn't need the daily chain adjustments.

The required adjustment amount on our chains was surprising. I was moving my rear wheel one full index mark on the swingarm each day. Usually when you adjust a chain the amount of movement required with respect to the swingarm index marks is trivial, but I wasn't finding that to be the case here. One full index mark. Wow. I had never experienced that before.

The first time I had to move the wheel this much, I thought about it while riding the entire day. I wondered if perhaps I had not tightened the rear axle enough and the rear wheel had eased forward again after the adjustment. At the next adjustment, I made a mental note of the wheel position with respect to the index marks. That day the chain had again loosened so much that it again required a full index mark of adjustment. I had counted index marks at the last adjustment, so I knew the rear wheel had not moved during the day. Nope, this was all in the chain. It was stretching that much.

I wondered if Baja John, Joe, and I would make it home on our chains. We had spare chains in the truck and I thought it was becoming more likely that the three of us would need to put new chains on our bikes. I wasn't worried about the other guys and their chains; they did not yet have the kinds of miles the three of us did.

Joe Gresh mentioned his chain again that morning in Willits, and this time, he told me he thought he would need to replace the chain. I joked with him again about the Port Orford burnout. He smiled.

"Every bad thing that ever happened in the world is due to that burnout," Joe said.

"Global warming is occurring because of you doing that burnout," I answered.

Hugo rounded up the guys and I gave the morning briefing. I covered the same topics I did every morning. Keep 30 meters between the bikes. Use a staggered riding formation. Don't try to take pictures while you're riding the motorcycle. It was the standard stuff I reiterated every morning, and then I pulled the map out of my jacket pocket and showed the group our route for the day.

The Chinese guys had been waiting for this. When I pointed to and said that we were riding into San Francisco, they all broke into the classic 1960s Scott McKenzie song...

> *If you're going to San Francisco*
> *Be sure to wear some flowers in your hair*
> *If you're going to San Francisco*
> *You're gonna meet some gentle people there*

They sang it well. We all laughed and enjoyed it. It was another one of those moments that will stick with me forever. The Chinese guys' ability to seize on these quintessential American things and create moments like this was simultaneously emotional and invigorating. I had been a bit tired that morning, but their singing fixed that. I was ready to roll, chain be damned.

We were on the road, we stopped for gas, and we continued our journey south on Highway 101. It was a cool morning and I was enjoying the ride.

About an hour later I noticed an interesting little town below us. It was Geyserville and it looked like it would make for a good place to take our morning break. Geyserville it would be, and it was a good call. Geyserville was a great stop. It was a cool little town with awesome photo ops.

We parked the bikes by a little general store and I told the guys we would be in Geyserville for half an hour. I figured we could take about an hour, but I knew if I told everybody to be back in 30 minutes, it would end up being about an hour. Lester, Baja John, and I went into the general store for a cup of coffee. The lady who worked there was a character and we chatted with her. The guys were out and about taking photos. I walked outside and did the same.

I found a hardware store that I could have spent an entire day photographing. I started photographing some of the things on display on the sidewalk and then moved inside. There was an older man and a younger woman behind the counter and I asked if I could take photos. They were cool with that.

A dog was sleeping in front of the counter and I took a few photos of him. He opened one eye to check me out, appropriately concluded I was harmless, and drifted back to sleep.

Willie, the Geyserville marathon man.

"That's Willie," the woman behind the counter said. "He ran a marathon."

"Excuse me?" I said.

She took a framed newspaper article off the wall behind the counter and showed it to me. "Willie is famous around here," she said. "A few years ago we ran a marathon starting in Geyserville. Willie heard all the commotion and before we realized what was happening, he took off with the runners. It was 26 miles, but Willie actually did more than 26 miles because every time he saw a rabbit he spun off and chased it for a while before rejoining the group."

The newspaper story was about Willie. I thought about what it must be like to be a dog running a marathon. Oh boy oh boy oh boy! Yep, I'm going for a run with the people! Whoa, there's a rabbit! Be back later, people! There's a rabbit that needs chasing! Gotta chase that rabbit! Okay, that's enough, I showed that screwy rabbit who's boss! Can't let the people get away! Okay, I'm back, people! Oh boy oh boy oh boy this is fun!

It must have been a grand adventure for old Willie. For me, that encounter in the hardware store in Geyserville was another Western America Adventure Ride memory bank moment.

I snapped a few more photos and then walked back to the general store. Our group was starting to reconvene. When everybody was back, I looked at my watch. We had been in Geyserville exactly one hour.

John the truck driver had used his iPhone and located an independent motorcycle repair shop in Petaluma another 40 miles down the 101. He had been looking for a place that could put one of our spare chains on Joe Gresh's bike. I was surprised that he had done that and my thought was that if we were going to put a chain on Joe's bike, we could have done it ourselves, but I only thought that because I didn't know what kind of chains we had.

We left Geyserville and rode to Petaluma. Finding the cycle shop was easy. At that point, just as we pulled to a stop in front of the place, Joe Gresh rolled up to me.

"I'm getting a flat tire," he said.

I looked at his rear tire. It was very low. "It must have been that burnout," I said.

"I always get a flat tire," Joe said. I'm the only one in the group who gets flats in any group I've ever ridden with. It's something that's been following me for years."

"Did you do burnouts all those years?"

John had the truck open and he pulled out the chain and a new rear tire. I met Paul, the proprietor, and John handed him the chain. He looked at it for an instant and said "It's a continuous chain. I'd have to pull the swingarm to install this chain. I can do that but it will take at least a couple of hours. Or I can sell you a chain with a master link in it."

I was surprised. I couldn't believe we left Azusa with a continuous chain. Paul took the chain out of its plastic bag, and sure enough, it was continuous. One big long loop with no master link.

"Let's do the one with the master link," I said. I toyed with the idea of having Paul put new chains on my bike and on Baja John's bike, but Paul told me he only had the one chain.

Paul told me when we first arrived he wasn't keen on working on Chinese bikes. I had heard it all before. The typical reaction to the thought of Chinese bikes in the motorcycle community is not good. It's bunk, because most people don't realize that their Japanese, American, German, and Italian bikes already have significant Chinese content. But hearing anti-Chinese sentiments in the motorcycle community is not unusual. Ignorance is bliss, or so the saying goes. Some of these folks must be the happiest people in the world.

When Paul finished working on Joe's bike, he took it for a short test ride to make sure everything worked.

"It's not bad," Paul said when he came back. That's what he said, but the smile on his face indicated his true feelings. The bike was a lot better than "not bad." Paul had been impressed by the RX3 while he was working on it, and that short ride solidified his feelings. In fact, as I write this, I can tell you that Paul's repair facility is on its way to becoming our first CSC Authorized Service Center.

A new tire, a new chain, and 90 minutes later, we were back on the 101 headed to San Francisco. The traffic on the 101 was heavy. It was moving, but there were a lot more cars around us now. I thought back to my earlier conversations with Joe Gresh about the Chinese wondering where all the people were (you know, when we were rolling through the vast openness that is the American West). Well, here they are, boys!

San Francisco and the Golden Gate Bridge were just ahead. I wanted to stop in the Marin highlands above the Golden Gate so the guys could grab photos of the bridge, but I couldn't find the exit to do that. Traffic was heavy and we were zooming. I had 10 motorcycles and the chase vehicle in our group, and I didn't want to make any sudden moves. It all became moot, though. I never saw the exit for the Marin highlands and suddenly, the Golden Gate Bridge was just a few hundred yards in front of us.

Now I had a new challenge: I couldn't find the lane to pay the toll. There were signs for all kinds of sensor-based payments (you know, the deal where the toll gantry picks up your signal and it's added to your bill automatically), but there were no signs indicating which lane to enter to pay the toll with actual money. We were sucked into the toll plaza's venturi and we were suddenly on the bridge.

I flipped my helmet video cam on, and then we were across the Golden Gate Bridge. It was over before I realized it.

Silly me. I didn't know you don't pay the toll at the Golden Gate Bridge any more. You used to be able to do that, but the times, they are a changing. The Golden Gate Bridge has a "pay by plate" billing scheme. You just roll across, a camera captures your license plate, and a couple of weeks later you get a bill in the mail. That's what happened. We received a bill. It cost $7.25 for each motorcycle to go across the Golden Gate Bridge.

After we crossed the Golden Gate Bridge we were in San Francisco. We pulled over to get our bearings. Baja John had his GPS and he had the hotel's address, so he hopped up front and led us from there.

When we arrived at the Van Ness Hotel, I was amazed yet again. Once more, John had done an amazing job. We were in great location, the hotel was reasonably priced, and we could park the bikes in a courtyard just outside our rooms. I wouldn't have thought all that was possible (especially the part about being reasonably priced) right there in the heart of San Francisco.

Once we were settled into the hotel, Hugo collected the motorcycle keys from the Chinese guys. There were a lot of ways to get lost and a lot of ways to get in trouble in San Francisco, and I guess he didn't want to take any chances. Juan Carlos and Gabriel took off on their motorcycles; they wanted to get photos in some of the classic San Francisco photo spots. I saw some of Juan Carlos' photos the next day and they were superb. He had photos of the bikes with the Golden Gate Bridge in the background, and several other RX3 shots with similar San Francisco icons.

The two Johns, Joe, and I had no desire to ride the bikes in the city or even to hire a cab to drive us around. We were only three or four blocks from Ghirardelli Square, the Embarcadero, and the center of San Francisco's tourist zone, so we hoofed it.

While we were walking there (it was already 3:00 p.m.), Joe Gresh asked about Alcatraz. We had a clear view of San Francisco Bay and I pointed to it. Joe wanted to go, but I told him it was unlikely he'd be able to get tickets on such short notice and it was already late in the day. Seeing Alcatraz is a very worthwhile thing to do, though. I've taken the tour twice. If you ever have an opportunity to visit San Francisco, go online and get your Alcatraz tickets early. They are always sold out a few days in advance.

We continued to walk and our conversation turned to where we might eat. With the events of the morning, Joe's chain and flat tire issues, and all the rest, we had not had lunch yet. A guy walking by heard us. He recommended a barbeque spot we would see as soon as we passed Ghirardelli Square. It sounded good and it was. It wasn't just good, it was fantastic. We had a leisurely lunch and a cold beer. It's hard to say which was better: The food, or the conversation.

Joe wanted to walk further into the Embarcadero area and look at the ships docked there. I would have liked to have done that, too, but my leg was bothering me. I'm not complaining. Leg pain is a fairly constant reminder of the motorcycle accident I told you about in Chapter 1, and this was the first time it had given me any grief on this trip. The fact that it was bothering me a little in San Francisco was no big deal. I figured I was way ahead of the game having gone the entire ride up to this point with no pain at all. Anyway, I wasn't up for continuing our stroll deeper into the tourist zone, so Joe left us to continue his exploration.

The two Johns and I walked back toward our hotel and I grabbed the obligatory tourist photos. Hell, I was a tourist and I was carrying my camera. I thought I might as well put it to good use. John the truck driver saw a gift shop. He ducked into it to buy souvenirs for his kids. Baja John and I waited outside for a while. When it looked like our truck driver was going to be in there for the duration, we split for Ghirardelli Square.

San Francisco. The left-wing lunacy has been commercialized, as evidenced by this flower power tour bus. We never met the gentle people.

I felt the urge for a cup of coffee so we stopped in a coffee shop and soda fountain kind of place and took a seat at the counter. It was relaxing. My old riding buddy Baja John and I spent an hour talking and nursing our coffee. John ordered a piece of apple pie. He really liked San Francisco, and he mentioned that he thought it would be cool to live in the city.

I have mixed emotions about San Francisco. It's an interesting place to visit, but in my opinion San Francisco is an expensive left-leaning tourist trap, and those are three strikes that make it an "out" in my book. The place has an ultra-liberal hippy edginess that I don't care for, and I think the people there are not friendly. Joe Gresh made a comment while we were walking together earlier. He said no one would make eye contact. He was right. Everyone was looking wherever they had to in order to avoid establishing eye contact. It's part of the edginess and unfriendly vibe that I think defines the place.

Here's another thing I find troubling: San Francisco is a so-called sanctuary city. That means the city's law enforcement community is restricted from working with the federal government in enforcing US immigration laws. I'm not a right wing fanatic about illegal immigration; I just find it preposterous that a city government can override federal laws. I never understood how such a situation can be allowed to exist, yet it does.

And one more thing: San Francisco has a lot of homeless people and panhandlers, and they are aggressive. I don't care for that, either.

I just don't feel comfortable in San Francisco. But, it is an iconic American city and I would feel remiss had I not shown it to our visitors, warts and all.

John and I walked back to the hotel (it was uphill going back, so it was a lot harder for a couple of old geezers like us). The hotel wasn't the fanciest place I'd ever seen, but it was clean and it had good connectivity. I posted a blog on the CSC site that night, and before long it was too late to go to dinner. Our late lunch at the barbeque place had been huge, and we weren't hungry. We called it a day early that evening, eager to continue our journey south the next morning.

Chapter 30: Santa Maria

The ride out of San Francisco the next morning was stressful because of the traffic. It would be easy for the group to get separated in that city. Even for a guy like me who lived in California, negotiating the streets of San Francisco was tricky (forgive me, Karl Malden). John led us out of the confusion, relying on his GPS to get us back on the 101.

I adjusted my chain again before we left and I noted that I was nearly out of adjustment range. We had to go about 450 miles to get to Azusa. I thought my bike could do that, but it was clear that my RX3 needed a new chain. It would have to wait until I got back to the plant. My rear tire was worn, but I had over 8000 miles on it. The tread was just starting to touch the wear bars. I was confident I'd get home on that tire and I was feeling good about it. I had never been able to get that kind of tire mileage on any motorcycle I had ever owned.

Traffic in the city and on the 101 was heavy. We were leaving at rush hour and I expected it to be rough in the city. I was surprised at how heavy it was on the 101 heading south, though, as people should be coming into the city at that hour (not leaving it). It lightened up a bit as we went past San Francisco's airport (which is on the 101 about 6 miles or so south of downtown). It intensified once again as we approached San Jose.

We were in the right lane, and I noticed that Highway 101 has a car pool lane. We could legally ride in the car pool lane with our motorcycles, but the trick would be getting across the several lanes of traffic it would take to do that.

Baja John was bringing up the rear, and his thinking was already way ahead of mine. When I checked my rear view mirror, John had moved over one lane and was blocking traffic so that we could move to our left. We repeated this move four more times, made it to the car pool lane, and squirted right through San Jose.

After San Jose, it was an easy and scenic roll down the 101. We approached San Luis Obispo and I saw the sign for the Highway 58 exit. That's the road we had discussed taking east to hook up with Interstate 5. We rejected that idea because it would be too hot in the central California desert. Highway 58 is a nice road, though. I wrote a piece on it for *Motorcycle Classics* a few years ago. My geezer buddies and I have done a few weekend rides in this area. We like to come up here on the 101, spend the night near San Luis Obispo, and then take Highway 58 home. It's full of twisties and great scenery until it approaches Interstate 5. Then it gets boring. For most of its length, though, Highway 58 is an awesome run. If you're ever planning a ride in this area, you might want to consider putting Highway 58 from San Luis Obispo to Interstate 5 on your list.

The temperature along Highway 101 was cool, and it was a comfortable ride. We passed San Luis Obispo, Pebble Beach (yes, that Pebble Beach), and we were rolling through Arroyo Grande when a gray Toyota pickup truck rolled up next to me. The truck was in the fast lane, and there was a young guy in the passenger seat smiling and waving. He wasn't just giving us a wave, though. These guys were keeping pace with me, smiling, making eye contact, beeping, and waving excitedly.

I smiled and waved back. We had experienced this several times during the Western America Adventure ride, where folks were excited to see ten motorcycles of the same type riding in formation. But there was something more to it this time. The two guys in that pickup were seriously enjoying seeing us.

The Highway 101 Hi Joe sign.

The young fellow in the passenger seat couldn't have been more than 18 or 19 years old. He stopped waving and was doing something. A couple of seconds later, he held up a hand-written sign that said, "Hi Joe."

I was flabbergasted. I didn't know who the guy was, but he clearly knew who I was. I had a good laugh over it and it made my day.

That night, I posted about it on the CSC blog and asked whoever it was to let me know who they were. I figured that whoever it was had been following our adventure, and he would see the request from me. It didn't take long for an email from my good buddy San Marino Bill to pop into my computer with an answer:

> Joe:
>
> My son just called me from the Paso Robles area and wanted to know where the CSC group was riding today. He is up there picking up his son. He was following a group of good looking bikes (10 or 12). I told him to make a sign that said HI JOE and show it to the leader. I hope it was you.
>
> Bill

I got a laugh out of that. Bill sent along a digital photo of the "Hi Joe" sign. It was pretty cool. Nothing like it had ever happened to me before.

We arrived in Santa Maria and checked into our last hotel of the trip. Our guests left to find a shopping mall in their continuing quest to find something to bring home that was not made in China.

John the truck driver, Baja John, Joe Gresh, and I walked to a restaurant across the street and enjoyed another one of the best dinners of the trip. It was an Asian fusion place that features dishes from the Philippines (the place is called Cre-Asian, and it is worth a stop). Maria, the owner, chatted for a while with us. We didn't know what the different things on the menu were and Maria explained them to us. In the end, we asked her to order for us, and the food was outstanding. So was the conversation.

Chapter 31: Sweet Home, Azusa

On our last morning of the Western America Adventure Ride, we had breakfast in a Carl's, Jr. restaurant across the street from our hotel. We had a mere 175 miles to ride that day, and then we'd be home in Azusa, where we had started our journey 18 days earlier.

Breakfast was surprisingly good. We were all excited and feeling good. Today was our last day. It was as if we were graduating. One of the guys told us that he had been propositioned by a hooker in the hotel parking lot the night before, and you can imagine the joking and ribbing accompanying that revelation.

South of Santa Maria, Highway 101 runs right along the edge of the Pacific Ocean. It was Saturday, so the traffic was light in the morning and the ride was awesome. Cool weather, a clear sky, and the magnificent Pacific on our right. We were on our way home after 17 long days in the saddle. Deserts, mountains, plains, pine forests, geysers, bison, elk, antelope, freeways, dirt roads, national parks, rivers, dams, a parade, the Continental Divide...we'd seen it all.

We didn't stop for gas when we left the hotel, and we rode for about an hour before we refueled just north of Santa Barbara. As we approached Santa Barbara, the gas gauges were on the last bar and I was looking for a place to refuel. Tony, who had been out on his bike the night before, had run a few more miles since our last refueling stop than the rest of us. He pulled alongside and pointed to his tank. I nodded my head. I know, Tony. I'm looking.

I saw a Union 76 station and we exited the 101. It was to be our last refueling stop of the Western America Adventure Ride.

Santa Barbara is a college town, and there were young folks in a Toyota SUV at the edge of the gas station's parking lot. I assume they were students. A young woman in the back seat had the door open as she leaned out of the vehicle and vomited. Her friends watched. Hard partying the night before, I suppose. Ah, to be young again.

A woman at the opposite end of the age spectrum stepped out of her car at the pumps. She wore a bright red knit body sock, a pink and purple floppy hat, and tons of makeup. She was doing her best to look younger, but it wasn't working. She struck up a conversation with Tony, reached into her car, brought out a book, and handed it to him. I'm not sure what her scam was (religion, politics, save the whales, outlaw the pigeons, vote for whomever), but she was working Tony like a Republican working a room full of donors. I gave my horn three long beeps, and Tony had the excuse he needed to escape her grasp.

Barfing, parking lot trolls, whatever. Welcome to La La Land. As we approached Los Angeles, we were re-entering the realm of the ridiculous, the world of the whack-a-doodles in the place I call home. We were almost there.

The ride through Santa Barbara saw a bit more traffic (it's a city of some size), but it thinned out for a little while as we continued south. As soon as we were past Santa Barbara, the Pacific was again to our immediate right. We could see the oil rigs out in the ocean and the surfers at the water's edge.

Traffic grew considerably heavier as we approached Ventura, and it took us a good two hours to go the next 60 miles to Burbank. The car pool lane would have made no difference on this stretch; it, too, was feeling the burn of too many vehicles and too little space. We were getting closer to home, and we had the traffic to prove it.

I was concentrating on the traffic, looking for an edge or an open lane, but it wasn't happening. Joe Gresh pulled up alongside and told me that Baja John and the truck had stopped. I grabbed the next exit onto a crowded Burbank street, turned right again, and we pulled into a Denny's parking lot. It was noon already, and I reasoned it was good time for lunch. Our last few miles were going to be hard ones.

I pulled out my cell phone. It had all of the bars showing. We're back in the world, I thought. Heavy traffic but great cell phone reception. Everything is a tradeoff. I called Baja John.

"What's up?" I asked.

"My chain came off the rear sprocket," John said. I told John where we were. "We'll catch up with you in 5 minutes," he said.

True to his word, Baja John pulled into the Denny's parking lot a few minutes later. The big yellow submarine was right behind him. We had a leisurely lunch. The restaurant was packed and we were lucky we found a table. To my surprise, even with the crowd the service was excellent. I found myself wishing for the first time during the previous 18 days that it wasn't. I wanted to hang out for a while at Denny's. Denny's wanted to turn tables.

I know the Los Angeles area well, and I knew that the traffic on the 101 had to be due to an accident or some other roadside anomaly further south. The heavy traffic we had experienced was unusual on a Saturday. I wanted to wait and allow it to clear.

I paid for our lunch and returned to the parking lot. My chain was droopy again. Of the three bikes that had worn out chains, mine was the last man standing. We had replaced Joe Gresh's chain in Petaluma, John was now on one of the demo bikes, and my RX3 was still on its original chain. I had nearly 8700 miles on it. I looked at the adjusters. I had maybe one thread left.

Baja John's bike had thrown its chain and I didn't want to have the same thing happen to me. As Willy Shakespeare once wrote, to adjust or not to adjust, that is the question. Should I adjust it for the remaining few miles, or should I just ride it? John's chain had come off, but John is what we call a full-figured rider. His size and the incessant stop-and-go nature of the last 15 miles undoubtedly contributed to his chain departing controlled flight.

I decided to err on the side of caution. I pulled my tools out of the panniers and took that last thread of adjustment. The chain was still fairly loose after the adjustment.

After we left Denny's the traffic on the southbound 101 lightened in just a few miles. There had evidently been an accident, or a police officer had pulled someone over, or someone stopped to change a tire, or any one of a dozen other things occurred that should have little effect on traffic but always brings things to a standstill. Whatever it was, it was no more, and the freeway was flowing again.

Highway 134 spun off to the left and we took it through Glendale to Pasadena, where we picked up the eastbound 210. This was good. The 210 freeway. We were on the road that would run us right into Azusa a scant 20 miles to the east. It was hot again, but we weren't noticing it. We were almost home.

We rode those final 20 miles and took the Vernon Avenue exit. Vernon wound through the blue collar homes of Azusa, built a half century ago during one of our many defense industry buildups. We had one final traffic light to get through to put us onto Foothill Boulevard (old Route 66), but our motorcycles were too light to trip the sensor. All 10 of us and the chase truck waited as the signal ignored us. We were sweltering, baking in the heat, and eager to roll that literal final mile to the CSC plant.

The traffic light had other ideas. It ran through a complete cycle without changing for us. This isn't right, I thought. Doesn't that light know we've just ridden 5000 miles at 8000 rpm?

I stepped off my bike, walked over to the curb, and pressed the pedestrian button to make the signal change, and it did.

We rode one more mile on Route 66, my right blinker went on, and we turned into the CSC plant.

Folks, we were home. 5000 miles at 8000 rpm! What a ride!

The boys in the band (the Western America Adventure Ride Band, that is), home in Azusa after riding 5000 miles. From left to right, Joe Gresh, Baja John, Lester, Gabriel, Juan Carlos, Tony, Da Jiu, Tso, King Kong, John the truck driver, and Kyle. Hugo was behind the camera, photographing this moment. Photo by Ying Liu.

Susie was waiting for me in the parking lot. I felt good and I felt bad. I felt good about completing the ride, and I felt bad knowing I wouldn't be seeing most of these guys any time soon. As I pulled into the parking lot, I realized I didn't want the ride to end. I wanted to ride another 5000 miles on my RX3.

Epilogue

Being the engineer that I am, as I was wrapping up this book I calculated how many revolutions an engine turns running 5000 miles at 8000 rpm.

It's 55 million.

Multiply that by the 10 motorcycles we had on this grand adventure and that becomes a half-billion crankshaft revolutions for our little run around the American West.

We did this ride to showcase the RX3 motorcycle's reliability. I teach reliability engineering at Cal Poly Pomona, and I know that the best way to demonstrate reliability is to get out there and actually demonstrate it.

I think that's what we did.

It was a gutsy move on our part. Yes, I'm patting myself on the back, and I'm doing the same for the other great guys who rode the entire Western America Adventure Ride 5000 miles with us (Joe, John, Kyle, Gabriel, Juan Carlos, Tony, Lester, King Kong, and Tso). I have the same respect for the guys and one gal who rode the 1700-mile CSC Inaugural Baja Run with us (Justin, Juddy, Tiffany, Pete, both Gregs, all three

Johns, Jay, Keith, Eric, Abe, and Reuben). We didn't know when we started either of these rides how the bikes would perform racking up these kinds of miles. It would have been really, really bad if they had not done well.

But they did. The rides were a success.

As much as we did these rides to demonstrate that the bikes could go the distance, we also wanted to find out what would break, and I believe we succeeded there, too. We could have simply sat back and watched the warranty claims roll in after selling a bunch of them, but we wanted to get ahead of the curve and fix the things that needed fixing before our customers experienced problems.

We found a few improvement opportunities. I'll summarize those with you now.

- The batteries in the first shipment of CSC RX3 had a high infant mortality rate on both of our adventure rides. We had two batteries conk out in Baja, and three on the Western America Adventure Ride. There's no nice way to say it: The first shipment of motorcycles we received from Zongshen had cheap batteries. If you have a bike from that first shipment and your battery hasn't failed, you're okay (they fail quickly if they're bad). Zongshen upgraded the battery (they turned to a higher-quality supplier), and all subsequent shipments will have the better battery.

- I'm not happy with the RX3's chain life. The chain is basically a goner at the 6,000-mile mark. I eked 8,700 miles out of mine, but it should have been replaced at 6,000 miles. The RX3 deserves a better chain; it's too good a world class adventure bike for the chain it has from the factory. As I said in this book, a chain ought to last 15000 miles in normal use. The reality of the situation is that most riders won't roll up the kinds of miles we did. But if you're launching on an adventure that will see you roll through 6,000 miles, you'll need a better chain.

- Two of the rear view mirrors failed on the Western America Adventure Ride (the reflective surface fell out of the plastic frame on one, and the ball joint pivot failed on another). We had experienced both of these issues on earlier rides. Zongshen knew of the issue when we surfaced it to them. They are incorporating an improved rear view mirror design on the next shipment of motorcycles to us.

- We had a few headlight bulbs fail. It's always the low beam that goes. We replaced the bulbs on those and we haven't experienced any failures with the replacement bulbs. The bike comes with a 35/40 watt bulb; when we replace these, we always use the 55/60 watt bulb. I installed the 55/60 watt bulb in my bike. I like the better illumination.

- We had what I consider to be fewer instances of threaded fasteners loosening or falling off than I have experienced on other motorcycles, but we did have a few things shake loose. Keeping an eye on nuts and bolts is a normal part of maintaining any motorcycle (this is not an RX3-unique issue). On the RX3, the fasteners to watch are the exhaust pipe heat shield screws (we had two of those unscrew), the countershaft sprocket nut (we lost one on the Baja trip), the exhaust header nut (we lost one on the Western America Adventure Ride), the gear shift lever bolt (those loosen on all brands of bikes and they do so occasionally on the RX3, although we did not have any fall out), and the muffler mounting bolts (we had three bikes experience this on the Baja trip, and none since).

That's about it for what went wrong. We didn't have a single engine failure on either trip. The engines on these bikes are bulletproof (that's an expression, folks...don't fire a .44 magnum into your engine and call us with a warranty claim).

I told you what went wrong. Let me tell you what went right and what I like about the RX3:

- Our ten RX3 motorcycles rolled up 50,000 miles during the 18-day Western America Adventure. Other than the few issues identified above, we had no other problems. No engine failures, no clutch failures, no cable failures, no brake failures, no overheating, and no other failures. You might not think that's significant. I've taken enough motorcycle rides and covered enough miles on other motorcycles to know that it is. I would estimate that on one out of two long rides on my other motorcycles something always went wrong (this includes Harleys, Triumphs, Suzukis, Yamahas, Hondas, and Kawasakis). I had the instrument cluster loosen on my Triumph Tiger on a ride through Baja. I had the rear brake caliper come off on a recent ride on my KLR 650 (on that motorcycle, the windshield fell off on the ride home from the dealer when I first bought it). I had the backrest fail on my '92 Softail and its rear fender bolts loosened constantly, even with Loctite. I couldn't ride 100 miles on my '79 Electra Glide without something major breaking. Things happen on motorcycles, folks.

- Our 15 RX3 motorcycles similarly accumulated 25,500 miles during the CSC Baja Inaugural Run. Same thing there, folks. The bikes performed magnificently. We didn't even have a flat tire on that ride.

- The rear tire on my RX3 went 8700 miles. That's phenomenal mileage on a rear tire. It's the best I've ever experienced. I have no idea how long the front tire will last on the RX3, but it's going to be a big number. At 8700 miles on my bike, the front tire is not showing any wear.

- All of the bikes shifted smoothly and finding neutral was a snap. I've read some criticism about the RX3's ability to find neutral. We didn't see any of that on either trip. The trick here is to adjust the clutch and the chain. If those things are where they need to be, you won't have any problems finding neutral.

- The RX3's handling is so good it's hard to describe. I could give you all the cliché phrases (you know, it's planted, it corners like it's on rails, it shreds, and all that), but you really need to ride the bike to understand what I am telling you here. It's the best-handling motorcycle I've ever owned,

- None of the riders on either trip (Baja or the Western America Adventure Ride) complained about the RX3's comfort. The ergonomics and natural seating position on this motorcycle make it easy to ride all day long. I've read criticism about the seat, but I don't have an issue with it on my bike and nobody raised it as an issue on our rides. I use our optional sheepskin cover on my RX3, just as I have on my other motorcycles, and it made for a comfortable ride (although I will admit I got a few dirty looks from those Bighorns in Zion). That said, I recognize that some people may not like the stock seat. If you find you don't like the stock seat, we have accessory seats from Seat Concepts. These get high marks from the folks who have them, and they are a lot less expensive than what you'd pay other custom seat makers.

- On that same ergonomic note, the RX3 windshield is phenomenal. Joe Gresh observed that it was the best windshield he's ever used on any motorcycle. It keeps you in still air all the way up to the bike's top speed of 84 mph. I found it did an amazing job in the rain, too.

- Fuel economy was phenomenal. On both rides, our RX3s averaged around 70 mpg. Fuel economy drops a little bit on the freeways when you're running 75 mph all day long, but it's still in the 65 mpg range or better. On a couple of legs on the Western America Adventure Ride, my bike did over 80 mpg.

- The engine is smooth. It has a counterbalancer, and on long trips like our adventure tours, that smoothness greatly increases comfort and reduces fatigue.

- The bike's luggage is a high point for me. Yeah, all you Internet trolls, I know it's not aluminum, but I also know it comes with the bike at no extra charge, it works well, and it's durable. I carried all of my camera gear, my computer, my tools, my maps, and other assorted odds and ends in the stock luggage during the entire Western America Adventure Ride. On the Baja run we did not have a chase vehicle, and I carried all of that plus my clothes. I've opened and closed those bags a lot of times and I've crammed a lot of stuff in there. They're still working fine. As an aside, the optional Tourfella aluminum bags are nice, and they offer significantly increased carrying capacity. If you were to buy aluminum luggage for a BMW GS similar to our Tourfella bags, the luggage alone would cost as much as the RX3 (and the RX3's price includes its luggage). I think that's pretty cool.

- The RX3 is a visually arresting motorcycle. We had people approach us wherever we stopped and the comments were all good. Many people were certain it was a BMW. The fit, finish, and styling are that good.

- The RX3 is not intimidating. It's not ridiculously tall and getting on and off the bike does not induce anxiety. It's light compared to other fully-equipped adventure touring motorcycles. The fact that it's a 250cc motorcycle never left me wanting for more power. In fact, I liked using 90% of what the engine has to offer. On my earlier performance bikes, I doubt I used 50% of what those machines could do, and I always had to worry about too much throttle. Those high performance machines sucked me into riding over my abilities. I don't do that on the RX3.

On that thing about the bike being a 250cc motorcycle, one of my geezer riding buddies who rides a Triumph Sprint asked me what it was like riding a 250 all those miles. My answer surprised me not because of what I said, but because I didn't have to think about it to formulate an answer. I told him you have less power so you have to plan how you pass slower vehicles, but other than that, it really made no difference. You quickly forget you're riding a motorcycle that's "only" a 250.

Regarding the trip itself, I made a few mistakes in planning and I will do a few things differently on our future rides. The daily mileage will be lower, and we'll take more photo stops. We'll probably take advantage of the lower daily miles on these future trips to leave at 9:00 a.m. instead of 8:00 a.m., too.

The bottom line? Folks, the RX3 is one hell of a motorcycle at any price, and our CSC adventure rides are magical. Everyone who rides with us will remember these adventures the rest of their lives. I sure will.

About the Author

This is my 11th book, and this is the part I've hated writing for every one of them. I imagine the drill is to write this part so that everyone thinks you are a swashbuckling character, one with revelations everyone should feel both compelled and privileged to read. The underlying subliminal message, of course, is that that every inhabitant of our planet should buy at least three copies of this book.

Nah, I'm not going to do that. I'm a guy who likes to ride and write. I've been riding motorcycles since I was 14, and that makes this my 50th year in the saddle. I've been writing for a while, too. I had my first story published by *EasyRiders* magazine when I was in my early 30s (I rode a Harley-Davidson back in those days). The best part about being published in *EasyRiders* was that it influenced the young lady I was dating. I think it convinced her that maybe I was interesting enough to keep seeing. We've now been married 32 years.

Ah, let's see, what else...I'm a father, I'm an engineer, I'm a shooter and a reloader, I'm a teacher, I write the blog for CSC Motorcycles, and I'm what some people would consider to be a guy who leans to the right. I think of that last item as being someone who thinks about things rather than some someone who simply swallows slogans. But I don't want to ignite any political debates or kill any book sales, which is why this "about the author" thing is buried at the end of the book.

If you'd like to connect, my email address is jberk@cscmotorcycles.com. Drop me a line. I'd love to hear from you.

Made in the USA
Lexington, KY
03 November 2015